AT THE WIRE

WIRE

Horse Racing's Greatest Moments

AT THE
WIRE

Horse Racing's Greatest Moments

By Edward L. Bowen

EP
ECLIPSE
PRESS

Lexington, Kentucky

Library of Congress Control Number: 2001088514

ISBN 1-58150-070-X

Printed in Hong Kong
First Edition: October 2001

a division of Blood-Horse Publications
PUBLISHERS SINCE 1916

- Table of Contents -

CONTENTS

- INTRODUCTION -

Great moments in racing history savor of varied emotions and tastes. On the one hand, there are the obvious choices, races that seemed important as they neared and fulfilled the ideal of matching outstanding horses at their best in fierce competition. Such races demand inclusion in any retrospective of memorable moments, events such as the 1920 Dwyer between Man o' War and John P. Grier, the 1988 Breeders' Cup clash of Amazons Personal Ensign and Winning Colors, or — the ultimate — the 1978 Triple Crown conclusion between Affirmed and Alydar.

Then, too, there are the moments when one horse reached such exalted heights that the event bespoke a towering achievement despite being bereft of a competitive struggle. Secretariat's thirty-one-length victory in heroic time in the 1973 Belmont Stakes is easily cast as the apogee of this sort of event.

Less definable — and subject to differences in the personal preference of the observer — is what makes other moments cherished in the recalling. The unexpected and inexplicable vie for their place. How could one predict the 1944 triple dead heat in the Carter Handicap, in which the otherwise unremarkable Brownie, Wait a Bit, and Bossuet earned a lasting place in lore for themselves — and for racing secretary John B. Campbell, who lived the handicapper's dream of weighting them down to the wire together?

There are those exalted moments when horses from which greatness is expected find themselves in mortal struggles in which courage outstrips brilliance in defining their depths — Equipoise and Twenty Grand, Citation and Noor, Kelso and Gun Bow, Sunday Silence and Easy Goer.

The years tick on, rhythmic and inexorable. Most of yesterday's cheers dissolve, hugged to the heart only in personal specifics — I was there with my dad; she was my favorite filly; we cut class to go; it was my first exacta.

Sometimes, though, the greatness of the Thoroughbred and his sport is transcendent. Some few moments rise above the ordinary into a life of their own. Following is a recounting of twenty-seven such events, plus Breeders' Cup highlights. They run their gamut, but each might be addressed with respect — and fondness.

Edward L. Bowen
Lexington, Kentucky, 2001

Dead heat in the Metropolitan Handicap on Belmont Park's opening day: Sysonby (rail) and Race King.

- CHAPTER 1 -

Grandeur and Grit

Although the age of grandiose New York race-tracks was four decades old, Belmont Park took the Turf to a glamorous new level. It was, in the words of Walter Vosburgh, "a revelation. People were in ecstasies over it."

The sprawling plant opened May 4, 1905, inducing superlatives at every level. "It was by far the most extensive racing property that had been opened," the historian and racing official averred, and he could back up that statement with reference to its 650 acres of grounds and a racetrack of one and a half miles. Moreover, "the saddling paddock was the most beautiful seen anywhere in this country." This observation entailed a certain interpretative license, of course, but was buttressed by talk of "stately oak and chestnut trees" that "shaded the ground where the ladies and gentlemen could roam about and inspect the candidates for the great events…and where the horses were put through their toilets" — perhaps not the way we would describe either pre- or post-race routine today, but who's to argue with Vosburgh?

As historian, Vosburgh did justice to Belmont with such extolment, and as racing secretary he had given his hand print to the occasion of opening day by assigning weights so as to emit a dead heat in the great Metropolitan Handicap. This opening-day feature found the highly acclaimed young star Sysonby struggling to the wire on even terms with the older Race King, the class/age differential divined precisely by Master Vosburgh at ten pounds of actual weight.

Belmont Park was devastated by fire in 1917 but was restored and over the years revamped from time to time. The racetrack became so instrumental to the sport that it has been called respectfully "the headquarters of the Turf," just as Newmarket is so known in England.

By 1963 the plant had been worn down by the years to the extent that it was condemned. By then its grandeur and its embodiment of the spirit of American racing were strong enough that racing men would not let it go and simply transfer all their Gotham activities to the new and shining Aqueduct. Belmont Park rose anew, and in time for the hundredth running of the venerated Belmont Stakes, in 1968.

>━•━◆━•━O━•━◆━•━<

Precedent for grand and elegant structures as the backdrop for American horse races included Jerome Park on Long Island. This was masterminded by Leonard Jerome, who would go down in history not only for his roles on the Turf and in business, but as the father of Jenny Jerome, she, in turn, the mother of that singular statesman Sir Winston Churchill.

cial club as sporting arena. The clubhouse of Jerome Park was on the opposite side of the irregular track — more or less kidney shaped — from the grandstand. It "was equipped with spacious dining rooms, ornamented by a gallery of pictures of all the famous English and American race horses of celebrity," Vosburgh recorded in *Racing in America*, published by The Jockey Club.

Jerome Park was joined by Morris Park, Sheepshead Bay, Brighton Beach, Jamaica, Yonkers, and Aqueduct, as New York City/Long

A throng of people attended opening day of the new Belmont Park on May 4, 1905.

The Civil War had halted racing in the South for the most part, and when the war ended, the impoverished situation in the South precluded it from regaining its leadership of the Turf. Northern tracks, always important, took on new stature, and they became fancier. Saratoga began racing in 1863, and in 1864 the first New Jersey Derby was run at Paterson. Jerome's image of a racecourse was as much so-

Island tracks, while across the state line Monmouth Park in New Jersey gave a similar gilt to the conduct of the sport.

This proved to be too much of a good thing, and by 1889 the competition among the tracks had created disgruntled factions among the leaders of racing's upper echelon. Morris Park was located so close to Jerome Park that in 1890 there was no racing at the latter, and what action that would later take place there over the next few years was done under lease by other associations. The final meeting at Jerome Park was held in 1894, the track being still not quite thirty years old.

In 1895 August Belmont and James R. Keene, along with some other members of the fledgling leadership organization, The Jockey Club, organized the Westchester Racing Association. The purpose of this group was to lease Morris Park in order to continue race meetings there. The lease was up in 1905, by which time the Westchester Racing Association purchased the land on which Belmont Park would be built. Racing at Belmont continued under the auspices of that association until New York racing was consolidated under the New York Racing Association in the middle 1950s.

Belmont Park's luxuries lacked nothing in imaginable amenities of the time, while the utilitarian aspects of its design were also first-rate. A quaint old mansion on the property became the Turf and Field Club, which Vosburgh rhapsodized as "embowered in woods and shrubbery, rendering it an abode 'fit for Juno and her peacocks,' as an enthusiastic lover of nature described it."

Although brand-new, Belmont Park was immediately a savior of traditions, for it provided a home for many important races begun at the other area tracks. In addition to the Belmont Stakes itself, today recognized as one of the United States' three classics, other well-established events transferred to Belmont

THE BLOOD-HORSE

The Metropolitan was inaugurated at the elegant Morris Park in 1891.

from disbanded New York tracks included the Withers, Jerome, Metropolitan, and, later, the Suburban, Futurity, and Lawrence Realization. All of these are extant in 2001.

Nearly a century after its first day, Belmont Park is still, and again, magnificent.

The feature race of its first meeting, the Metropolitan Handicap, had been inaugurated at Morris Park in 1891. Its winners already included some distinguished runners, such as Ramapo, Ethelbert, Gunfire, and Irish Lad, while the quality of its fields was illustrated by such as Tenny, Henry of Navarre, Imp, and Beldame having been beaten in the event. It was run at a mile and one-eighth through 1896 and then was switched to one mile, and today it is one of the most important races of that route in the country.

The 1905 Metropolitan marked the debut at three of Sysonby. Although seen as a brilliant colt,

CHAPTER 1

Sysonby had a black mark near the end of his two-year-old season, so it was difficult to know just what to make of him in the spring of 1905. Wall Street tycoon James R. Keene, owner of a great stable of the day, bred Sysonby, although the circumstances that produced the colt were set into motion by Marcus Daly. Himself a wealthy owner, courtesy of the Anaconda copper mines in Montana, Daly owned Apperfield Stud in England as well as the sumptuous Bitter Root Stud out West. In 1901 Daly bred one of his English mares, the Orme five-year-old Optime, to Melton. Daly died later that year, and his English stock was imported for auction in New York, where Keene bought Optime for $6,600. The following spring, the mare foaled a colt at Keene's handsome Castleton Farm in Kentucky.

Keene's son, Foxhall, leased a lodge named Sysonby Hall in Melton Mowbray, an English village at which life centered around spirited horses, foxhunting, sporting gentry, and artists to record the richness of their existence.

The connection to the name of the sire, Melton, suggested the name Sysonby, and the colt was so named.

Sysonby was not impressive as a youngster, but by the time he was scheduled to be part of the Keene string sent to England, the Silver Fox of Wall Street's trainer turned foxy himself. James Rowe Sr. had seen in Sysonby's trials that this was one of the good ones, so he wrapped him in blankets and bandages and convinced the owner that the colt was too sick to make the arduous trip.

Thus retained for Rowe's further delight, Sysonby won his first start by ten lengths and went on to three more consecutive triumphs, in major stakes, with similar panache. Then, in the Futurity, he was

beaten by three and a quarter lengths as the filly Artful first unleashed an ability that would lead to her own acclaim for greatness. Artful won by daylight, with Tradition a neck ahead of Sysonby for second.

Several days later, Sysonby's groom was seen to be wielding the sort of money roll more likely associated with a Silver Fox of Wall Street or a Western copper miner. This led to an interrogation, during which Keene elicited the confession that the employee had administered bromidian (a tranquilizer) to the horse before the race. Presumably, as matters transpired, the incident cost Sysonby the opportunity to retire unbeaten in fifteen starts and thus match exactly the record to be established a few years later by Colin. (In fairness to Artful, it perhaps should not be taken as a given that a healthy Sysonby could have beaten her in the Futurity.)

Sysonby suffered no lingering effects, apparently, for he came back three weeks later to win the Junior Champion Stakes. He was not seen under colors again until that glorious opening day at Belmont Park, when a great crowd converged in fine carriages and with their elegant ladies in their own fine livery.

A field of twelve showed up for the Metropolitan. Sysonby, as a three-year-old early in the year, was assigned 107 pounds, with the four-year-old Race King in at only 97. This was a difference of ten pounds of actual weight, but a difference of thirty pounds according to the scale of weights for the season and distance. The field also included the great filly Beldame. One of Beldame's two defeats from fourteen starts at three had come in the Metropolitan of the previous year, at Morris Park. Although she would win only two races from ten starts as a four-year-old, one of them was the Suburban Handicap. Beldame was the top weight in the 1905 Met, at 122 pounds. The weights ranged down to ninety-five pounds.

Despite the severity of the challenge in his first race at three, and despite the defeat in the Futurity, Sysonby was the favorite at 2-1, Beldame second choice at 4-1. Race King, a son of Tenny—Orderlette, by Order, bred by Edward Frazer, was a 20-1 shot.

Conjectured *The Thoroughbred Record*, "Race King's position in the race was undoubtedly due more than anything else to his being fit. He had already participated in a number of races this year, and should be at his best, whereas the Metropolitan was a first-out for Sysonby."

O.L. Richards' Race King won fourteen of ninety-nine races in a career spanning from 1903 to 1907. His winning races included the Nursery Handicap and Columbia Handicap, as well as the Metropolitan. The hardiness of the horse is illustrated even more strongly by his individual slates at two and four. As a juvenile, he ran thirty-four times, winning eight races. At four, the year he met Sysonby, he ran thirty-nine times, winning four. During 1905 he had won two of six starts prior to the Met.

The writer, identified oddly as "No. 10," went on to quote himself from the previous autumn as having observed, "It is not well to be making excuses for beaten horses, nor is it wise policy to condemn them

on one defeat, and we shall have to wait until another year before we are able to gauge accurately the true merits of Sysonby."

The Metropolitan began that process. Sysonby took the early lead and had a length over Race King after a quarter-mile, although the chart noted that Sysonby "did not have the dazzling early foot that

Courtesy Ken Grayson

Sysonby won fourteen of fifteen races.

characterized him last season."

Sysonby and Race King ran first and second almost the whole way. After a half-mile, Sysonby had edged out to one and a half lengths, but Race King was to show "rare gameness" in the words of the chart caller, and he began to cut into the lead. By the furlong pole, Sysonby's margin had shrunk to a half-length, and Race King continued to creep up. In a furious final furlong, Sysonby strove to hold him off, but the older, lightly weighted runner came to what the judges could only discern to be even terms. The first great race at Belmont Park had produced a dead heat.

The six-year-old Colonial Girl was third, six lengths behind.

"What a marvelous capacity Mr. Vosburgh, the Official Handicapper, has for accurately gauging the capability of any race horse was well brought out by the finish of the Metropolitan Handicap," No. 10 observed. "I cannot quite see how the pencilers can make out one horse a favorite over the other when one of Mr. Vosburgh's handicaps is down for decision."

Racegoers at the turn of the century.

He chose to make no mention of top weight Beldame's having finished ninth, beaten about seven lengths.

No. 10 was correct in his observation that Sysonby "will from now on be a hard one to beat." In eight subsequent starts, he won eight times, giving him a record of fourteen wins in fifteen starts. So brilliant was Sysonby that at least one generation of horsemen for many years generally ranked him with Man o' War, Citation, and Colin as the top four horses of the century.

Sysonby was meant to race on at four, but he contracted what was diagnosed as a liver disease along with the blood malady known as variola. He died in his stall on June 17, 1906. A crowd of 4,000 was reported at his burial the following day. Sysonby was later exhumed, and his skeleton was placed on display the following year at the American Museum of Natural History. (The skeleton is no longer on public display, having been stored off site by the museum.)

Nearly a half-century later, this somber turn of events was treated lightheartedly from the comfort of distance in A.J. Liebling's book *The Honest Rainmaker* (Doubleday & Co., New York, 1953). Liebling recounts that a compatriot he identified as "The Colonel" told him, "Mr. Keene was by then a valetudinarian, swathed in thick-carpeted luxury and surfeited with attendance in the old Waldorf-Astoria, on the site of the present Empire State Building. The triumphs of his horses were to him the most potent of tonics, accountable, according to his physicians, for his continued survival. But the doctors adjured the members of his suite to cushion him against shock as much as possible."

This self-same "Colonel" was a reporter for the *New York Evening Journal*, and acting on the tip of a racetrack contact, rushed to Rowe's stable, where a veterinarian told him that Sysonby was "a goner for certainty." Whereupon, The Colonel reported to his paper that "the great race horse Sysonby was fatally stricken by illness…this evening," and the paper saw fit to publish the headline "Sysonby Dead." Because of the instructions to protect Keene from any bad news his employers could ward off, attendants at Keene's suite denied the allegation. Thus was set into motion a series of rival headlines such as "Turf Scoop Proves Hoax," consigning The Colonel to a long night of despair over how he might continue to support his wife and children. When he arrived next at his employer's office, expecting to be banished, he was embraced instead by the proprietor and greeted with another headline, "Sysonby Died Saturday Night, Trainer Admits." The subterfuge to protect old Mr. Keene had not, of course, continued for long.

The Colonel confessed to Liebling that, "In my memories of equine immortals, Sysonby holds a special place. I sometimes dream of him…charging down upon me as I lie flat on my back on an unidentified racing strip. As he comes thundering down upon me I hear him singing, "Alive, Alive-o," to the tune of "Cockles and Mussels," an air I never hear in my waking moments without a shudder of grim association."

Metropolitan Handicap
Purse: $10,000 Added

4th Race Belmont Park - May 4, 1905

Purse $10,000 added. Three-year-olds and upward. 1 Mile. Main Track. Track: Fast. Net value to winners $5,655 each.

P#	Horse	A	Wgt	Med	Eqp	*Odds	PP	St	1/4	1/2	3/4	Str	Fin	Jockey
12	Sysonby	3	107		w	3-1	12	2	1^{1}	$1^{1\frac{1}{2}}$	$1^{1\frac{1}{2}}$	$1^{1\frac{1}{2}}$	$1^{\dagger}$	Shaw
3	Race King	4	97		wb	20-1	3	1	$2^{1\frac{1}{2}}$	$2^{1\frac{1}{2}}$	2^{2}	2^{h}	$1^{\dagger 5}$	L Smith
9	Colonial Girl‡	6	111		w	‡10-1	9	9	5^{h}	5^{h}	6^{h}	3^{h}	3^{4}	A W B'ker
5	Oxford	3	100		w	12-1	5	6	$7^{1\frac{1}{2}}$	$7^{1\frac{1}{2}}$	7^{h}	6^{h}	4^{1}	R McDan'l
10	Dolly Spanker	4	114		wb	10-1	10	8	$6^{1\frac{1}{2}}$	$6^{1\frac{1}{2}}$	5^{h}	5^{h}	5^{h}	Redfern
7	First Mason‡	5	117		wb	‡10-1	7	3	8	8	8	8^{h}	6^{2}	Lyne
6	Kehailan	3	95		wb	50-1	6	12	10	10	10	9	7^{2}	Kent
8	Wotan	4	98		w	8-1	8	5	$4^{1\frac{1}{2}}$	$4^{1\frac{1}{2}}$	4^{1}	4^{h}	8^{1}	J Kelly
4	Beldame	4	122		w	3-1	4	4	$3^{1\frac{1}{2}}$	3^{1}	3^{h}	$7^{1\frac{1}{2}}$	9	F O'Neill
2	Ormonde's Right	4	108		wb	15-1	2	11	12	12	12	10	10	W Davis
1	Santa Catalina	3	98		w	12-1	1	10	11	11	11	11	11	W Miller
11	Jacquin	4	100		w	15-1	11	7	9	9	9	12	12	C'mmins

† Dead heat; purse divided. ‡Coupled in betting.

Off Time: 4:15 **Time Of Race:** :12⅖ :25⅗ :49 1:41⅗
Start: Good For All but Ormonde's Right **Track:** Fast
Equipment: w for whip; b for blinkers

Winner: Sysonby, b. c. by Melton—Optime, by Orme (Trained by J. Rowe); bred by Marcus Daly in Ky.
Race King, ch. c. by Tenny—Orderlette, by Order (Trained by J. McLaughlin); bred by Edward Frazer in Ky.

Won driving; second the same.
SYSONBY quickly took the lead and showed the most speed, but RACE KING held to him all the way. Both came to the extreme outside and fought it out. SYSONBY might have won had Shaw used his whip, as it was, the weight told on him in a hard finish and they passed the judges on even terms. RACE KING was lucky and finished gamely. COLONIAL GIRL closed up courageously in the stretch and was best of the others. DOLLY SPANKER closed a big gap and saved ground on the turn. BELDAME showed speed, but tired in the deep going after six furlongs had been run. WOTAN was a sharp contender to the final furlong. ORMONDE'S RIGHT got off poorly. OXFORD ran a high-class race.
Scratched—Delhi, 124; Tanya, 99; Leonidas, 105; Pasadena, 104; Siglight, 93; Roseben, 111.
Overweight—Race King, 3 pounds.

Owners: (12) J R Keene; (3) O L Richards; (9) C E Rowe; (5) J McLaughlin; (10) R T Wilson Jr; (7) C E Rowe; (6) J L Holland; (8) S Deimel; (4) A Belmont; (2) S Paget; (1) Albemarle Stable; (11) D C Johnson

©DAILY RACING FORM/EQUIBASE

* Because bookmakers were used during this era, this chart does not show all available odds.

*Man o' War showing his mettle
against John P. Grier in the
Dwyer Stakes.*

- CHAPTER 2 -

The Challenge of the Myth

At the conclusion of the twentieth century, various polls voted Man o' War as that era's best horse. Man o' War flashed and flourished as a racehorse from 1919 to 1920 and then for more than a quarter-century presided over a legacy-enhancing stallion career as the monarch of Kentucky tourism at Faraway Farm in Kentucky.

Man o' War won twenty of twenty-one races in his two seasons on the Turf. Not surprisingly, his one loss is perhaps his most famous race, for the sake of sheer disbelief. Man o' War was two years old at the time and had won six races before he met enough traffic problems and front-running speed that he missed catching Upset by a half-length in the Sanford Memorial.

If that race stands as a prototype of a Thoroughbred contest gone awry, the Dwyer Stakes of the next summer stands as a beacon of horse racing's sheer *mano a mano*. In this case, it was Man o' War versus John P. Grier, and the results echo over more than eighty years into the realm of great moments.

For here was a champion tried and tested, and not found wanting — fact and fable incarnate.

><→>∘<←≺

Man o' War was a child of the post-World War I euphoria of American society. His final racing year was at the dawn of the roaring twenties, a decade that produced immortals in numerous sports — Babe Ruth in baseball, Red Grange in football, and Jack Dempsey in the boxing ring. Although the Kentucky Derby had for the last five years or so achieved a status perhaps unique on the Turf, Man o' War had become the most famous of horses before he even reached the age to be seen as a Derby contender. The racing historian John Hervey observed that "…it was from his victory in the Hopeful Stakes (at two in Saratoga) onward that the career of Man o' War began to be followed by a largess of praise that soon became unprecedented…Publications of all kinds, in which ordinarily no notice whatsoever was paid to such an animal as a race horse, featured him conspicuously…He was dubbed 'the

17

Man o' War easily held off John P. Grier in the Travers Stakes some weeks after the Dwyer.

most photographed horse in the world,' and that he deserved the title is beyond contradiction."

Samuel D. Riddle, the Pennsylvania country squire and sportsman who had purchased Man o' War as a yearling for five-thousand dollars, did not allow trainer Louis Feustel to prepare Man o' War for the Derby. Riddle felt one and a quarter miles in May was too much to ask of a three-year-old, and did not run a horse in the race until many years later when he was persuaded to let Man o' War's most noted son, War Admiral, have his chance for the Triple Crown. That series of races had become crystallized in the intervening years, whereas when Sir Barton had won it in 1919, the series of races was not even known as the Triple Crown.

The other two races that became part of the Crown, the Preakness and Belmont Stakes, were on Man o' War's schedule, however. He galloped

home in the Preakness in his debut at three, eight months after the Futurity Stakes had occasioned his ninth victory in ten starts as a two-year-old.

Upset, who had lowered Man o' War's colors in the shocking Sanford Memorial, finished second. That he was back to try again in the Preakness was part of a pattern of his trainer, James Rowe, knocking his head against the wall that Man o' War constructed. Rowe trained for a top stable of the day, that of Harry Payne Whitney, and ran relays of horses at Man o' War. At the end of Man o' War's career, Rowe still had only the Sanford to show for his and his boss' stubbornness — or sportsmanship.

After the Preakness, Man o' War trod happily through victories in the Withers Stakes, Belmont Stakes, and Stuyvesant Handicap. "New American record" was a frequent footnote to his victories.

There was one colt of rising acclaim that he had

not yet met at three, however. This was Whitney's and Rowe's John P. Grier.

John P. Grier (Whisk Broom II—Wonder, by Disguise) had finished second to Man o' War, beaten two and a half lengths, in the Futurity at the end of their two-year-old season, but had convinced observers that he had continued maturing at a significant rate. John P. Grier had won twice at three, and

War's dance card would need: "Man o' War had been referred to as the champion throughout this season, but all the while there was one colt which he had not met…John P. Grier was the last of the good ones of his age to be sent after the mighty son of Fair Play." (Man o' War was by Fair Play—Mahubah, by Rock Sand, and was bred by August Belmont II, a great owner-breeder and racing leader who sold a

SUTCLIFFE

John P. Grier, a worthy opponent.

Rowe had made no secret that he had his eye on the Dwyer Stakes, a one and one-eighth-mile event for three-year-olds run at Aqueduct in New York. Riddle and Feustel saw no reason to dance away from a collision course.

Fred Van Ness of *The New York Times* verified that a meeting with John P. Grier was an event Man o'

number of yearlings while serving the U.S. war effort in an administrative post abroad.)

Rowe had finessed this meeting to perfection, for conditions based on earnings, etc., dictated that John P. Grier got in with 108 pounds, while Man o' War would tote 126! Clarence Kummer, who would ride Man o' War in the Dwyer, had also ridden the other colt and observed that John P. Grier was "marvelously fast." He expressed confidence, however, that the Whitney colorbearer could not beat Man o' War. Eddie Ambrose would be aboard John P. Grier.

BROWNIE LEACH

Samuel D. Riddle and Man o' War.

Owner Riddle sought to dictate the race in some detail, and his manner bespoke his confidence in Man o' War. "Lay along with Grier all the way," he told Kummer, "and if you find you can win, don't try to ride him out, but win by a length or two lengths."

Ambrose, too, had the thought to "lay along," but it would not be a casual outing. The two broke together. The larger Man o' War, on the inside, blocked the sight of John P. Grier from the stands to an extent that some of the 25,000 witnesses had the impression the Whitney colt had been left at the post.

Even considering that there was nothing else in the race to come along and pass tiring horses, the pace was indiscriminate. They raced through a quarter-mile in :23⅖. Man o' War had a half-length lead. John P. Grier was capable of better, and after another quarter-mile in :22⅗ the pair were virtually nose to nose.

On they sped. The next quarter-mile was recorded at :23⅗, for six furlongs in 1:09⅗. The Dwyer has often been inaccurately described as the only time a horse went with Man o' War from the start. In fact, the big colt dropped off the early pace several times. What was true, though, was that Grier was the one horse that went with Man o' War early and was still around after a number of furlongs to continue to contest the issue.

The fourth quarter-mile saw the inevitable slowing of the pace, to :26⅖. Man o' War had weathered Grier's early bravado, but the same was true of the other. Not only was John P. Grier still there, but he got his head in front!

The prospect of the defeat of a great champion — an idol, a staff of consistency — swamps the senses. It is shocking, but compelling. You may be repulsed, but you cannot look away. The crowd engrossed in the 1920 Dwyer had to face the stomach-kick thought that Man o' War was about to be defeated. Then Kummer reached back and smacked Man o' War with his whip — a brazen violation of the colt's prevailing image of easy superiority. Trainer Feustel said years later that he had taken up a position in the infield and he began to scramble down toward the finish line shouting "Come on, Big Red! Come on, Big Red!"

Big Red — Man o' War' s immortal public nickname thereafter — felt the urgency. He charged back into the lead. Grier had been repelled. But no! Here he came again for one final rush. There were but fifty yards to cover, and the race was still hot. Then, finally, Grier stared into the abyss of reality. Nature had decreed that there was but one Man o' War at a time, and Grier was not the anointed. He didn't like it, but he couldn't change it.

In the final yards, Man o' War drew out, winning by one and a half lengths. What was all the excitement about?

The final furlong was run in :13⅕, and the composite time of 1:49⅕ was another new American record.

Man o' War continued unbeaten at three, his career concluding with a galloping victory over Sir Barton in a match race in Canada. He had won twenty of twenty-one and earned an unprecedented $249,465. Grier and Upset were sent to try again, in the Travers, but were no longer competitive.

Man o' War became a leading sire as well as a public hero. John P. Grier was neither, although with ten-percent stakes winners he was a very good stallion. Man o' War lived to the age of thirty. He died in 1947 at the Faraway Farm of Riddle and his family near Lexington, Kentucky. His likeness was executed in bronze by Herbert Haseltine, and this heroic-sized statue today stands at the Kentucky Horse Park in Lexington.

For the most part, Man o' War's speed as a racehorse was unassailable, but courage is something we admire in the Thoroughbred, too. Man o' War passed that test on a summer day in 1920. He had John P. Grier to thank for that.

Dwyer Stakes
Purse: $6,000 Guaranteed

4th Race Aqueduct - July 10, 1920

Purse $6,000. Three-year-olds. 1 1-8 Miles. Main Track. Track: Fast. Net value to winner $4,850; second, $700.

P#	Horse	A	Wgt	Med	Eqp	*Odds	PP	St	1/4	1/2	3/4	Str	Fin	Jockey
1	Man o' War	3	126		w	1-3	1	2	1½	1h	1h	1½	1 1½	C Kummer
2	John P. Grier	3	108		w	2-1	2	1	2	2	2	2	2	E Ambrose

Off Time: 4:07 **Time Of Race:** :23⅗ :46 1:09⅗ 1:36 1:49⅕ (new American record)
Start: Good For All **Track:** Fast
Equipment: w for whip

Winner: Man o' War, ch. c. by Fair Play—Mahubah, by Rock Sand (Trained by L. Feustel).
Bred by Mr. August Belmont in Ky.

Start good and slow. Won easily; second driving.
MAN O' WAR set a great pace under steady restraint for the first three-quarters, then responded gamely when called on in the race through the homestretch and drew away under hard riding in the last sixteenth. JOHN P. GRIER ran lapped on the leader to the last eighth and had a slight lead between calls in the homestretch, but tired in the last seventy yards and was eased up in the closing strides.

Owners: (1) Glen Riddle Farm; (2) H P Whitney

©DAILY RACING FORM/EQUIBASE

* Because bookmakers were used during this era, this chart does not show all available odds.

*Exterminator holds off Grey Lag in the
1922 Brooklyn Handicap.*

- CHAPTER 3 -

Old Bones Supreme

American racing has been elevated by an honor roll of horses that excelled at the exacting discipline of handicap racing. Racing secretaries assign weights with the theoretical intention of equalizing the field. In the earlier decades of the twentieth century, weight spreads of thirty or forty pounds were not unheard of, and valiant weight carriers took up well over 130 pounds without a complaint.

The true great weight carriers are perhaps a thing of the past, lost to modern racetrack management's need to compete for the best horses and perhaps by a general fear that the Thoroughbred is less hardy than before. In the last two decades or so, some few horses have breached the 130 pounds threshold successfully, including Spectacular Bid, John Henry, Cigar, Skip Away, and Sky Beauty. While these deserve respect as outstanding handicappers within the context of their own times, when we speak of great weight carriers, the tendency is to start at Forego and look back.

The last truly astonishing weight-carrying feat

was Forego's drive from seeming defeat to catch Honest Pleasure in time to win the 1976 Marlboro Cup, then one of the most important races in the land. Forego was a familiar and well-beloved old fellow by then, a six-year-old about to secure his third Horse of the Year title. In the signature handicap achievement in a career laced with 130-plus-pound victories, Forego hefted 137 pounds that day! Honest Pleasure, a three-year-old, carried 119.

The decade of the 1960s had also seen a great gelding in Kelso, whose sweep of the New York Handicap triple crown included his Brooklyn Handicap score under 136. Weights of 130-plus were a staple in Kelso's life as he toured through an unmatched five Horse of the Year titles.

Damascus, Dr. Fager, and Buckpasser also were among distinguished weight carriers of the 1960s, and the previous decade had seen similar achievements by such as Tom Fool, Bold Ruler, and Round Table.

The 1940s had been a time of great vitality in the

handicap ranks. Generally, the economics of racing and breeding mean that great colts are retired to stud after relatively short racing careers, and so in the nature of things many of our long-lasting handicappers are geldings. In the middle 1940s, however, consecutive leading money-earners Assault and Stymie were entire males whose racing careers spanned sev-

Grey Lag with Earl Sande up.

eral years. A personal favorite among handicaps from history was Assault's head triumph over Stymie, with the grand mare Gallorette third, in the 1947 Butler Handicap. Going one and three-sixteenths miles, Assault toted 135, giving nine pounds to Stymie and eighteen to Gallorette.

The decade of the 1940s had begun with the conclusion of the career of Seabiscuit, another distinguished weight carrier. During the 1930s he had been joined by the likes of Equipoise and, perhaps

the greatest weight carrier of all, Discovery. In the third of his three consecutive triumphs in the Brooklyn Handicap, Discovery carried 136 pounds. He also won under as much as 139 and once was tried under 143 pounds!

The earlier decades of the century had seen the startling victory of Whisk Broom II under 139 pounds in the 1913 Suburban Handicap. His victory in record time of 2:00 under that weight for one and a quarter miles was so sensational as to be, well, unbelievable. At least there was doubt as to the accuracy of the timing, which stood as a record in New York until matched by Kelso and eventually broken by Gun Bow in 1964.

The sprinters Pan Zareta and Old Rosebud had seen their assignments edge into the 140-pound category, and the great Man o' War had carried 138 pounds in winning a handicap as a three-year-old.

Chosen to represent such great weight-carrying feats for this volume is a race from 1922. An early version of Kelso and Forego, the great gelding Exterminator took up 135 pounds for the Brooklyn Handicap. He was giving nine pounds to the champion Grey Lag, a four-year-old, and thirty-two pounds to the filly Polly Ann. A thrilling stretch run ensued, perhaps stroking the emotions of Exterminator's fans in a similar manner of Forego's last-gasp victory in the 1976 Marlboro.

Exterminator was bred in the name of F.D. (Dixie) Knight and was foaled in 1915 at the Knight family farm near Nicholasville, Kentucky. He was by the stallion McGee, who had the happy distinction of being the only foal sired by White Knight before the latter was gelded. The dam of Exterminator was Fair Empress, whose sire, Jim Gore, was a son of the great Hindoo.

Over the name of Charles Brossman, this female family was described in a 1922 article in *The Thoroughbred Record* as "the old-fashioned American type; the kind that produces winners that race year after year, rugged, stout-hearted and dependable." Brossman took the occasion to lecture a bit on the subject, with an acerbic Anglophobic slant: "…American breeders have been advised by the so-called English experts to quit breeding mares with bloodlines like Exterminator's dam, Fair Empress. [Some of which were then ineligible to the *General Stud Book*.]…The only thing Exterminator lacks is a number [an apparent reference to the Bruce Lowe System of numbering foundation female families in the *General Stud Book*]. Kentucky breeders can be proud of the fact that numerous mares, bred along the same lines as Fair Empress, are owned in the state…As long as this condition prevails, Kentucky will continue to breed winning race horses. If by any chance these mares should be discarded, it would be a national calamity, and Kentucky, as a breeding state, would degenerate into the same condition that England is now."

While the English Thoroughbred was hardly in decline, Brossman's eulogizing of such qualities as dependability and ruggedness was appropriate, and it certainly fit Exterminator's case. The horse campaigned from two through nine. By including a special exhibition race against time, his record traditionally has been described neatly as an even one hundred starts, with an even fifty wins — easy to remember. Less easily recalled would be the names of the nine trainers Exterminator had over the years. Such a revolving door of horsemen is a commentary on Exterminator's adaptability — and perhaps an insight into what it was like to work for a snake-oil salesman. Well, maybe that designation is needlessly unkind, but the owner in question, Willis Sharpe Kilmer, had made his fortune as a patent medicine purveyor and at one point in his career conjectured that he was "the most unpopular man in the country."

Kilmer was a combination of P.T. Barnum, W.C. Fields, and Bill Gates. He oiled his way into a family business and soon cast out his brethren. With a combination of audacity and an early understanding of saturation advertising, he turned a "kidney specific" known as Swamproot into a fortune estimated at $30 million. Journalism of the day was perhaps not as pervasive as it is now, with television added to the mix, but it could be lethal if not met with resolve. Reportage about Swamproot at one stage was harassing Kilmer even in his hometown of Binghamton, New York. According to Gerald Carson's history of patent medicine, delightfully entitled *One For A Man, Two For A Horse*, Kilmer eventually concluded that he must do the only manly thing available: he started a rival newspaper, which drove the previous one into bankruptcy, effectively silencing the criticism.

Upon the foundations of wealth initiated by Swamproot, Kilmer began to pay back the public. Donning a flaming red cloak, he popularized the game of golf in his section of New York, and he supplied many a dollar to many a charity. In time he was a respected publisher, as the motivation for his original investment in that field faded in the bonhomie of the country club. Moreover, he had a passion for speed, in a sporting sort of way. He drove trotting horses as a youth and moved on to automobile racing to pilot the "Green Demon" in the Vanderbilt Cup, one of the first great races for internal-combustion four-wheelers. Then, in 1916, Kilmer bought his first Thoroughbred racing prospects. Exterminator was not among them, but he was to follow rather soon.

Having been bought at Saratoga as a yearling for $1,500 in 1916, Exterminator began racing for J. Cal Milam. He won two of four races at two. The following spring Exterminator caught the eye of Henry McDaniel, trainer of the top colt of the day, Kilmer's Sun Briar, but McDaniel wanted him as a workmate. For that humble role, Kilmer was willing to pay a high price for Exterminator — reported from $9,000 to as much as $15,000 in some accounts. Whatever the exact figure, it seems certain that Milam made a tidy profit on the gelding.

Sun Briar did not train well enough to run in the Kentucky Derby, for which Kilmer had been pointing, but since Exterminator, the new sparring partner, was around, he was entered instead. At 30-1, he closed in the stretch to win by a length. American fans take Kentucky Derby winners to their hearts, but their love affair with this upstart did not warm in earnest for some time. He lost his next five races, giving little hint of what was to come. By the end of his career, however, Exterminator had shown all that ruggedness and dependability, and he had done it winning races from six furlongs to two and a quarter miles. He carried up to 138 pounds to victory

and accepted as much as 140. He carried 130 pounds or more thirty-five times and won twenty. He was around a long time, winning the Saratoga Cup four straight years and the Pimlico Cup three times. Exterminator's angular frame gave rise to the affectionate nickname Old Bones, which also had been employed three decades before in salute of another gallant gelding, Raceland.

Nevertheless, the challenge in the 1922 Brooklyn Handicap was so severe that many of his ardent supporters were just hoping for, rather than expecting, victory. He was giving nine pounds to Grey Lag. That this foe was an exceptional animal is quickly demonstrable in the opinion expressed by his breeder, John E. Madden: Grey Lag was the best horse he ever bred. This placed him above the Triple Crown winner Sir Barton in the estimation of the great horseman.

Grey Lag was by the five-time leading sire Star Shoot, out of the Meddler mare Miss Minnie. Max Hirsch, then a young trainer and wheeler-dealer on the way up, bought him along with a filly for $10,000 from Madden. Grey Lag was named for a type of wild goose in Northern Europe, a somewhat threatening name for a pedigree with a sire named "Shoot." He won the Champagne Stakes by six lengths at two, and Hirsch was able to sell him that fall for $60,000. The buyer was one of the high rollers of the era, Harry F. Sinclair, who gave his name to his oil company and who owned the great Rancocas Farm in New Jersey. Sam Hildreth trained Grey Lag for Sinclair. By the time of Grey Lag's showdown with Exterminator in the 1922 Brooklyn, the chestnut colt had developed into a champion. Historians tend to rate him the best three-year-old of 1921, co-champion with Exterminator as best older horse of 1922, and champion alone again at five. If there had been a Horse of the Year voting, Grey Lag most likely would have been that horse in 1921 and Exterminator in 1922.

At three in 1921, Grey Lag was forced to miss the Derby because of a stone bruise, but he later got rolling and won eight consecutive races. This skein began with the Belmont Stakes and also included victory in his first Brooklyn Handicap battle with Exterminator. As a three-year-old in the summer, Grey Lag got in with 112 pounds to Exterminator's 129. The top weight at 132 was Mad Hatter, and in with 124 was John P. Grier, the only horse to push

ments were up to as much as 135 pounds, under which he won the Knickerbocker Handicap.

He tailed off late in the year and was rested from September until the following June. He came back with a win in a handicap, under 126 pounds, and was ready for the next Brooklyn Handicap. Exterminator had already run seven times as a seven-year-old that year, winning six, including the Kentucky Handicap under 138 pounds. He went into the Brooklyn with a winning streak of five races.

Still, Exterminator was carrying 135 pounds and giving nine pounds to a younger champion of spe-

Exterminator working with stablemate Sun Briar (on rail).

Man o' War in a cleanly run race. Moreover, the field included another Kentucky Derby winner, Paul Jones, in addition to Exterminator. Grey Lag dashed them all, pulling away by one and a half lengths over John P. Grier, with Exterminator third. By the end of the year, Grey Lag's weight assign-

cial brilliance. The smart bet was to go with youth, it seemed, and Grey Lag was favored at 7-10. Polly Ann, Captain Alcock, and Bersagliere formed the short supporting cast in the field of five.

Polly Ann dashed off to a lead of about a length with a half-mile in :47⅗. Laverne Fator on Grey Lag and Albert Johnson on Exterminator trailed closely in second and third, respectively. Leaving the backstretch, Polly Ann drifted out enough for Fator to bring Grey Lag through on the inside. Grey Lag turned for home in front, running strongly. Nevertheless, he was just wide enough that the gallant old Exterminator had room to come through on the rail. It was a grinding, demanding effort for the oldster to wear down the younger champion, but neither age nor weight dissuaded him. Exterminator got up in time to win by a head in 1:50. Polly Ann held on for third, beaten four lengths.

The *Record*'s reporter was ecstatic:

"In a stretch duel that will be long memorable to racegoers, the ever-youthful Exterminator — greatest gelding of them all — shouldering 135 pounds like a Titan, wore down the lighter weighted Grey Lag and outgamed him in the final furlongs of today's renewal of the historic Brooklyn Handicap…the two giants settled down for that long, hard stretch battle. Polly Ann finally weakened and dropped back. Then the fight was on, and they were both game and fit. With that bulldog courage that has carried him to victory so often, the old son of McGee stuck to his task under Johnson's urging and, though he threw his tail in the air once, as though indicating that he was giving up his last ounce, he never faltered…Right to the finish they charged closely lapped, but old Exterminator had finally earned a lead of a head, and it was his to hold.

"There was a big opening day (at Aqueduct) throng on hand to witness the duel between Exterminator and Grey Lag, and while these two were given an ovation as they stepped on the track, it was mild compared to the reception accorded the Willis Sharpe Kilmer star when he jogged back to the scales after his victory."

The case might be made that the Brooklyn took a little out of Exterminator that he never got back, but the evidence is far from conclusive. After the race his trainer at the moment, Gene Wayland, went to the barn to check on him and was advised by his foreman, Blink McCloskey, that "he looks as if he's all through, boss. He turned his tail to the feed box, and won't eat. He never did that before."

Exterminator did get a month's rest, but thereafter was not gingerly treated, either by Wayland or racing secretaries. His next start found him struggling home sixth under 140 pounds, but a month later he won the Saratoga Cup to launch a brief, three-race winning streak (including the aforementioned exhibition). From there, he was to win five of the remaining fourteen races of his career, last competing on June 21, 1924, when he finished third as a nine-year-old in the Queen's Hotel Handicap at Canada's Dorval Park.

His earnings of $252,996 exceeded those of Man o' War by a small margin and stood second to the all-time record in that era, Zev's $313,639.

Kilmer had a variety of places to house a pensioned champion. Exterminator lived in retirement for twenty-one years, attaining the age of thirty, and he was stationed from time to time at Remlik (Kilmer spelled backward) Hall in Virginia, Court Manor, also in Virginia, and finally at Sun Briar Court in Binghamton, New York. The last name was ironic, and had he been human Exterminator might have wondered why, years later, the name of an admirable, but less-distinguished old stablemate was so honored instead of his own. Kilmer would have had the ready response that "Exterminator Court" would hardly be an inviting name, nor would "Old Bones Manor," while "Rotanimretxe Hall" would be linguistically and aesthetically prohibitive. Moreover, Sun Briar became a foundation stallion in Kilmer's successful breeding enterprise.

Although a gelding, Exterminator was not overshadowed as a sire by his Brooklyn foe Grey Lag to the extent one might assume. Grey Lag proved virtually sterile and was brought back to the races by Hildreth. He won three of six starts at nine and ten before being retired again and given away as a riding horse. The new owner died, and his estate sold off the horse, who, amazingly, showed up back in training in Canada at the age of thirteen, placing once in four races to earn $40. Sinclair heard of this travesty and sent an agent to buy the old champion and return him to the splendor of Rancocas.

A postscript to the 1922 Brooklyn was a poem published in the *Chicago Tribune* in honor of Exterminator, written by a fellow named, like Old Bones' sire, McGee — Guy McGee:

Exterminator — That's All

Who is it laughs at the years that flow?
Who it is always gets the dough?
Whose only creed is go and go?
                    Exterminator

Who's never ridden for a fall?
Who is it tackles one and all?
Who meets and beats'em, great and small?
                    Exterminator

Who is it ever just the same?
Who is it never shames the game?
Who is it sticks close to his name?
                    Exterminator

Brooklyn Handicap
Purse: $10,000 Guaranteed

4th Race   Aqueduct - June 16, 1922
Purse $10,000. Three-year-olds and upward. 1 1-8 Miles. Main Track. Track: Fast. Net value to winner $7,600; second, $1,500; third, $750.

P#	Horse	A	Wgt	Med	Eqp	*Odds	PP	St	1/4	1/2	3/4	Str	Fin	Jockey
2	Exterminator	7	135		w	6-5	2	5	3²	3³	2³	2³	1ʰ	A Johnson
1	Grey Lag	4	126		wb	4-5	1	4	2¹	2¹	1½	1ʰ	2⁴	L Fator
3	Polly Ann	4	103		wb	30-1	3	3	1²	1¹	3²	3¹	3ʰ	C Lang
4	Captain Alcock	5	116		ws	20-1	4	2	4¹	4¹	4⁸	4⁸	4¹⁰	C Ponce
5	Bersagliere	5	105		wb	20-1	5	1	5	5	5	5	5	J Callahan

Off Time: 3:50   **Time Of Race:**   :24   :47⅗   1:12⅗   1:37   1:50
Start: Good For All   **Track:** Fast
Equipment: w for whip; b for blinkers; s for spurs

Winner: Exterminator, ch. g. by McGee—Fair Empress, by Jim Gore (Trained by E. Wayland).
          Bred by Mr. Frederick D. Knight in Ky.

Start good and slow. Won driving; second and third the same.
EXTERMINATOR raced in close pursuit of the early leaders under restraint and close to the inner rail all the way and, improving his position gradually, outfinished GREY LAG in a grand finish. The latter was well ridden and took the lead when entering the stretch and tired in the last eighth, but held on with splendid courage in the final drive. POLLY ANN rushed into the lead and displayed fine speed, but tired in the last quarter mile. CAPTAIN ALCOCK showed early speed and finished resolutely. BERSAGLIERE was outrun all the way.
Scratched—Mad Hatter, 128; Sennings Park, 122; Devastation, 102.

Owners: (2) W S Kilmer; (1) Rancocas Stable; (3) S L Jenkins; (4) Quincy Stable; (5) G A Cochran
©DAILY RACING FORM/EQUIBASE

* Because bookmakers were used during this era, this chart does not show all available odds.

Equipoise, the mud-splattered Pimlico Futurity victor.

- CHAPTER 4 -

The Grand Young Soldiers

"Prodigal wasters of speed" was how the late Joe Estes described Equipoise and Twenty Grand in a poem in *The Blood-Horse*, of which he was the erudite editor for many years. It was an apt description for these two, who represented one of the best foal crops in American history and who blazed down the stretch at one another's blue-blooded throats thrice in succession in the autumn of 1930.

Equipoise and Twenty Grand were produced by two of the grand Eastern stables of their day, and theirs was a day when grand Eastern stables were collectively far more dominant than can be the case today. Their breeders and owners were relatives. Equipoise was bred by Harry Payne Whitney, who assumed the mantle of leadership of the Whitney clan from his father, William Collins Whitney. The latter had a brief but productive soiree on the Turf, and Harry Payne Whitney took full advantage of having an earlier start as a sportsman and led America's breeders eleven times and the owners' list six times. Twenty Grand was bred and raced by Harry Payne Whitney's sister-in-law, Mrs. Payne Whitney. (Yes, the family loved the name Payne.) This Mrs. Whitney was the owner of Greentree Stud, and while her numbers could not match the brother-in-law's, she did lead both America's breeders' and owners' lists in 1942.

Equipoise was by Pennant—Swinging, by Broomstick. He was a dark liver chestnut colt of such surpassing handsomeness that veteran observers rhapsodized over his physical perfection: "…a living harmony in horseflesh" was what the historian John Hervey regarded him. The public nicknamed him "The Chocolate Soldier," after the title of a Broadway play enjoying a revival at the time. At two, Equipoise was trained by Fred Hopkins.

Twenty Grand was a son of St. Germans—Bonus, by All Gold. He was trained at two by Thomas W. Murphy. This bay colt's physical presence also elicited praise, such as racing official and historian Walter Vosburgh's comment that he had "not observed a better looking youngster in several seasons."

Equipoise and Twenty Grand met in their final three races at two. Long before that, Equipoise had established himself as a sprightly contender in a juvenile crop that also included Jamestown and Mate. Before their concluding series, Equipoise had won a

rail and won by a length. Equipoise's followers had the ready excuse that he was giving eleven pounds to the less-established colt.

Both were shipped to Kentucky, still regarded as "the West" insofar as Thoroughbred racing was concerned. They hooked up again on October 16,

Equipoise, known as "The Chocolate Soldier."

half-dozen stakes, while losing the Saratoga Special and Futurity to Jamestown and the Champagne to Mate. Twenty Grand had run only four times, with two allowance victories to show for them.

On October 4, Equipoise and Twenty Grand met at Aqueduct, going a mile in the Junior Champion Stakes. Equipoise rallied in the stretch and seemed to take control, but then Twenty Grand, working his way up from last place, dashed through along the

again at a mile, for the Kentucky Jockey Club Stakes at Churchill Downs. "By all accounts," wrote Kent Hollingsworth in *The Great Ones* in 1970, it "was the greatest 2-year-old race ever run in Kentucky."

That time they were carrying equal weight of 122 pounds each, and Equipoise was again the favorite, at 3-4 to the Greentree colt's odds of 5-2.

Sonny Workman on Equipoise allowed rival Don Leon the early lead, but then nudged his colt to a clear margin with five furlongs to go. At that point, "Equipoise stopped racing and began galloping," Charlie Hatton observed a short time later in *The Blood-Horse*, "increasing his lead going around the turn to a good three lengths, running easily and with clocklike precision. Twenty Grand had extricated himself from the pack and was quickening his stride…As they swung into the stretch, Charlie Kurtsinger on Twenty Grand stole a march on Workman and rushed his mount past him ere…he knew what was happening."

Twenty Grand, observed Hatton, "was a length to the good in a jiffy. Workman sensed that he must do something and quickly, if he was to save the day, and his whip arm traveled in the well-known Workman circle three times in rapid succession. By the time they had reached the eighth pole, Equipoise was back on his stride and gaining with every jump on the inside. Both riders were driving to the limit and their mounts responding as only great horses can. It was wonderful to see, and the crowd rose to its feet. The din was deafening."

Neil Newman, writing in Derrydale Press' *Famous Horses of the American Turf* for 1930, recorded that "Equipoise began to creep up on his rival inch by inch, and the distance between the two gallant Thoroughbreds slowly shortened. There was no diminution in the efforts of the horses or riders as they swept under the wire. Instinctively all eyes were riveted on the numbers board."

Again to quote Hatton: "It was nip and tuck, and 70 yards out…it looked for a moment that it might come tuck and nip."

The interval between the end of a great race and the winning number's being posted is one of Thoroughbred racing's most engulfing, albeit maddening, gifts to its followers. In this case, the tension lasted ten minutes, according to Hatton, before being emptied by the number of Twenty Grand appearing on top, he having won by a nose. The time was 1:36, then the fastest time for a mile ever recorded by a two-year-old and a track record as well. The third horse, Knight's Call, was beaten ten lengths.

Estes stipulated that his poetry was meant "to be recited by an old man in 1980" — or a half-century later, a furlong pole he, sadly, did not reach. He captured much of the visceral feel of those special horse races when one comes away not so much thinking of oneself as a fan, but as a privileged witness: "I remember the day, I can see them still/In the Churchill paddock, I hear the shrill/and quickening refrain…And how they shot from the starting gate/and scudded down the backstretch straight/Prodigal wasters of speed…"

About three weeks later, on November 5, the Twenty Grand—Equipoise road show appeared at yet another venue, in Maryland, for the Pimlico Futurity. Human sorrow had intervened. Harry Payne Whitney died on October 26. His young son, C.V. Whitney, was urged by racing leaders to take the mantle of the family tradition. The Pimlico Futurity marked his debut as the owner of a horse in an important race. Photos of the day indicate an unsure and edgy young man, but in time Whitney worked the Turf in among his many business, artistic, and philanthropic interests to become an enduring figure of importance to the sport.

The Pimlico race was run at one and one-sixteenth miles, and again the colts were at level weights. The Futurity was run during a transition

Twenty Grand, who later won the Derby and Belmont.

have control, but Equipoise and Twenty Grand both came calling. Stride for stride, they rallied, and they got to Mate deep in the stretch. Equipoise got there first, and best, and as all three horses scudded under the wire within a length of each other, it was the novice Whitney's colt by a half-length. Twenty Grand got up for second.

Workman was pumped: "My greatest race? Hell, it may have been the greatest race anybody ever saw."

There was no voting for championships, or even an Experimental Free Handicap,

phase of American racing. Maryland had adopted the starting stalls system to begin its races. Starter Jim Milton had a devil of a time getting the field organized, and it was fifteen minutes before the race commenced. Equipoise was away awkwardly, and then horses cut in front of him, the effect being virtually the same as being left at the post. Workman considered whether calling it a day and protecting his colt in the sea of mud that prevailed would be the prudent course.

"When we got shut off and left, I was ready to fold up," he said. "I didn't want to make a good horse work for nothing. Then I looked up through the slush and saw that Twenty Grand was way back, too, and I said to myself that if I could catch him we might have a chance."

Mate was rolling happily in front and seemed to

in 1930, so listings that place Jamestown and Equipoise as co-champions of the division have to be recognized as a retroactive evaluation of an unofficial consensus — hardly the stuff of fact. Nonetheless, the later careers of leaders of 1930 ratify the quality of the foal crop. Equipoise's shelly feet — he lost both front plates in the Pimlico mud lark — and quarter crack problem cost him most of his three-year-old season. In his absence, Mate won the Preakness, run before the Kentucky Derby. Then, Twenty Grand was so brilliant in winning both the Derby and Belmont, plus the Travers and Jockey Club Gold Cup, etc., that some observers were willing to regard him as the best since Man o' War. (That meant only eleven years at the time, but still suggested that Twenty Grand was better than the likes of Sarazen, Crusader, Zev, and Gallant Fox!)

Equipoise eventually would be regarded as the greatest of the lot, with his impressive weight-carrying ability and courage over the next three years. His stallion career was cut short by death after only four crops, but he got Greentree's Derby-Belmont-Travers winner Shut Out and was the leading sire of 1942. Twenty Grand's stallion career was eliminated by sterility, and various efforts to return him to the races, both here and abroad, proved more or less pointless.

A remarkable series of events occurred in 1935. Five years after their brilliant races at two, Equipoise and Twenty Grand, the old "wasters of speed," showed up as seven-year-olds aiming for the Santa Anita Handicap. Their old mate Mate was still around, too. In a prep Equipoise gave nine pounds to Twenty Grand and beat him by a length, only to be taken down by disqualification, Twenty Grand thus getting in the last victory. Then, in the Santa Anita Handicap itself, there was not sufficient speed, or soundness, left to waste, and the three old rivals all finished unplaced. It was not an indication of owners' indifference to their welfare, but perhaps a romantic reluctance to admit to the reality and the rigors of time.

The late failures slide easily from the escutcheons of Equipoise and Twenty Grand. The robust sap of youthful valor is their everlasting image.

Pimlico Futurity
Purse: $40,000 Added

5th Race   Pimlico - November 5, 1930
Purse $40,000 added. Two-year-olds. 1 1-16 Miles. Main Track. Track: Muddy.
Net value to winner $50,360; second, $5,000; third, $2,500; fourth, $1,500.

P#	Horse	A	Wgt	Med	Eqp	Odds	PP	St	1/4	1/2	3/4	Str	Fin	Jockey
2	Equipoise	2	119		wb	.95	2	6	8	8	5^h	2^{nk}	1$^{\frac{1}{2}}$	R Workman
8	Twenty Grand	2	119		w	3.40	8	5	6^h	6^4	6^{12}	4^3	2^{nk}	C Kurtsinger
6	Mate	2	119		w	5.30	6	1	1^{nk}	1$^{1\frac{1}{2}}$	1^1	1^2	3^4	L McAtee
1	Aegis	2	119		w	19.60	1	7	4^3	3^h	2^2	3$^{\frac{1}{2}}$	4^5	F Col'letti
7	Gigantic	2	119		w	34.80	7	4	2$^{1\frac{1}{2}}$	2^1	3$^{1\frac{1}{2}}$	5^{15}	5^{12}	M Garner
3	B'ar Hunter	2	122		wb	72.15	3	8	7^2	5^{nk}	4^{nk}	6^4	6^6	W Cannon
4	Tambour	2	114		wb	14.55	4	2	5^{nk}	7$^{\frac{1}{2}}$	8	8	7^8	L Schaefer
5	Backgammon	2	122		wsb	88.20	5	3	3^{nk}	4^{nk}	7^1	7^1	8	J Bejshak

Off Time: 3:34   **Time Of Race:** :23$\frac{2}{5}$:48$\frac{3}{5}$ 1:14$\frac{2}{5}$ 1:42   1:48$\frac{3}{5}$
Start: Poor out of machine   **Track:** Muddy
Equipment: w for whip; b for blinkers; s for spurs

Mutuel Payoffs
2	Equipoise	$3.90	$2.40	$2.30
8	Twenty Grand		3.30	3.60
6	Mate			2.80

Winner: Equipoise, ch. c. by Pennant—Swinging, by Broomstick (Trained by F. Hopkins).
     Bred by Mr. H. P. Whitney in Ky.

Start poor out of machine. Won driving; second and third the same.
EQUIPOISE began sidewise and horses crossed in front of him, causing him to be left at the post; was an early trailer, but gradually improved his position on the far turn while racing wide, but closing with splendid courage under punishment, got up to outfinish TWENTY GRAND and MATE in the last twenty yards. TWENTY GRAND, outrun early, saved ground entering the stretch and finished next to the rail. MATE began free of interference, was rushed to the front in the run to the first turn, raced GIGANTIC into early defeat and drew away into a good lead, only to tire in the last sixteenth. AEGIS was a contender to the eighth post after being responsible for the long delay at the post. TAMBOUR had a rough race in the early stages.
Scratched—Vander Pool, 122.

Owners: (2) C V Whitney; (8) Greentree Stable; (6) A C Bostwick; (1) W M Jeffords; (7) J E Davis; (3) E R Bradley; (4) P M Burch; (5) Sagamore Stable
©DAILY RACING FORM/EQUIBASE

CALIFORNIA THOROUGHBRED

Phar Lap's lone North American
start fueled his legend.

- CHAPTER 5 -

"The Red Terror" of the Antipodes

Phar Lap raced only once on this continent and defeated a rather modest field, and yet he left the impression of being one of the greatest horses of all time. This was expressed by various individuals, possessing various levels of credibility. The immediate reaction of horseman Pat Knebelkamp that "Phar Lap is the best horse I have ever seen," immediately after the singular performance can be easily discounted, since it was he who had sent out one of the vanquished in Spanish Play. More indicative of the universal awe Phar Lap engendered were testimonials made from memory years later, such as the great trainer Charlie Whittingham's comment during a lifetime of association with champions: "I never got to see Man o' War, but he'd have had to be a helluva horse to be better than Phar Lap."

Then, too, the distinguished international Turfman Paul Mellon in 1996 submitted a list of what "I consider the 10 greatest Thoroughbreds of my lifetime," and he penned in Phar Lap's name alone at the top. When *The Blood-Horse* convened a history-savvy panel to rank the best of the twentieth century, the 1932 Agua Caliente Handicap winner was rated highly, twenty-second in a list of one hundred. (Imagine how great he would have been regarded if he had never raced here at all!)

Phar Lap was enormous, had a long, raking stride and the dignity of a champion, and he clearly had a great deal of charisma. What he also had was good press, and, of course, his lasting reputation was not actually dependent on one day in Mexico. Indeed, he personified in Australia the cliche "legend in his own time."

For the horse-savvy Australians, his emergence had created a tug of emotion similar to that which many Americans would feel when Secretariat came along. In the latter case, we had embraced an acceptance of Man o' War as the greatest of all time, for more than a half-century, and the thought we might be seeing a horse to equal or surpass him created some nostalgic resistance even in its enthralling possibilities. In the case of the Australians, as they watched Phar Lap brighten their morale in the face of a nation's doleful economic picture in the early 1930s, they were being nudged to alter the precept held for forty years. This was that dear old Carbine was and would remain the greatest horse in their history.

Like such later day public heroes as Stymie, Carry Back, and John Henry, Phar Lap presented the sort of ragamuffin-to-regent motif that easily seduces

Phar Lap's imposing presence inspired all of Australia.

the public heart. He was bred in New Zealand, then, as now, a spawning ground of great horses. His were modest enough credentials that he brought but 160 guineas, about eight-hundred U.S. dollars, when offered as a yearling. Foaled in 1926, Phar Lap was bred by A.F. Roberts, who stood his sire, Night Raid, at his modest Seadown

Stud at Timaru. The sire also had started life as a 160 guineas yearling, but in a different currency. He was an English foal by Radium, he a son of the great Bend Or, and was out of a Spearmint mare. Night Raid was unimpressive at two and was sold to an owner in Australia, where he won two races before breaking down. The *Bloodstock Breeders' Review* of 1929 reported that Roberts purchased him for stud "for a few hundred dollars."

The dam of Phar Lap was Entreaty, she by a stallion stuck with the non-macho name of Winkie. That beast, however, was by the St. Simon stallion William the Third. Entreaty had several other winners and so did her dam, but not of the sort to create much impression in a sale catalogue. The next dam, Catherine Wheel, however, had foaled the champion Treadmill.

The trainer Harry Telford was a scuffling sort of horseman who had not yet had a big break, and Phar Lap's was the sort of pedigree he looked for, which is to say, nothing close up to elicit a high price, but with stamina and class influences further out on the page. He induced the American businessman David J. Davis to purchase the yearling. Davis, however, had little interest in racing, and he leased the horse to Telford for three years, the trainer to pay all expenses and reap two-thirds of earnings.

The exact reason the horse was named Phar Lap is unclear. The phrase means "lightning strike" in the Javanese language, but it was also said that Davis chose the name because he was told that it was a scientific term for lightning. (Other accounts of Phar Lap's name list the meaning as Thai for "emitting light from the sky" and Senagalese for "wink in the sky." Maybe Winkie had some influence there, too.)

The gaunt young chestnut gelding made little impression in his early starts. Then he blossomed suddenly during his three-year-old season, winning the Rosehill Guineas, Australian Jockey Club Derby, Victoria Derby, AJC St. Leger, Victoria St. Leger, and other important races. He was third in his first assay in Australia's most revered race, that holiday known as the Melbourne Cup. By the time the Cup came around again during Phar Lap's four-year-old season, he had a winning streak of seven races and had won sixteen of his last seventeen starts.

Perversely illustrative of his public standing by that time was a plot by three journalists, apparently aimed at poking fun at the nation's "Phar Lap hysteria." They concocted a report that a motorist had fired a gun at the horse as he returned from training, and then sped away, suggesting a bookmaker about to lose a packet was trying to frighten the horse into injuring himself. While this was a hoax, it induced extra precautions, and Telford spirited Phar Lap off to a different yard and transported him to the Flemington racecourse in a steel-sided van.

(There is, sadly, some credibility in fears of horses being accosted prior to a race. While this type of crime often involves drugging either to kill or compromise form, an example of a different sort occurred in 1966. The South African hero Sea Cottage was shot in the hindquarters while training for the Durban July Handicap. He came back to race successfully the next year, carrying extra lead both under and behind the saddle!)

Phar Lap won his two-mile Melbourne Cup amid rousing cheers. He carried 138 pounds, giving fourteen pounds to the runner-up, twenty-two pounds to the third-placed finisher, and thirty-one to the Sydney Derby winner Tregilla.

His seven-race winning streak grew to fourteen, during which he won with as much as 143 pounds while taking a seven-furlong race to underscore his versatility. The next year, he authored a new winning streak of eight races before finishing unplaced under 150 pounds while trying for a second Melbourne Cup. (That time, he was accompanied to the post by four attendants, a reflection of a lingering, although perhaps paranoid, memory of the earlier hoax.)

Telford's lease had run out, but Davis allowed the trainer to purchase an interest in the horse, who had become known in some circles as "the Red Terror." The Melbourne Cup of 1931, in which he ran well most of the way, was his last race in Australia. He had won thirty-six of fifty races there in total, but even more impressive was that once he had found himself he had won thirty-one of thirty-four starts!

Owner Davis had visited America sometime prior to Phar Lap's third run in the Melbourne Cup and had signed an agreement for the great horse to run in the Agua Caliente Handicap in Mexico the following winter. Phar Lap was sent to New Zealand for a rest, then sailed for California. Reports later surfaced that Phar Lap might contest an earlier race at California's Tanforan. However, the Caliente management released a statement that their agreement with Davis guaranteed five-thousand dollars, but that amount would be

CHAPTER 5

waived should the horse race on this continent prior to the March 20 Caliente.

Not all had gone well for the track, located not far south of the California-Mexico border. The $100,000 purse for the event was reduced to $50,000, and racing secretary John B. Campbell gave horsemen an opportunity to withdraw. The weights were announced just prior to Campbell's resignation from his post at that track. Phar Lap was assigned 129 pounds, giving from nine to thirty-nine pounds to the forty-two other horses nominated for the mile and a quarter event. Given that his rider, William Elliott, weighed 102 pounds, a total of twenty-seven pounds was to be made up by lead pads, although the horse was undoubtedly accustomed to far more so-called "dead weight" at home.

Phar Lap, accompanied by assistant trainer Tommy Woodcock, arrived at Caliente and had his first work on February 19, going six furlongs in a casual 1:26. His first really serious effort found him working six furlongs again, but knocking more than a dozen seconds off the earlier time. Finally, the singular day arrived. So many things could have gone wrong, but there was the great red gelding in superb condition, many days and 10,000 miles from his last competition.

Charlie Hatton, writing for *The Blood-Horse* under the name Old Rosebud, remarked upon the sheer size of the invader. American horsemen of recent years had regarded Man o' War and Gallant Fox as large Thoroughbreds, he noted, but Phar Lap's essential measurements eclipsed them each as he stood 16.2¼ hands tall and girthed seventy-five and three-quarter inches. Race fans, 15,000 strong, were surprised to see the Australian arrive in the paddock to begin walking after the tenth

race, although the Caliente was the thirteenth race on a fifteen-race program that had started well before noon.

Of his ten rivals, only two were given much chance against him and Phar Lap started the 3-2 choice. Spanish Play (117) was coming off a victory in the New Orleans Handicap eight days before, while Reveille Boy (118) had been training at Caliente and was a recent winner there. The 1929 Preakness winner, Dr. Freeland, was also in the hunt, at 120 pounds.

Reveille Boy's antics held up the start, and he, at length, was assigned to start outside the starting stalls then in use. When the break came, Phar Lap was dilatory in commencing the event, but there was no sense of urgency.

The horseman Kimball Patterson was later quoted to the effect that Woodcock's instructions to Elliott were: "When you leave the gate, canter down the front side, and when you get to the backside, gallop on home."

Elliott more or less followed that pattern, but with an added dramatic flourish. Early in the backstretch, Cabezo was earnestly racing along in front under his one-hundred pounds, but about halfway down that side of the track, Elliott gave Phar Lap his head. The great red strider rushed past his field and was three and a half lengths in front by the time they came again to a turn.

"After such a withering burst of speed, jockey Elliott figured that he must have squelched the hopes of his opposition," reported *The Blood-Horse* of the following week. "He once more took the champion in hand."

Reveille Boy, however, was not yet convinced, and he rallied brazenly until he was lapped on the distinguished visitor, only a head off the lead with a furlong to run! Elliott then let out Phar Lap again, and he cruised away to win drawing out, setting a record for the track at 2:02⅖. The winning margin was two lengths, and Reveille Boy had three more lengths over the third-placed Scimitar, a former claim.

Phar Lap was unperturbed by the event, but then bruised a leg when he became annoyed by the prospect of having a wreath of roses foisted upon his neck during the post-race ceremonies.

There were different interpretations of how easily he won. *The Blood-Horse* report of the race noted that "he came away with such ease that it was apparent that Elliott had never taken Reveille Boy's challenge seriously."

The following week, however, the publication quoted various descriptions, one of which was tendered by the English horseman and writer Harry Sharpe: "As to the race itself, I got the impression that at the finish Phar Lap was giving of his best. My neighbors in the grandstand seemed to think that, if required, he could have drawn away another length or two. I am very doubtful that he could have done so. I think that impressive burst up the backstretch took its toll from him. May I add that jockey Elliott came through the testing ordeal with flying colors."

Sharpe had praise for the physical being of the Red Terror, and his attitude:

"Phar Lap is typical of all the Australian horses I have seen. Fine, sloping shoulders, great girth, perfect loins with great length from hip to hock. As to horse sense, well, this fellow has it. He seemed the coolest actor in the drama being unfolded, in fact, almost nonchalant compared with his rivals

A worthy victor in his last visit to the winner's circle.

who were all on edge...he quietly lifted each foot in turn, for his trainer's precautionary quiz for a possible picked-up stone, with his jockey already on his back..."

Such was the headline worthiness of the Caliente spectacle that responses included a message from England's King George V: "Heartiest congratulations on great victory of Phar Lap." Messages were also conveyed by the premiers of

CHAPTER 5

both Australia and New Zealand.

Writer Hatton admitted to having become "quite steamed up" over Phar Lap. Years later, it would be the self-same Hatton who was most incisive and eloquent among the elder observers about Secretariat's new supremacy. Of Phar Lap, he wrote of "what a surprise (American star) Twenty Grand will get when and if, as we all hope…he meets Phar Lap at a big distance. The Australian will loaf along with the Greentree Stable crack until the latter moves, then, for once in his blithesome young life, Twenty Grand will find himself in company of a racer capable of giving him all the argument he wishes in the last

Phar Lap: "He doesn't run. He bounds."

quarter-mile. If either gallops to the finish that afternoon, it will be the invader!"

Hatton also referred to a colorful description of Phar Lap in a New York paper that the Australian was "a leaper on the flat. He doesn't run. He bounds."

The success and aura of Phar Lap and his owner's apparent appetite for further international adventure led to a glut of fantasy among racetrack executives. Various plans were cast about. The great impresario Colonel Matt Winn was said to be planning a meeting with such American cracks as Equipoise and Twenty Grand, while throwing in the best England, Ireland, and France had to offer as well. (It would be more than two decades before anything remotely similar in international racing seemed practical.) Meanwhile, the great English jockey Steve Donoghue was musing on how the Cambridgeshire and Cesarewitch at Newmarket would fit the horse and how he would like to ride him in those events.

Tragedy interrupted such intoxications.

After the mishap of the rose garland in the Agua Caliente winner's circle, Phar Lap was sent to Edward Perry's ranch at Menlo Park, near San Francisco, to recuperate. Sixteen days after the glories of Caliente had echoed, the shocking news came that the great horse was dead. The reason was thought at first to be colic, but tests indicated arsenic. The source of the deadly material was traced to insecticide, sprayed by a farm employee and apparently carried by the wind to the field where Phar Lap was turned out.

At the time of his death, he was the second leading money earner of the world of Thoroughbred racing, his thirty-seven wins in fifty-one races translating into American dollars of $301,402. (Sun Beau was the leading money earner with $376,744.)

Naturally, death by arsenic led to the darkest of suspicions. To this day, Australians raise eyebrows over the explanation of an accidental death. They tend to muse that some nefarious jealousy in America led to Phar Lap's intended demise. Admittedly, the perversity of some individuals knows no bounds, but to destroy a champion racehorse because he is a foreigner is hardly supported by the traditional response of either country to champions past or present.

Phar Lap's heart was said to be of extraordinary capacity, although successive reports tended to embellish this fact more strongly with time. The animal was submitted to a taxidermist, who articulated the great body for display at the Museum of Victoria (now Museum Victoria) in Melbourne.

Perhaps to a stronger degree than any other racehorse of yore, Phar Lap remains a treasure to a nation — inseparable from Australians' self-image and pride in their homeland.

Agua Caliente Handicap
Purse: $50,000 Added

13th Race Agua Caliente - March 20, 1932

Purse $50,000 added. Three-year-olds and upward. 1 1-4 Miles. Main Track. Track: Fast

Net value to winner $50,050; second, $5,000; third, $2,500; fourth, $1,250.

P#	Horse	A	Wgt	Med	Eqp	Odds	PP	St	1/2	3/4	1m	Str	Fin	Jockey
9	Phar Lap	6	129		s	1.50	9	7	6^{h}	$1^{1½}$	1^{3}	1^{h}	1^{2}	W Elliott
4	Reveille Boy	5	118		wb	7.20	4	11	9^{5}	6^{1}	2^{h}	2^{3}	2^{3}	R Wholey
2	Scimitar	8	100		w	28.20	2	6	7^{h}	8^{5}	5^{2}	4^{3}	3^{3}	G Smith
6	Joe Flores	3	90		wb	†6.50	6	2	2^{2}	$3^{½}$	4^{2}	3^{h}	4^{h}	S Coucci
10	Marine	6	114		w	18.60	10	8	11	$10^{1½}$	9^{2}	6^{1}	5^{h}	F Mann
1	Good and Hot	5	102		w	59.60	1	3	$5^{½}$	5^{h}	6^{3}	7^{h}	6^{h}	W Moran
7	Seth's Hope	8	112		wb	41.40	7	10	10^{1}	11	8^{1}	8^{8}	$7^{1½}$	C Turk
3	Spanish Play	4	117		w	3.00	3	9	$8^{½}$	4^{1}	3^{h}	5^{2}	8^{10}	C Landolt
8	Dr. Freeland	6	120		wb	14.80	8	4	4^{nk}	7^{h}	7^{h}	9^{5}	9^{4}	L Cunningham
5	Bahamas	3	99		wb	10.60	5	1	3^{1}	9^{h}	11	10^{3}	10^{15}	J Longden
11	Cabezo	3	100		w	†	11	5	1^{1}	2^{h}	10^{4}	11	11	A Fischer

† Coupled as S. H. Lee and Mrs. W. T. Anderson entry.

Off Time: 4:55 **Time Of Race:** :22⅘ :46⅗ 1:11⅗ 1:36⅘ 2:02⅘ (new track record)
Start: Good For All but Reveille Boy **Track:** Fast
Equipment: w for whip; b for blinkers; s for spurs

Mutuel Payoffs

9	**Phar Lap**	**$5.00**	**$6.60**	**$2.80**
4	**Reveille Boy**		**6.20**	**5.40**
2	**Scimitar**			**6.00**

Winner: Phar Lap, ch. g. by Night Raid—Entreaty, by Winkie (Trained by T. Woodcock).
Bred by Mr. A. F. Roberts in New Zealand.

Start good for all but Reveille Boy out of machine. Won easily; second and third driving.

PHAR LAP, taken under restraint soon after the start and guided to the middle of the track, moved up resolutely on the outside of the others entering the back stretch and, taking a clear lead, drew away from REVEILLE BOY when the latter challenged on the stretch turn and won with ease. REVEILLE BOY, showing exceptional gameness, challenged boldly entering the stretch, but was not good enough. SCIMITAR improved his position gradually and finished fast. JOE FLORES, close up early, tired in the stretch. MARINE closed a big gap. SPANISH PLAY was in close quarters at the half-mile post and dropped back. DR. FREELAND met interference on the far turn. BAHAMAS saved ground on the first turn, but was cut off after going a quarter. CABEZO showed early speed, but dropped out of it after half a mile.

Overweight—Good and Hot, 2 pounds; Bahamas, 1.

Owners: (9) Davis & Telford; (4) J A Best; (2) J D Mikel; (6) S H Lee; (10) Mount Royal Stable; (1) J Toplitzky; (7) Mrs J A Parsons; (3) Knebelkamp & Morris; (8) B Creech; (5) Oak Tree Stable; (11) Mrs W T Anderson

©DAILY RACING FORM/EQUIBASE

*Wallace Lowry's photo of the 1933 Kentucky Derby
shows Don Meade on Brokers Tip (right) battling
Herb Fisher on Head Play.*

- CHAPTER 6 -

"I Blowed My Top"

Selecting events to include in this book, in the main, involved sifting among races in which champions or near champions engaged in thrilling struggles with a great deal on the line. Almost invariably, in the way of things, this also meant great jockeys, and jockeyship, were also involved. What we did not set out to ennoble were races involving otherwise forgettable horses, reprehensible behavior by the riders, and laissez faire stewards. Yet each of those elements was described by one or more commentators as bespoiling the 1933 Kentucky Derby.

Why, then, do we pause to retell this tale? Lore. It is simply a matter of lore.

Even in that steaming burgoo of tales that gives the Kentucky Derby its unique flavors of history and myth, few runnings were as spectacular as the battle between Brokers Tip and Head Play — and their grasping and slashing riders.

Instrumental in the longevity of this Derby in folklore is a picture taken by Wallace Lowry, a pho-

tographer for the *Louisville Courier-Journal* and *Louisville Times*. Lowry sprawled under the inside rail near the Churchill Downs finish line and pointed his lens toward two horses doing their best and two jockeys doing their worst. The photo of what often is recalled as "The Fighting Finish" froze for all time a unique moment. Each time it is reprinted, those in the know gawk and smirk, the uninitiated gasp and point. There was also film footage of the race, to be perused through the years.

Many races are remembered for their greatness. The 1933 Derby, however, has everlasting fame for its negatives. So, omit the 1933 Derby from this volume and we would invite the indignant query: "How did you happen to miss one of the most famous races of all time?"

><del>+</del><del>+</del><del>O</del><del>+</del><del>+</del><del><</del>

In 1915 Harry Payne Whitney decreed the Derby to be America's greatest race. The self-same Whitney had just won the event with Regret. Such intimate connection with a happy result would ordinarily disqualify one as a judge, but the declaration was highly significant in Whitney's case. He was the son and heir of one of the great Eastern stables, and for that echelon of sportsman, in that time, New York's grand prizes were held as the aristocracy of Ameri-

Depression-era economics, plus bad weather for the fledgling industry of commercial flight, reduced the crowd to perhaps 30,000 for 1933. Nevertheless, by that time the Kentucky Derby was sweetly safe in the arms of the public's sporting affections.

Head Play's rider Herb Fisher: "I hit him (Meade) across the head with my whip once or twice..."

can horse races. That racetrack impresario Colonel Matt Winn had nurtured and hawked a race in Kentucky — still referred to as "the West" by racing writers — to the extent that one of the swellest of the New York swells was now decreeing it supreme among Turf contests was a badge of high gloss. The ensuing years had polished that status.

In a manner whose definition is elusive, the Derby had become a part of America's self image, along with the World Series, the Indianapolis 500, and the Rose Bowl.

Thus, a poor edition engendered indignation.

"Looking at the matter dispassionately, I think it can be asserted that it was the worst field that has gone to the post in a Kentucky Derby for a generation," wrote Neil Newman under the name Roamer in *The Bloodstock Breeders' Review* of 1933. The avowal of the latter part of that sentence brings into question the claim to be "dispassionate" in the introductory clause, but never mind. If challenged afterward, Newman had a ready-made answer: The race was won by a maiden who never won another race in his life. "It is questionable whether any of the starters had any pretensions to real class," was Newman's parting slap.

Favored in the thirteen-horse Derby was W.R. Coe's 3-2 entry of Ladysman and Pomponius, and the Catawba Stable entry of Good Advice and Mr. Khayyam was the 4-1 second choice. Mrs. Silas Mason's Head Play was next at 11-2, and the R.M. Eastman Estate's Charley O. was 6-1.

Brokers Tip was a maiden after five races, but he carried the most fashionable designer silks of the day. His owner, Colonel E.R. Bradley, had already won three Kentucky Derbys, including the 1932 running with Burgoo King. The Bradley colors proffered a cachet upon a horse in Kentucky, especially a Derby horse. "Kentuckians and many others invariably back the Bradley colors in the Kentucky Derby," observed Newman.

In later years, the devil's red and blue Calumet Farm silks would engender a similar sense of familiarity, comfort, and confidence in the Bluegrass State, as do the Claiborne Farm silks of orange-gold today. In New York, the Belair Stud colors of white with red polka dots once had the same magic, and, in more recent times, a special aura has accompanied to the post horses carrying the Phipps family silks of black and cherry. Casting this net toward the West, one suspects that the silks of Mr. and Mrs. John

Mabee or Mr. and Mrs. Robert Lewis have been current counterparts of the eras of Charles S. Howard and Rex Ellsworth. Every part of the country probably has its version of that special connection of owner and fan.

Unlike those other stables, however, the Bradley mystique was undoubtedly tied to the owner's reputation as a high roller. The fact that Brokers Tip had been 50-1 in the first winter-book odds released for the Derby could be read by the average bettor as "the good Colonel has something going, and I'll go along for the ride." A colt named Boilermaker had been identified as the best hope for the Bradley stable early but did not make the fifty-ninth running of the race.

However important the Bradley silks might or might not have been, the maiden Brokers Tip was at respectable odds of nearly 9-1. While he had never won a race, he was once stakes-placed at two and had worked the full mile and a quarter Derby distance in 2:08⅗ on Wednesday of Derby Week. He also had been second in his only start at three.

The remaining four betting interests in the Derby, including three field horses, were all 25-1 or higher. No fewer than nine horses were listed as having been scratched.

The art of the chart caller is specific and trying. It involves recording, or estimating, the exact positions of all horses in a race at various points. The year 1933 was a quarter-century before instant replay video for sports was introduced with Tim Tam's Preakness of 1958. There was not even a photo-finish camera to help placing judges at Churchill Downs in 1933. Thus, the official *Daily Racing Form* chart of the 1933 Kentucky Derby, understandably, is bereft of the drama that attended the stretch run. It reads: "BROKERS TIP, much the best, began very slowly, saved some ground when moving up leaving the backstretch, but lost some on the stretch turn, then went to the inside and, responding to urging and overcoming interference, was up to win in the final strides after a long and

Don Meade: "It was the survival of the fittest."

rough drive. HEAD PLAY, rated close to the pace, went to the front easily, came out when increasing his lead on the stretch turn, and bumped the winner when holding on stubbornly."

For starters, how a horse that wins in the final stride could be called "much the best" is difficult to fathom. Then, too, "bumped the winner" seems rather an understated description of a race in which

two jockeys were grabbing and grappling with one another, but, again, the chart caller did not have the advantage either of still photography or moving pictures.

A common syndrome in legendary sporting events — be they pre-designated home runs in baseball or long counts in boxing — is that the drama of controversy tends to telescope in the retelling. Yet even before the 1933 Derby became part of racing lore, spontaneous reports gave particulars of something amiss. *The Blood-Horse* dated a week after the Derby printed the melee in some detail:

"…(Herb) Fisher brought Head Play into the straightaway some distance out from the rail. But now a new threat appeared. The colors of Col. Bradley had been seen moving up rapidly on the turn…(Don) Meade was cutting the corner, saving ground, and gaining on the leaders at every stride. Briefly it looked as if the finish was to be fought out by Charley O., Head Play, and Brokers Tip. But a sixteenth of a mile in the homestretch was enough to show that Charley O. was weakening. Fisher accordingly turned his attention to beating Brokers Tip, which had slipped through on the inside and now was bidding for the lead and running so strongly that there seemed no question he would take it.

"Then ensued one of the most regrettable incidents in the history of the Kentucky Derby. Fisher took Head Play over toward the rail and toward Brokers Tip until he had the latter in close quarters. Through the last three-sixteenths of a mile the contest was not a horse race so much as a hand-to-hand combat between the jockeys. Just what happened cannot be told for certain, though it took place in view of thousands. According to Meade's charge, Fisher leg-locked him. Meade attempted to fight off his rival, but had little success. While the two horses ran neck and neck through the last furlong, their jockeys battled above them. As they flashed past the finish line four lengths ahead of Charley O., Head Play's head was visibly pulled sidewise toward the grandstand and Brokers Tip was straining straight ahead. The reason Head Play's head was pulled out toward the right — and, in all probability, the reason he failed to finish in front — was the fact that Fisher was leaning far over to the left, grasping the saddlecloth of Brokers Tip. In so doing, he loosened Head Play's left rein and tightened the right. Brokers Tip's margin of victory could have been no more than two or three inches. After the horses had passed the finish, Fisher, realizing his defeat, viciously slashed Meade across the face with his riding bat."

The reporter, who by the time of that report was aware of the Lowry photograph, continued that while Meade was taking a floral horseshoe aboard his mount's withers, Fisher "clicked up the steps to claim foul. Judge C. F. Price wouldn't listen. Other

THE COURIER-JOURNAL

Herb Fisher: "I kinda lost my head. I blowed my top."

stewards (Thomas C. Bradley, C. Bruce Head, and Elijah Hogge) showed little interest. Evidently, they had seen something of what happened and had already made up their minds there was to be no disqualification. The claim of foul was dismissed immediately. Fisher's first reaction was to sit down and cry; his second to rush for the jockeys' room and attack Meade when the latter entered. Several blows were passed before the two were separated."

Two days later, Bradley's fourth Derby safely in hand, a ruling was issued that "…after careful investigation, including a hearing of jockeys H.W. Fisher and D. Meade, (the stewards) have suspended each of the latter for 30 calendar days for rough tactics during the stretch running of the Kentucky Derby. Each boy, according to the evidence and observation, was guilty of grasping the equipment of the other. Jockey Fisher was given an additional five

Joe Palmer upgraded the pugnacity of this affair to say that "...the famous rodeo finish ensued, with Fisher and Meade fighting, grabbing, and slashing at each other down the stretch to the very finish."

Fifty years after the race, *The Blood-Horse*'s report

THE BLOOD-HORSE

Brokers Tip — one win, one Derby.

days for assaulting jockey Meade while in the jockeys' quarters after the running of the race."

A week or so later, *The Blood-Horse* summarized the event as follows: "The Kentucky Derby of this year was an elaborate story in which romance, villainy, vituperation, and frenzied action combined to make an elaborate plot, long in the telling."

Not quite a decade later, the revered racing writer

of the death of jockey Fisher quoted a previous report of his personal explanation of the famous skirmish on horseback. As is often the case in fights, he laid blame for the initial blow on the other principal:

"I wanted to stop Brokers Tip from coming through. I took my horse to the inside. Meade grabbed my saddlecloth at the three-sixteenths pole and I blew my cool. I reached over and pushed him away. He grabbed my shoulder. I grabbed his leg. There was no danger of either of us falling off. We both rode with longer stirrups than the boys do today."

Various articles agree that Fisher and Meade did not speak to each other for some fifteen years after the incident. Their careers were inevitably linked back to that one immortal moment, however, and so they eventually became friends. Fisher died in 1983, and Meade outlived him — not by a narrow margin this time — by thirteen years.

The gentle gentleman Jim Bolus loved the lore of the Kentucky Derby, and he devoted a good deal of his career to describing it. For Bolus, interviewing Meade for a chapter in one of his books, *Derby Fever* (Pelican Publishing, Gretna, La., 1995), must have been an especially gratifying experience — history in the retelling, and straight from the saddle:

"If it wasn't for (Lowry's) photo, no one would have ever known actually what happened," Meade said. "…It would be a guess and guess thing…I actually was the one that grabbed first, but I only grabbed him to protect myself. I thought he was going to shut me off or bump me real hard. That's why I put my hand out to keep him off. I wasn't going to have him put me through the fence…I pushed him off me to get running room, and then he took a hold of me.

"Now, I'm not going to sit there and let him lead me down to the finish line…So from there down to the finish line that's what it was — we grabbed, grabbed, grabbed all through the stretch.

"It was the survival of the fittest. I couldn't sit there and let him rough me around and he had to retaliate, too. Really, it was just a man to man thing

that he couldn't help and I couldn't help."

Bolus quoted the beaten rival Fisher as having expounded further: "When I put him in tight quarters, he reached over and grabbed my saddlecloth at the eighth pole and held on to me. I tried to shake him loose by squeezing him against the fence, and he just held onto me. I was so amazed to think that he had the nerve to have a hold of me that I kinda lost my head. I blowed my top. I hit him across the head with my whip once or twice before the finish, and then after the finish."

This concept of sportsmanship, and a result left standing, aggrieved the writer Newman. The case could be made that two horses, well out of the way of others and with misconduct adjudged to have been equal, should be left as they stood at the wire. The judges quickly came to that conclusion, but Newman was indignant at the thought of even the Derby being held sacrosanct in the face of what he saw as racing's responsibility toward its rules.

"This was probably the most asinine ruling ever promulgated by a body of stewards," he wrote, deciding understatement was not called for in the circumstances. "(The stewards) completely stultified themselves. If both jockeys were guilty of improper practice, both horses should have been disqualified, and in view of the importance of the race, and the disfavor racing was brought into by their actions, both should have been suspended for the balance of the season."

❧━◆━◦━◆━❧

A week later, Head Play won the Preakness under Charlie Kurtsinger, as Brokers Tip ran last, ridden by Jimmy Smith. Brokers Tip had broken his maiden in the Kentucky Derby, and he would not win again. Head Play came back at five to win five important stakes from coast to coast, including the San Juan Capistrano and the Suburban Handicap (over the great Discovery).

For Fisher and Meade, there would always be the inevitable task of explaining themselves, and the Derby, over and over. "I was greatly disappointed in myself," Fisher said some years later. "I had got beat on the best horse, and had got outroughed — and I was pretty rough myself."

"If Fisher hadn't started grabbing me, he would have won," Meade was quoted as saying years later. "He had the better horse."

Neither Meade nor Fisher was close enough to the winner to have an effect on any other Kentucky Derby finish. Each had only two other mounts. Fisher had been eighth on Bobashela in 1928 and was sixth on Holl Image three years after the Fighting Finish Derby. Meade finished ninth on Col. Bradley's Bazaar the year after his win on Brokers Tip and then sixteenth on the same stable's Boxthorn the year after that.

Fisher, who was born in England and raised in Canada, battled weight throughout his riding career, which he had begun as a teenager at Montreal's Blue Bonnets racetrack in 1926. He was about twenty-two at the time of the 1933 Derby and rode until 1940. He then became a trainer, having modest success and winning stakes with four horses.

Meade's career proscribed that of the archetype of a Hollywood sports movie — great ability, great glamour, wasted talent, sad conclusion. He was only eighteen when he won the raucous Kentucky Derby of 1933. Six years later he led the nation in races won, and he repeated as the leader in that category in 1941; moreover, Meade also led all riders in earnings in 1941. In 1937 and again in 1943, however,

Meade was banned for betting against his own mounts, as recorded in an article in *The New York Times* in 1997.

In 1944, after he was reinstated to ride in New York, Meade had one more excellent opportunity. Captain Harry Guggenheim, owner of Cain Hoy Stable, regarded Meade as "a brilliant natural jockey, a master at getting his horse off at the start, rating his mount in front, and at getting everything out of a horse at the finish line."

Meade rode well for Guggenheim until late that year. The good Cain Hoy mare Good Morning was to run in the Lady Baltimore Handicap at Pimlico, and, as Guggenheim later recorded, "a famous race track figure warned that the word had passed that Star Copy would win, which seemed incredible."

Guggenheim supplied the following for an unpublished private history of Cain Hoy Stable: "I was at the races with one of my dearest and warmest friends, Rozier H. Dulany Jr. …When the race was over (Star Copy indeed first, Good Morning second), I told him I was going into the jockey's room to talk with Meade. Rozier went with me. When Meade saw Dulany, a great figure of a man six feet two without an ounce of fat, bearing down on him, he immediately burst out — 'I couldn't help it. I was out all night and weak, and I gave her a bad ride!'

"Meade's contract with me was up. He went to Mexico, where he very shortly got into serious trouble again with the stewards, and has had his license revoked…"

Indeed, in 1945 Meade was effectively banned for life. Called before the stewards in Mexico City for rough riding, he went beyond defensive. He reportedly wound up swearing at his judges. Their ban was recognized in U.S. jurisdictions. By the time the ban was rescinded, in 1950, it was too late to do Meade much good. Moreover, the Florida Racing Commission was harshly criticized for its decision to grant him a probationary license that year, and Meade eventually withdrew his own application.

Like a Mickey Rooney movie character, Meade had married a showgirl during his heyday, but that connection was one of the constants of his life. At the end, she was still with him, having raised a family and suffered through the accidental death of a grown son. Meade trained for a while, owned a grocery store at one point, and put out a tip sheet. He owned a couple of taverns at the time of his death in 1996.

He was eighty-three, an old man, but still frequently defined by one perilous furlong from his youth.

Kentucky Derby
Purse: $50,000 Added

6th Race Churchill Downs - May 6, 1933

Purse $50,000 added. Three-year-olds. 1 1-4 Miles. Main Track. Track: Good.
Net value to winner $48,925 and gold trophy; second, $6,000; third, $3,000; fourth, $1,000.

P#	Horse	A	Wgt	Med	Eqp	Odds	PP	St	1/2	3/4	1m	Str	Fin	Jockey
11	Brokers Tip	3	126		wb	8.93	11	11	11^{1}	$8^{\frac{1}{2}}$	4^{2}	$2^{1\frac{1}{2}}$	1^{n}	D Meade
7	Head Play	3	126		w	5.64	7	5	$3^{\frac{1}{2}}$	$1^{\frac{1}{2}}$	1^{1}	1^{h}	2^{4}	H W Fisher
1	Charley O.	3	126		wb	6.02	1	6	7^{h}	6^{1}	$2^{1\frac{1}{2}}$	3^{4}	$3^{1\frac{1}{2}}$	C Corbett
4	Ladysman	3	126		wb	‡1.43	4	7	$5^{\frac{1}{2}}$	7^{3}	$5^{1\frac{1}{2}}$	$5^{1\frac{1}{2}}$	4^{n}	R Workman
12	Pomponius	3	126		w	‡	12	12	$10^{\frac{1}{2}}$	$9^{1\frac{1}{2}}$	$6^{\frac{1}{2}}$	6^{3}	5^{3}	J Bejshak
9	Spicson	3	126		wb	†25.85	9	13	13	12^{3}	$10^{1\frac{1}{2}}$	7^{1}	$6^{1\frac{1}{2}}$	R Fischer
5	Kerry Patch	3	126		wb	26.89	5	1	$6^{1\frac{1}{2}}$	$5^{\frac{1}{2}}$	3^{h}	4^{h}	7^{2}	L Schaefer
13	Mr. Khayyam	3	126		w	§4.09	13	9	9^{1}	11^{3}	9^{h}	9^{2}	$8^{\frac{1}{2}}$	P Walls
6	Inlander	3	126		wb	44.27	6	8	8^{2}	10^{2}	8^{1}	8^{2}	$9^{1\frac{1}{2}}$	D Bellizzi
8	Strideaway	3	126		wb	†	8	4	$12^{\frac{1}{2}}$	13	12^{3}	10^{3}	10^{5}	A Beck
3	Dark Winter	3	126		wb	†	3	10	4^{2}	4^{h}	7^{2}	11^{8}	11^{12}	R Jones
10	Isaiah	3	126		wb	66.86	10	2	$2^{1\frac{1}{2}}$	$3^{\frac{1}{2}}$	11^{2}	12^{8}	12	C McCros'n
2	Good Advice	3	126		wb	§	2	3	1^{h}	2^{h}	13	13	P. up	E Legere

† Mutuel field. ‡ Coupled as W. R. Coe entry; § Catawba Stable entry.

Off Time: 5:18 **Time Of Race:** :23⅕ :47⅕ 1:12⅘ 1:40⅖ 2:06⅘
Start: Good For All **Track:** Good
Equipment:: w for whip; b for blinkers

Mutuel Payoffs

11	**Brokers Tip**	**$19.86**	**$6.28**	**$4.54**
7	**Head Play**		**5.52**	**4.08**
1	**Charley O.**			**3.84**

Winner: Brokers Tip, br. c. by Black Toney—Forteresse, by Sardanapale (Trained by H. J. Thompson). Bred by Idle Hour Stock Farm in Ky.

Start good out of machine. Won driving; second and third the same.
BROKERS TIP, much the best, began very slowly, saved some ground when moving up leaving the back stretch, but lost some on the stretch turn, then went to the inside and, responding to urging and overcoming interference, was up to win in the final strides after a long and rough drive. HEAD PLAY, rated close to the pace, went to the front easily, came out when increasing his lead on the stretch turn and bumped the winner when holding on stubbornly. CHARLEY O., well in hand for three-quarters, challenged gamely, then tired, but held LADYSMAN safe. The latter raced wide most of the way, was under restraint for seven-eighths and failed to rally when hard urged. POMPONIUS closed resolutely. SPICSON began slowly. KERRY PATCH tired. MR. KHAYYAM was never a factor. ISAIAH and DARK WINTER showed early speed. GOOD ADVICE quit badly and was pulled up.
Scratched—Pompoleon, 126; Sarada, 126; Fingal, 126; Warren Jr., 126; Captain Red, 126; Boilermaker, 126; Silent Shot, 126; At Top, 121; Fair Rochester, 126.

Owners: (11) E R Bradley; (7) Mrs S B Mason; (1) R M Eastman estate; (4) W R Coe; (12) W R Coe; (9) L M Severson; (5) L Rosenberg; (13) Catawba Stable; (6) Brookmeade Stable; (8) Three D's Stock Farm Stable; (3) W S Kilmer; (10) J W Parrish; (2) Catawba Stable

©DAILY RACING FORM/EQUIBASE

Seabiscuit taking the 'Big Cap.

- CHAPTER 7 -

Sensational Seabiscuit

Seabiscuit was a beloved little bay colt who was bred by a prominent stable but, nevertheless, had much of the appeal of the "rags to riches" motif. He was bred by the Wheatley Stable, which had been established by Mrs. Henry Carnegie Phipps and her brother, Ogden Mills. From the vantage point of the year 2001, the Phipps generations have been so long a mainstay of the best in racing that it would be inconceivable that a Phipps-bred would be of indifferent pedigree. In 1933, however, when Seabiscuit was a foal, the Wheatley operation, while having had some success, was not yet so exalted.

Seabiscuit was by Wheatley's Hard Tack, a stakes-winning son of Man o' War. Hard Tack was closely inbred to Rock Sand, and his hot temper engendered a wary response from breeders. Horace N. Davis Sr., to whom he was leased, was finding no outside mares for him, and Seabiscuit was one of but four foals in Hard Tack's first crop. The colt was out of Wheatley's unraced Swing On, a Whisk Broom II mare from the female family of Equipoise.

Sunny Jim Fitzsimmons trained for Wheatley, as well as for William Woodward Sr.'s Belair Stable. For the latter, he was busy winning the Triple Crown with Omaha in 1935, the year Seabiscuit was two. Nonetheless, he found time to race Seabiscuit no fewer than thirty-five times that season! The colt had lost seventeen times, frequently for claiming prices as low as two-thousand-dollars, before he broke his maiden. In those days there were a number of claiming stakes, so Seabiscuit was able to be a claimer and a stakes winner at the same time. Later in the year he did win a more legitimate stakes, the Ardsley, and, all told, won five races. He was ranked below twenty-seven other two-year-olds on the Experimental Free Handicap.

The following year he won another claiming stakes and some handicaps. By Saratoga time, however, he was still of such modest rank in the stable that when trainer Tom Smith was shopping for a prospect for Charles S. Howard, Fitzsimmons sold him Seabiscuit for $7,500.

Seabiscuit at that time had started forty-seven times and won nine, earning $18,465. Through the age of seven, he was to start forty-two more times, but in that phase he won twenty-four and became the world's leading money winner.

Smith shipped Seabiscuit around the country, and the colt immediately began winning a series of

was voted national champion older horse for 1937, the second year such balloting was conducted.

At five, Seabiscuit was not only champion older horse again, but Horse of the Year. His campaign included two races that could fairly represent separate chapters in any volume reviewing special moments of the century. One was a match race with a horse

Seabiscuit wearing his workout clothes.

stakes. The Howard horses were based in California, where big-time racing had been rejuvenated only a few years before. As a four-year-old, Seabiscuit began winning stakes at Santa Anita. Mrs. Phipps' son, Ogden Phipps, once remarked that the success of the cast-off colt was interpreted initially as indicating California racing was not too competitive, but Seabiscuit came East and continued winning. He

co-owned by Charles Howard's own son! Ligaroti raced for the Binglin Stable, which was a partnership of the famous crooner Bing Crosby and Lindsay Howard. Moreover, Lin Howard trained the Argentine import himself.

Ligaroti had won several West Coast stakes when he was matched with Seabiscuit in a $25,000 event. The race was staged at the new resort track of Del

Mar, in which Crosby was a major investor and which still broadcasts daily his rendition of "Where the Surf Meets the Turf at Old Del Mar." The match race was at nine furlongs, Seabiscuit to carry 130 and Ligaroti 115.

Match races between horses with common or familial ownership seem destined to arouse cynicism.

as he climbed toward Sun Beau's all-time money record. The California Horse Racing Commission declared there would be no pari-mutuel betting on the race.

As it unfolded, only the most obstinately cynical could deny it was a true horse race. Seabiscuit and Ligaroti dashed through quick fractions, neither

Kayak II ran well to finish second in the Big 'Cap.

Many years later, when the initial Marlboro Cup was conceived as a match between Meadow Stable champions Secretariat and Riva Ridge, the reaction was so skeptical that the organizers quickly recast the race and opened it to others. Likewise, in 1938, the Howard vs. Howard/Crosby match drew comment that it would not be a true race and was a bogus way to add $25,000 to Seabiscuit's earnings

able to shake loose from the other, and at the wire the great Seabiscuit prevailed by only a nose. In the stretch, mischief had been afoot. Ligaroti had a tendency to lay over on horses, and he apparently did so on this occasion. His rider, Noel Richardson, was seen to reach over to grab the saddlecloth of Seabiscuit's rider, George Woolf. Woolf responded by flailing the other rider with his whip. Stewards

JOE FLEISCHER

Trainer Tom Smith (right) leads Seabiscuit into the winner's circle.

suspended both jockeys for the remainder of the meeting but found the horses blameless, and the finish order stood.

The other highlight of Seabiscuit's 1938 campaign had been perhaps more sensational but less controversial. As the year had unfolded, many racetracks coveted a meeting of Seabiscuit and the previous year's Triple Crown winner, War Admiral. The last attempt to get them together was successful when young Alfred Vanderbilt, then the head of Pimlico, attracted both for his Pimlico Special. So great was public interest that Vanderbilt scheduled the race for a weekday, recognizing that on a weekend the crowd would have been so large that many would have come away with an unhappy experience of jostling, crowding, inability to bet or see, and more or less cross about the whole prospect of attending a horse race.

The presumption was that the speedy War Admiral would set the pace, and he was the 1-4 choice over 6-5 Seabiscuit. Setting a tenor that would reverberate through later match races, Woolf recognized that a two-horse race would most likely be won by speed from the outset. A walk-up start was employed, and a splendid photo of the initial strides shows Woolf ready to bring his whip down on Seabiscuit's right flank. The Western campaigner thus established the lead early and dominated, winning by four lengths.

Ironically for a horse that had validated the quality of West Coast form, Seabiscuit had been unable to win California's signature modern event, the $100,000-added Santa Anita Handicap — a race of virtually unique riches for the era. Twice he had lost the Big 'Cap in photo finishes, once nosed out by Rosemont and again while giving thirty pounds to the upstart three-year-old Stagehand. After the Pimlico Special of 1938, the 1939 Santa Anita Handicap was Seabiscuit's next designated target, but after he made one start in a prep race wearing bandages all around, he was diagnosed with suspensory ligament trouble. He missed not only the winter's big handicap but the rest of the year.

Seabiscuit was a public hero, but the announcement that he would come back a year later to attempt finally to win the Santa Anita Handicap was met by realism as much as sentiment. Here was a horse that had not raced in nearly a year, had served seven mares during his hiatus from the track, was trying to return from an injury, and would be seven years old. Beloved or not, Seabiscuit could be had at 10-1 in early betting for the 1940 Santa Anita Handicap.

An unlikely winter of consistent rain conspired to force Smith to scratch Seabiscuit four times from what was intended to be his first start in nearly a year. At the same time the taciturn trainer was forced to work the horse on off going on several occasions. Finally, Seabiscuit appeared in a seven-furlong event, and his third-place finish was satisfactory, given his lengthy absence. Again raced at seven furlongs in the San Carlos Handicap, however, he finished a dismal sixth. Pessimism abounded, even amid his legion of fans.

Thus, Seabiscuit's subsequent easy victory at one and a sixteenth miles in the San Antonio Handicap was as joyous as it was confusing. So, 74,000 sojourned out for the Santa Anita Handicap on March 2, 1940, hopeful but wary. Seabiscuit's entrymate was Kayak II, who had deputized in winning the event for Smith and Howard the previous year. The entry was made the 7-10 favorite. What proportion of support came from the heart and what from cold handicapping was, of course, a collective secret. Seabiscuit carried top weight of 130 pounds, giving a pound to Kayak II and up to thirty pounds to the remaining eleven horses. (Two Binglin entrants were allowed to be bet as a separate entity and went off at almost 17-1.)

Red Pollard had been Seabiscuit's jockey for his initial glory, but he had missed the campaign of 1938 due to an injury. He was reunited with Seabiscuit for the horse's seven-year-old campaign. On Big 'Cap Day, Seabiscuit appeared without bandages and was observed to seem tighter and less the rotund little fellow that he had been through most of his career.

Pollard got him away well from post position twelve, and he tracked Whichcee (114 pounds). Pollard spurted him out of pending traffic on the first turn, and he was right with the leader after a half-mile, after six furlongs, and after a mile. As they swung for home, the crowd let out a hopeful roar,

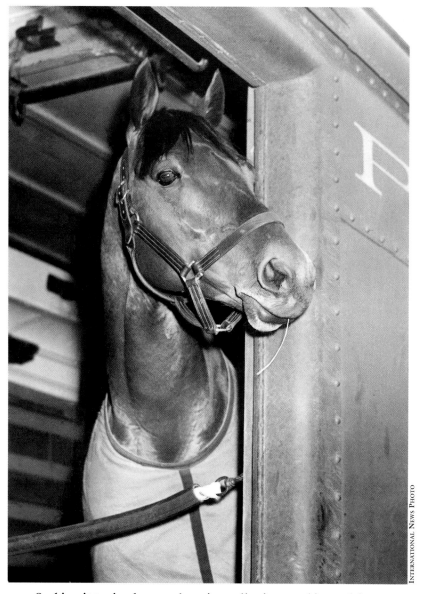

Seabiscuit trained across America, collecting trophies and fans.

Form's book, *Champions*, published in 2000, adjusts the margin to one and a half lengths in Seabiscuit's past performances.)

The time for the one and a quarter miles was 2:01⅕, a new track record. Basil James, rider of Whichcee, occasioned a collective gasp from the crowd when he claimed foul. He alleged that Seabiscuit had cut off his colt when he moved to the rail in the stretch. Since both the winner and runner-up Kayak II were from the same stable, a disqualification of Seabiscuit would mean a disqualification of both. The stewards, appropriately enough, had been watching the stretch run, and since the alleged incident took place very close to them were able to dismiss the claim as groundless.

The purse placed Seabiscuit's earnings above those of Sun Beau's as the one-time castoff became the all-time leading earner with $437,730. He had won thirty-three of eighty-nine races. It was soon announced that he would not be pressed further, despite his return to the highest form, but would be retired to Howard's California ranch. So much a public presence was Seabiscuit that a book on his life was immediately begun, and

for their hero was seen to put his gallant old head in front. Whichcee stayed on bravely to the furlong pole, but then Seabiscuit began to draw clear, eventually cutting over to the rail. In the final strides, he opened a safe lead, and he won by daylight from his stablemate Kayak II. (Photos show some distance between the two, although the chart apparently miscalled the margin as a half-length; *Daily Racing*

Hollywood came calling with a feature film. (In 2001 another biography, by Laura Hillenbrand, stayed atop *The New York Times* bestseller list for several weeks.)

John Hervey, writing in *American Race Horses of 1940*, described Seabiscuit's ascent to the top of the earners' list via the Santa Anita Handicap as having been done "in a manner so thrilling, against a background so eventful and romantic that nothing in the annals of sport can approach it."

Mrs. Howard had a similar feel for the occasion. She chose to stay in the barn area, able to see but a flash of the colorful field. "I just could not bear to watch the race from the clubhouse, among a crowd of people," she said. "I wanted to be alone, for I wasn't sure I could hold myself together."

Santa Anita Handicap
Purse: $100,000 Added

6th Race Santa Anita - March 2, 1940
Purse $100,000 added and gold cup to owner of winner. Three-year-olds and upward. 1 1-4 Miles (Out of chute). Track: Fast.
Net value to winner $86,650; second, $20,000; third, $10,000; fourth, $5,000.

P#	Horse	A	Wgt	Med	Eqp	Odds	PP	St	1/2	3/4	1m	Str	Fin	Jockey
12	Seabiscuit	7	130		wb	†.70	12	5	$2^{1/2}$	2^{h}	2^{h}	1^{h}	$1^{1\frac{1}{2}}$	J Pollard
2	Kayak II	5	129		wb	†	2	13	13	8^{1}	6^{h}	$3^{1\frac{1}{2}}$	2^{1}	L Haas
6	Whichcee	6	114		wb	3.90	6	3	1^{1}	$1^{1/2}$	1^{h}	$2^{1\frac{1}{2}}$	$3^{1\frac{1}{2}}$	B James
1	Wedding Call	4	108		wb	96.60	1	2	5^{h}	3^{h}	3^{2}	4^{1}	$4^{1/2}$	D Dodson
9	War Plumage	4	107		w	26.80	9	7	11^{1}	10^{2}	$8^{1/2}$	$8^{1/2}$	$5^{1/2}$	R Neves
10	Heelfly	6	114		w	10.10	10	10	12^{h}	$11^{1\frac{1}{2}}$	10^{5}	10^{1}	$6^{1/2}$	G Woolf
3	Viscounty	4	110		wb	28.20	3	4	$7^{2\frac{1}{2}}$	6^{1}	5^{h}	$5^{1/2}$	$7^{2\frac{1}{2}}$	E Rodriguez
7	Can't Wait	5	108		wb	34.00	7	9	8^{2}	$7^{1/2}$	4^{h}	7^{h}	8^{h}	J Longden
5	Specify	5	116		wb	16.10	5	1	3^{h}	$5^{1\frac{1}{2}}$	9^{2}	$9^{1\frac{1}{2}}$	9^{h}	H Richards
13	Royal Crusader	3	104		wb	50.10	13	8	$4^{1\frac{1}{2}}$	4^{3}	$7^{1/2}$	6^{4}	10^{3}	L Knapp
11	Don Mike	6	112		w	‡16.80	11	12	9^{h}	12^{5}	11^{5}	11^{7}	11^{15}	L Balaski
4	Ra II	5	118		w	‡	4	6	6^{2}	9^{h}	12^{5}	12^{6}	12^{7}	M Peters
8	Kantan	3	100		wb	55.10	8	11	10^{h}	13	13	13	13	N Wall

† Coupled as C. S. Howard entry; ‡ Binglin Stock Farm entry.

Off Time: 4:26 **Time Of Race:** :23 :47⅕ 1:11⅕ 1:36 2:01⅕ (new track record)
Start: Good For All **Track:** Fast
Equipment: w for whip; b for blinkers

Mutuel Payoffs

12	**Seabiscuit**	**$3.40**	**$2.80**	**$2.60**
2	**Kayak II**	**3.40**	**2.80**	**2.60**
6	**Whichcee**			**3.60**

Winner: Seabiscuit, b. h. by Hard Tack—Swing On, by Whisk Broom II (Trained by T. Smith).
Bred by Wheatley Stable in Ky.

Start good and slow. Won driving; second and third the same.
SEABISCUIT, close to the pace from the start, was urged forward and out of trouble when it seemed as if he might be caught in close quarters nearing the first turn, then came on to catch WHICHCEE entering the final eighth and was going in his best form to the finish. KAYAK II, slow to get going, ran a sensational race to make a very strong move in the back stretch and might have been closer to the winner had he been vigorously ridden in the last sixteenth. WHICHCEE had his speed going to the front early and set a fast pace, but was clearly not good enough for the first two. WEDDING CALL, showing an excellent effort, was close to the pace in the early stages, made a determined bid rounding the stretch turn, but was forced to race a trifle wide and, although seeming to lack the class of the first three, went in superb fashion to the end. WAR PLUMAGE made a strong move nearing the stretch turn and was in close quarters rounding the turn, but turned in a creditable effort. HEELFLY lacked early speed and was never a serious contender, although closing fairly well. VISCOUNTY made a couple of bids to reach the leaders, but was not good enough. SPECIFY was never able to get to the front and failed to run his best race. ROYAL CRUSADER showed fine early speed and was a strong contender for seven-eighths, then faded. CAN'T WAIT, DON MIKE, and RA II were never serious contenders. KANTAN was clearly out classed and did not belong in the race.
Scratched—Hysterical, 108.
Overweight—Royal Crusader, 4 pounds.

Owners: (12) C S Howard; (2) C S Howard; (6) A C T Stock Farm; (1) Gaffers & Sattler; (9) J C Brady; (10) Circle S Stable (3) Valdina Farm; (7) M Selznick; (5) Silver State Stable; (13) R C Stable; (11) Binglin Stock Farm; (4) Binglin Stock Farm; (8) W L Ranch

©DAILY RACING FORM/EQUIBASE

*Alsab, a seven-hundred-dollar yearling,
was one of racing's great overachievers.*

- CHAPTER 8 -

"A Photo In Excelsis"

Most of the ballyhooed, specially arranged match races of the twentieth century fell rather flat, or further. Papyrus was shod in smooth plates and could make little headway in his muddy 1923 match with Zev; the Man o' War-Sir Barton duel, the Armed-Assault match, and the Nashua-Swaps meeting were all accompanied by reports of one of the contestants being lame; and, worst of all, Ruffian suffered a fatal injury in her match against Foolish Pleasure. Even the great victory of Seabiscuit over War Admiral at Pimlico in 1938 was more sensational than competitive.

Against that backdrop, it seems perhaps puzzling that a race that fulfilled the greatest hopes of such contests — a fierce battle right to the wire — tended to establish fewer lingering memories than the disappointments. The most remarkable of such races was the 1942 showdown of the champions of two generations, both publicly acclaimed, when Alsab met Whirlaway. (Another match, thirty years later, that produced a photo finish was Convenience's

head triumph over Typecast in 1972, but those two were invested of less national stature.)

Perhaps the era in which Whirlaway and Alsab ran, and the type of campaigns their stables prescribed, worked against their two-horse meeting being revered. After all, the match was put together only a week after a meeting in a regularly scheduled race had come apart. A proposed meeting in the Narragansett Special was scuttled when Alsab's owner finally realized the colt needed a bit more time for freshening from his strenuous campaign. Moreover, within a month, these two hard-working champions had met twice again!

Whirlaway and Alsab presented the sorts of contrasts that energize sport, the Turf especially. Whirlaway was a son of Blenheim II, who had won the most important race in England, the Epsom Derby, and had become the leading sire in America after importation. Whirlaway's dam was Dustwhirl, by Sweep, also a leading sire. The chestnut was a homebred from Warren Wright Sr.'s Calumet Farm, just then emerging as one of the bright, newer names among the most important stables in the country. He was trained by Ben A. Jones and had won that horseman his second Kentucky Derby en route to a Triple Crown sweep in 1941. He had a dashing, late-charging way of racing and the added beauty mark of a tail so long that his public grasped it, figuratively, as a nickname — "Mr. Longtail."

Alsab, on the other hand, was the quintessential overachiever. At the end of the twentieth century, the one-time seven-hundred-dollar yearling still ranked with the $1,500 claim of Stymie and the erstwhile $1,100 purchase of John Henry as the

Alsab was named by and for his owner, Albert Sabath.

most idyllic of Cinderella stories.

Alsab was by the moderate stallion Good Goods and out of a Wildair mare, Winds Chant, once purchased for ninety dollars and winner of a total of $115 in maiden claiming races. Alsab was bred by Thomas Piatt, an old-time Kentucky agriculturist noted for horsemanship, integrity, and down-to-earth goodness, but not for high fashion in his Saratoga yearling consignments. Alsab's purchaser

was Chicago attorney Albert Sabath, the president of Hawthorne racetrack. (Here, too, was contrast. Calumet owner Wright was an investor in Arlington Park, the most social and glamorous of the Chicago tracks. Sabath's Hawthorne was important, but more working class in image.) Sabath, who raced the horse officially in his wife's title, looked no further than his own name in creating the colt's name. Alsab was trained by August (Sarge) Swenke, who plucked him from Piatt's Brookdale Farm consignment on Sabath's behalf.

Whirlaway and Alsab each emerged as a champion two-year-old male of his year, and each was subjected to heavy campaigning. Whirlaway won seven of sixteen races at two, then thirteen of twenty at three in 1941. The season Whirlaway was three-year-old champion male as well as Horse of the Year, the juvenile Alsab came onto the scene and won fifteen of twenty-two to rule as champion two-year-old.

In 1942, Whirlaway at four was again a power. By September, he had put together no great winning streak, but had won five important handicap races. Alsab had started his three-year-old campaign so poorly that he was booed on the track and carped at in the press. Moreover, his owner drew cynical comments when he at one point declared that the horse belonged to the public and only for that reason was he sent one and a quarter miles against older horses early on in the Widener Handicap! Eventually, Alsab lost his first eight races at three, but the last of those was a second to Shut Out in the Kentucky Derby. He followed with a breakthrough victory in the Preakness and then added the Withers and American Derby.

Interest was high in what was projected to be the first meeting of Whirlaway and Alsab, in the Narragansett Special on September 12. Whirlaway came up to the race off a four-week freshening followed by a victory in the Trenton Handicap. He was sent to the Narragansett in advance and appeared to be at his sharpest. Meanwhile, Alsab's campaigning was often accompanied by suggestion of an enthusiastic owner overruling the judgment of the trainer. He seemed to be force-fed into this meeting off four races in August and then a second against older horses in the Washington Park Handicap only a week before the Special!

Sabath backed off, with the good of the colt in mind, but he even did this in such a way as to maximize resentment. A crowd of 30,000 turned up, only to be informed that Alsab was scratched. Sabath claimed the horse had shipped poorly and that it would be unfair to those who might bet on him to run him that soon.

These were two wonderful and wonderfully sound colts, however, and the tenor of the time was such that the concept of more time meant a week. Narragansett reacted quickly and put together a $25,000 match race for the following Saturday, September 19! The race was to be the same distance as the Special, one and three-sixteenths miles, at weight for age (126 pounds Whirlaway, 119 Alsab), winner take all. The track's profits for the day were announced as headed to the war-relief program, there, after all, being dreadful events taking place in the world at the time.

<hr/>

The great jockey George Woolf played an ironic role in the match race, which was officially named the Narragansett Championship. It was Woolf, nicknamed "The Iceman," who had understood the dynamics of match races to the extent that he had driven the supposed stretch runner, Seabiscuit, to the early lead to run the supposed pacemaker, War Admiral, into defeat in the 1938 Pimlico Special. (Seventeen years later, this lesson was to be applied to the famous Nashua-Swaps Match Race, when

Courtesy Belmont News Bureau

Trainer Ben Jones posed aboard Whirlaway and feigned "the look of eagles."

Eddie Arcaro pulled a Woolf and put Nashua on the lead and dominated the race.)

In 1942, however, Woolf was the wrong man on the wrong horse — and apparently with the wrong attitude. He had ridden both colts recently, although with the frequent racing both undertook, no rider could be described as the "regular" partner of either. Woolf chose Whirlaway, asserting that the younger colt would be no match for him. Alsab's connections reverted to Carroll Bierman, who had not ridden their colt since his victory in the Champagne Stakes nearly a year before. Bierman expressed great confidence in his mount. The public sided with Whirlaway, making him the 3-10 choice over the 1.60-1 Alsab.

John Hervey, the racing historian known as "Salvator," recounted the events for *American Race Horses of 1942*: "The preliminary interest in the match…had almost entirely hinged upon the fact that both colts raced in the same manner, staying back in the early running and then coming from behind to do their work in the stretch. It would now be necessary for one of them to go out and set the pace, leaving the other to his habitual tactics. That this would favor the latter — be a great advantage — was the expert opinion…"

That a writer might fall for this line of thinking is excusable. That Woolf would ignore his own success on Seabiscuit is baffling. At any rate, it was Bierman

on Alsab who cried Woolf. They burst into the lead and assumed command. Woolf played into his hands, not only failing to push for the lead, but allowing Alsab to roll along in front at a moderate pace. After a half-mile in :50⅖, Alsab had a length and a half lead on the older colt. The pace quickened. The next quarter-mile was run in :23⅖, and Alsab had increased his margin to two lengths.

Rounding the turn, Alsab raced the next quarter-mile in :24⅖ and still had a length and a half lead. This had been a race from the beginning. Now, it became a battle of blood and courage. "It will be such a finish as seldom has been seen," observed Hervey. Woolf swung Whirlaway outside for the colt's signature rally. The horse who had thrilled the world with his charge to win the Derby by eight lengths the previous spring was back at it. Alsab, though, had not been without his crucible tests. Both horses leveled. Whirlaway charged on, Alsab fought back. It was no longer a question of one overwhelming the other, parading home with banners unfurled. It was a battle of inches, and Whirlaway was the one gaining them. Still, Alsab held on. The older horse perhaps gained even terms, perhaps not. At any rate it was Alsab with the more perseverance, but only by a nose.

"Alsab, unflinching, unyielding, unconquerable," rhapsodized Hervey, "…It is a photo finish, in excelsis, and the tension is almost unbearable…The number is flashed. It is Alsab's. He wins by the tip of his nostril."

For the record, the final time was

Alsab (left) and Whirlaway during training hours.

THE BLOOD-HORSE

1:56⅖, compared with the track record of 1:55 set by Discovery.

Calumet would have a hold on the public in the future, as when Alydar lost consistently to Affirmed but yet so often seemed the preferred hero. Of the Alsab victory, Hervey at the time observed: "The result is not popular, although Alsab receives rounds of applause...It had...been a Whirlaway crowd...but it was impossible to offer alibis, which rather aggravated the matter..."

Ten days after his noble victory, Alsab won the Lawrence Realization, whereas seven days after the match, Whirlaway was beaten into second in the Manhattan Handicap. Then, only four days after the Realization, they met again at two miles in the Jockey Club Gold Cup. Alsab led for much of the way, but Whirlaway came along to win by three-quarters of a length. Still, the battle raged. Only a week more passed before they met at two and a quarter miles in the New York Handicap. Alsab, getting nine pounds, won by a head over an abject long shot named Obash, while Whirlaway finished third.

NARRAGANSETT PARK

Alsab (rail) was "unflinching" in his match against Whirlaway.

Alsab had thus won two of three against the older horse. Such were stable strategies, though, that Alsab raced three more times, winning only once, while Whirlaway also raced on, winning four of five remaining starts. Alsab was voted champion three-year-old, but Whirlaway — having become the first earner of a half-million dollars — was older champion and repeated as Horse of the Year.

Narragansett Championship
Purse: $25,000

7th Race Narragansett Park - September 19, 1942

Match Race. Purse $25,000. Weight-for-age. 1 3-16 Miles. Main Track. Track: Fast. Net value to winner $25,000.

P#	Horse	A	Wgt	Med	Eqp	Odds	PP	St	1/2	3/4	1m	Str	Fin	Jockey
2	Alsab	3	119		wb	1.60	2	1	$1^{1\frac{1}{2}}$	1^{2}	$1^{1\frac{1}{2}}$	1^{1}	1^{n}	C Bierman
1	Whirlaway	4	126		wb	.30	1	2	2	2	2	2	2	G Woolf

Off Time: 5:36 Eastern War Time **Time Of Race:** :25⅖ :50⅖ 1:14⅕ 1:38⅗ 1:56⅖
Start: Good For All **Track:** Fast
Equipment: w for whip; b for blinkers

Mutuel Payoffs
2 Alsab $5.20
No Place or Show Mutuels Sold.

Winner: Alsab, b. c. by Good Goods—Winds Chant, by Wildair (Trained by A. Swenk).
Bred by Mr. Thomas Piatt in Ky.

Start good from stall gate. Won driving; second the same.
ALSAB went to the front at once, drew clear in the first sixteenth, was rated under slight restraint, increased his advantage nearing the far turn and, vigorously ridden when challenged in the stretch, had enough left to withstand WHIRLAWAY's game bid. WHIRLAWAY, steadied along in pursuit of the pace, came to the outside for the closing test and finishing stoutly, was slowly wearing down ALSAB at the finish.

Owners: (2) Mrs A Sabath; (1) Calumet Farm

©DAILY RACING FORM/EQUIBASE

AQUEDUCT 6R 6-10-44   AQUEDUCT 6R 6-10-44   AQUE 6R 6

TRIPLE DEAD HEAT
CARTER HANDICAP
1944
#5 – Brownie – Jockey – Guerin, E.
#4 – Bossuet – Jockey – Stout, J.
#6 – Wait A Bit – Jockey – Smith, G.L.

DEAD HEAT

PHOTO FOR WIN
BY D&S PHOTO

The Carter Handicap's triple dead heat, a handicapping wonder.

- CHAPTER 9 -

Triple Dead Heat

Racing secretaries can only aspire to the feat John B. Campbell accomplished in the 1944 Carter Handicap — a triple dead heat in a major stakes race. No one has been able to replicate this ultimate handicapping tour de force, earning it a deeper place in history as each year passes.

The essence of handicapping, we are always told, is to weight the horses so that theoretically they will all arrive at the finish at the same time. Bearing a title that smacks of jargon, the racing secretary is in charge of setting out the conditions under which every race at a given track will be run. These conditions include many elements, of which weight carried by the horses and the distance to be run are among the most important. In most races, a pre-set scale, or a formula based on recent earnings, dictates the weights to be carried. In a handicap, however, the racing secretary's judgment is more or less unfettered.

By deduction, fact, and intuition, he attempts to equalize the differences in ability among the runners to get them to the wire together — enhancing the competition. A great many factors other than weight, including the fact that the outside horses are running farther, preclude this ever from actually happening. Still, American racing fans have been treated to some marvelous performances with a boost from racing secretaries.

Handicaps came into vogue with the success of the Suburban Handicap, inaugurated in 1884, and for many years America's champions have been exposed to a stern test of superiority over and above the ability to win repeatedly at weight for age. While weight assignments of 130 pounds or more are rare today, for many years weight carriers such as Discovery, Assault, Kelso, Tom Fool, Bold Ruler, Dr. Fager, and Forego earned status that weight-for-age races could not alone bestow. Along the way, many a thrilling finish has replaced a procession — and, incidentally, made an attractive wagering proposition out of what otherwise would have been an exhibition. So, both the sport and the business of the Turf

William Ziegler's homebred Wait a Bit.

game to the extent that they rank with their employers in status from an historical perspective. John "Jack" Blanks Campbell was one of these. He also had a colorful past, having been born in New Orleans and named for "the cussingest captain on the Mississippi, Capt. Jack Blanks." While operating a cotton press as a young man, Campbell became enamored of horse racing, went on a long winning streak as a bettor, and then was pulled back into reality by a counterpoint losing streak. He caught on as a racing official, mutuel seller — whatever — and by 1914 had begun writing races, as the racing secretary's craft is described, at Douglass Park in Kentucky.

have been well served by handicap racing, as have the reputations of some of our best horses.

The uniqueness of the 1944 Carter Handicap came not from the exceptional quality of its participants, although it included a fine bunch of stakes horses, but from the success by racing secretary Campbell in assessing their relative merits and expressing them via the numbers 115, 118, and 127.

These were the weights assigned three horses whose names formed the lyrical phrase Brownie, Wait a Bit, and Bossuet. (The erudite racing writer and university instructor Joe Palmer anticipated the reader's curiosity over the last of those names: "What interest William Woodward Sr. of Belair Stud has in French religious thought of the period is not clear to the writer...[but] Bossuet got his name from a famous French pulpit orator and theological writer of the late 17th Century.")

Some few racing secretaries and other hired officials have achieved success and lent leadership to the

No one has matched John B. Campbell's feat.

Over the years, Campbell had assigned weights to the likes of Exterminator, Phar Lap, Equipoise, and Count Fleet. He was undeterred by the outraged

GARDEN STATE PARK

Brownie, a homebred who raced for Joe W. Brown.

cries of trainers or owners, and he once reckoned that 143 pounds was just what Discovery should carry in the 1936 Merchants' and Citizens' Handicap. Discovery's owner, Alfred Vanderbilt, was one sportsman who did not complain, and he went for it. Discovery was last, giving forty-three pounds to the mare Esposa, who won. Campbell was defensive, and defiant: "Without 143 pounds on Discovery, it wouldn't have been a horse race."

Thus, Campbell was respected, possibly feared, on the Turf long before he set about weighting

the 1944 Carter Handicap.

Belair Stud's homebred Bossuet was a 1940 foal by Boswell—Vibration II, by Sir Cosmo, trained by Sunny Jim Fitzsimmons and ridden in the Carter by Jimmy Stout.

Joe W. Brown's Brownie was a 1939 foal by Cohort—Dorothy B., by Diavolo, bred in the name of Mrs. Brown, trained by John B. Theall, and ridden by Eric Guerin.

William Ziegler Jr.'s homebred Wait a Bit was a 1939 foal by Espino—Hi-Nelli, by High Cloud, trained by Matt Brady, and ridden by Gayle L. Smith.

It is interesting to note that these three horses that were to be linked historically for their prowess at

Belair Stud's Bossuet, whose pedigree emphasized distance.

seven furlongs were not bred to be sprinters. Bossuet's sire, Boswell, had won England's one and three-quarters-mile St. Leger, and Wait a Bit's sire, Espino, had won the one and five-eighths-mile Lawrence Realization and one and three-quarters-mile Saratoga Cup. Brownie's sire, Cohort, also was the sire of the middle-distance stakes horse Roman Soldier, who had been second to Omaha in the one and a quarter-mile Kentucky Derby.

There was a field of nine in the 1944 Carter. The seven-furlong race carried a purse of $10,000-added, as one of the richest sprint races of the time, and had a field of appropriate merit. The topweight at 132 pounds was Belair's noted sprinter Apache, and the weights ranged down to the 109 assigned Bill Sickle.

Bossuet (127) won five of his nine starts that year, including two other $10,000-added stakes. Wait a Bit (118) won another stakes that year, placed in five others, and had won the Vosburgh and Bay Shore the previous year. He also held the track record of 1:22⅗, set in 1943 under 109 pounds. Brownie (115) won seven other races during 1944, including the Princeton and Bay Shore handicaps, and placed in ten stakes.

The Carter was run over sloppy going at Aqueduct on June 10. Apache gunned to the early lead, but was closely pressed by Bill Sickle and Ariel Lad. The early efforts discouraged Ariel Lad, but Bill Sickle replaced Apache in the lead. In the meantime, Brownie, Bossuet, and Wait a Bit had been fifth, seventh, and eighth in that order in the early going, but the first two were moving forward. In the final furlong, they all came along. Brownie struck the lead first and fought on bravely, as Bossuet gradually gained on him. Wait a Bit was still only seventh at the stretch call. In the imprecise art of the chart caller, he had about three and a half lengths to make

up; in the precision of the photo finish camera, he did exactly that, and nothing more.

The three hit the wire together in 1:23⅘.

Multiple dead heats of yore had involved close finishes and the inability of the human eye of judges to separate them. The Carter involved a close finish, and the photo finish camera. Even so, Palmer reported, the "judges took an extraordinarily long time to study it."

Unable initially to believe what they were seeing, they eventually found it unnecessary to look beyond reality — one major race, three winners.

Carter Handicap
Purse: $10,000 Added

6th Race   Aqueduct - June 10, 1944
Purse $10,000 added. Three-year-olds and upward. 7-8 Mile. Main Track (Out of chute). Track: Sloppy.
Net value to winners $3,623.33 each; fourth, $500.

P#	Horse	A	Wgt	Med	Eqp	Odds	PP	St	3/16	3/8	5/8	Str	Fin	Jockey
6	Brownie DH	5	115		wb	10.60	6	5	$5^{1½}$	4^1	3^{nk}	4^{nk}	$1^{1½}$	E Guerin
3	Bossuet DH	4	127		wb	a-1.05	3	6	7^3	$6^½$	5^1	$3^½$	$1^{1½}$	J Stout
2	Wait a Bit DH	5	118		wsb	6.65	2	8	8^4	8^2	7^h	7^1	$1^{1½}$	G L Smith
9	Bill Sickle	4	109		wb	8.65	9	3	2^h	$3^{1½}$	1^1	1^2	4^h	H Lindberg
7	Apache	5	132		wb	a-1.05	7	2	1^h	1^h	2^2	2^h	5^h	E Arcaro
1	Jack S. L.	4	112		wb	14.20	1	7	6^h	7^2	$6^{1½}$	6^{nk}	6^{nk}	R Permane
5	Alquest	4	120		wb	6.45	5	9	9	9	9	5^h	7^5	J Longden
8	Ariel Lad	5	112		wb	24.50	8	4	4^h	2^h	4^1	8^5	8^{20}	S Brooks
4	Doublrab	6	121		wb	12.45	4	1	3^{nk}	5^{nk}	8^{nk}	9	9	D Meade

Coupled: a-Bossuet and Apache.

Off Time: 4:36½ Eastern War Time   **Time Of Race:**   :22⅖   :44⅘   1:10⅕   1:23⅘
Start: Good For All   **Track:** Sloppy
Equipment: w for whip; b for blinkers; s for spurs

Mutuel Payoffs

6	Brownie DH	$4.30	$3.90	$3.90
3	Bossuet DH (a-entry)	2.40	2.30	2.30
2	Wait a Bit DH	3.50	3.40	3.70

Winners: Brownie, blk. h. by Cohort—Dorothy B., by Diavolo (Trained by John B. Theall); bred by Mrs. Joe W. Brown in Ky. Bossuet, dk. b. c. by Boswell—Vibration II, by Sir Cosmo (Trained by James Fitzsimmons); bred by Belair Stud in Ky. Wait a Bit, ch. h. by Espino—Hi-Nelli, by High Cloud (Trained by M. Brady); bred by Mr. William Ziegler, Jr. in Va.

Start good from stall gate. Won driving.
BROWNIE, well up from the start, assumed a slight lead inside the final eighth and held on gamely. BOSSUET was sent between the leaders in the stretch run and held on with good courage. WAIT A BIT, on the outside and sluggish in the early running, came with a rush at the end. The first three finished in a triple dead heat for first place. BILL SICKLE was sent into command rounding the far turn, drew away and then faltered. APACHE showed early speed and then quit under the weight. JACK S. L. could not keep up. ALQUEST moved up fast on the inside in the stretch and then faltered. ARIEL LAD had early speed. DOUBLRAB was eased up when impeded by a flopping hind bandage.
Scratched—Smart Bet, 97.

Owners: (6) Joe W Brown; (3) Belair Stud; (2) William Ziegler Jr; (9) W-L Ranch; (7) Belair Stud; (1) Mrs J S Letellier; (5) A C Ernst; (8) Selznick Stable; (4) Mrs T Christopher

©DAILY RACING FORM/EQUIBASE

SANTA ANITA

Noor (outside) prevails over Triple
Crown winner Citation.

- CHAPTER 10 -

The Nose of Noor, the Heart of Citation

Because the 1950 San Juan Capistrano was the second in a remarkable sequence that grew into four victories by an upstart over a Triple Crown winner, the suspicion is invited that its status was enhanced in retrospect. We have on the word of Robert Hebert, however, that it was recognized as a pip from the moment Noor and Citation hooked up with more than a half-mile to run. In the week after the race, the articulate, gentlemanly Hebert, who was to cover California racing for *The Blood-Horse* over some forty years, declared it "the greatest race ever run at Santa Anita" and "very easily the greatest race this reporter has ever seen, or expects to see."

So great a horse was Citation in his prime that he was probably the first to convince more than a few horsemen that there might be a fault line within Man o' War's rock of supremacy. At the end of the century, though, he was muscled aside by Secretariat for second place in *The Blood-Horse*'s ranking by a panel of experts, as Man o' War eventually retained top spot. Nevertheless, the Citation chorus remains proudly audible — both insistent and persistent.

We admit to discomfort at the irony of the great Citation appearing in a volume of "great moments" as a runner-up rather than a conqueror. Perhaps we might be permitted to suggest Citation himself shares the responsibility. Citation at his best did not allow "great moments," which for the most part suggests heated battles or astounding dominance. Citation tended to dictate more than titillate. As Joe Palmer's famous quote had it, Man o' War evoked thoughts of "a living flame," Citation "a well-oiled machine."

At two and three Citation lost but twice, and each time there was credible thought that a jockey choosing to persevere might have gotten him up to win. In one case, he was chasing a Calumet Farm stablemate, so what was the purpose of maximum effort? In the second case, jockey Eddie Arcaro was familiarizing himself with the colt and chose not to beat him up to win a minor prep for a larger prep for the ultimate prize, the Kentucky Derby.

Arguably, then, Citation could have been twenty-nine for twenty-nine at the end of his three-year-old campaign, although we must append that even the masterful trainers Ben and Jimmy Jones might have felt the pressure of a two-year unbeaten status and done at least a few things differently. Citation won the Triple Crown in a manner to suggest that the go and Kentucky and New York and New Jersey and Maryland and Florida. He was not big on flair, perhaps, but in race after race he demonstrated an authority that sorely tested any observer's ability to get worked up over wondering who was going to win.

Then he went lame, and things were never the same after that.

Noor and trainer Burley Parke (in white hat).

great, testing sequence was not really very difficult. He dashed older horses in a manner to suggest the weight scale was unnecessary, a joke, in fact. He once won the one-mile Sysonby on Wednesday and the two-mile Jockey Club Gold Cup on Saturday — of the same week. He won in California and Chica-

Citation won nineteen of twenty at three in 1948, standing up to a campaign begun on the East Coast in February and ending on the West Coast in December. He then came up with an osselet — a bony growth in a fetlock — for which he was fired, under the practice of the day. (Firing is a painful procedure in which hot needles or pins are inserted into the unsound area in an effort to hasten healing.) Citation did not get back to the races for more than a year. Jimmy Jones, the trainer of record of most of Citation's career, told Pohla Smith, author of *Citation* in Eclipse Press' Thoroughbred Legends series, that he was against firing Citation, preferring just to give him time. The owner, Warren Wright, prevailed, Jones eventually figuring that the difference was not worth getting fired over, in which case Citation would have been fired anyway and assigned a new trainer.

Having missed his entire four-year-old season, Citation returned at five at Santa Anita, winning an allowance race. This was his sixteenth consecutive victory, a fact that came into play nearly a half-century later when two-time Horse of the Year Cigar was able to match, but not exceed, that number. Thus "16 ones" endures as a modern record for major American racing.

In his next start at five, Citation was beaten by Miche in another overnight sprint designed to hone him back into stakes-class form. Next, in the San Antonio Handicap, he was beaten again, this time by, of all things, a Calumet stablemate, fellow Kentucky Derby winner Ponder. Third was an English-foaled import flying the colors made famous a decade before by Seabiscuit. This was Charles S. Howard's five-year-old Noor. It was an unrecognizable launch of an incredible relationship.

Noor's description above as an upstart is not meant to equate with being undeserving, or commonplace. He was in one of the early crops of Nasrullah and was conceived abroad before the great stallion's importation to Kentucky. Noor was bred by the Aga Khan, but from a mare some distance below His Highness' best, the unplaced Bahram mare Queen of Baghdad. Noor, who was also a three-year-old in 1948, won several lesser stakes and finished third in two very big races, the Epsom Derby and the Eclipse Stakes, that year. In neither his two-year-old nor three-year-old season was he ranked closer than eleven pounds to the top weights in official handicaps for his age.

Noor was imported by Howard as a sort of end link in a chain of events. The Aga Khan's Irish Derby winner Nathoo was brought over to New York in 1948 to contest a new event. James Butler, the owner of Empire City racetrack, had hoped to establish a successful international event. The first two runnings were staged in 1947 and '48 under the auspices of the Empire City Racing Association, but were held at Belmont Park. Nathoo did little in his International Gold Cup visit, save attract the interest of Howard, who pursued the deal after the horse had been returned abroad. (In an interesting side note, Citation won the 1948 Gold Cup.) Contemporary accounts had it that Nathoo was offered at $100,000 when he was in this country, and Howard eventually opted to purchase Nathoo and stablemate Noor for a price reported variously at $150,000 and $175,000.

In the autumn of 1948, the pair was flown to America, and it was discovered that Noor — like his rival of destiny — was developing an osselet.

In a virtual parallel to Citation's plight, he was fired and turned out for almost a year, making his American debut in October of 1949, as a four-year-old. He was trained by Burley Parke, who in later years was coaxed out of retirement by Louis Wolfson of Harbor View Farm, for which he trained champions Raise a Native and Roman Brother.

BERT CLARK THAYER

Citation (right) accompanied by trainer Jimmy Jones (center).

Noor took some races to get sharp, and then in the San Francisco Handicap was ridden for the first time by the great jockey Johnny Longden. The first moments of this partnership hardly created visions of a championship campaign the following year. Noor propped at the start, and Longden at first figured he should just let the recalcitrant beast gallop around the track. Then Noor began to pick it up on his own and came to within a head of catching the winner, Huon Kid. Longden was impressed.

Noor still had only an overnight victory to show for seven races in this country when he lined up for the San Antonio Handicap early in his five-year-old season, but he had come on late in enough races that

he was second choice to the storied Calumet stable-mates Citation and Ponder. Citation carried top weight of 130 pounds, and Ponder under 128 came along to beat him by a length going one and one-eighth miles. Noor, getting sixteen pounds from the Triple Crown winner, finished a half-length behind him in third.

Next came California's signature event, the Santa Anita Handicap. Weights had been assigned before the San Antonio, and Citation took the worst of them. Having finished ahead of Noor by only a half-length while giving him sixteen pounds at nine furlongs, he was now asked to give him twenty-three pounds at an extra furlong, 132 to 109. Longden stressed himself to get to the latter weight, but wound up a pound overweight, Citation thus giving away "only" twenty-two pounds.

Calumet ran a triumvirate that many a successful stable could not have assembled in a lifetime — Citation, Ponder, and distaff champion Two Lea. The female took the lead, Citation stalked, Ponder tarried. It was Noor, however, who finally wore down the pacemaker and got home one and a quarter lengths ahead of Citation, who had to be checked early in the stretch. Two Lea and Ponder finished third and fourth, respectively.

Only a week later Citation and Noor sallied forth for the San Juan Capistrano. At one and three-quarter miles, this handicap offered a challenge for a racing secretary, or perhaps an occasion for virtually total guesswork. Few races are run at that distance. Whether through wisdom or disorientation, racing secretary Webb Everett composed a classic. He gave Citation 130 pounds and Noor 117, reducing the weight spread from twenty-two to thirteen. Eight horses turned up, and although Citation this time had no Calumet teammates, he was favored at 3-5, with Noor second choice at just under 7-2. None of the other runners carried more than 108 pounds, and the lightweight, Rose Beam, was getting twenty-six pounds from Citation.

Eddie Arcaro, who had ridden Citation in the Triple Crown, had come back to ride the horse again in his last two races, but this event was left to another frequent partner, Steve Brooks. Longden was again on Noor. Brooks had Citation under a strong hold as they allowed Old Rockport and Moonrush to lead early. Then the Calumet charger took over. Longden, poised about four lengths back early, moved Noor to him. Citation and Noor

hooked into a bloody battle with slightly more than a half-mile to run.

On went the furlongs, with the great champion and his new antagonist locked together. "It was an unforgettable spectacle," recalled the *American Racing Manual.*

"Every step of the last five-sixteenths of a mile, Citation and Noor were together, stride for stride," exuded *The Blood-Horse*'s Hebert. "At the quarter pole, Noor, on the outside, had an advantage of perhaps a head. In mid-stretch, Citation had battled his way to the top by a quarter of a length. Ten yards from the wire, Citation still looked like the winner; then Noor, calling on some untapped reserve of speed and courage under an inspired ride by Longden, came along to arch his head under the wire in what surely must have been the last jump. Both horses were straight as a string at the finish. The camera caught them both with heads outstretched, as though they were reaching for that elusive finish line. The margin was a couple of inches, and it belonged to Noor."

Mocopo was third, a respectful twelve and a half lengths behind Citation.

The time was 2:52⅘, which was immediately recognized as a new American record. The world record at the time was attributed to Buen Ojo, who had been recorded in 2:52⅗ at Montevideo in Uruguay in 1922. Buen Ojo's race, however, had been measured in meters, giving him some fifty-three feet less to cover at one and three-quarter miles. By the time the 1952 *American Racing Manual* was published, Noor's effort had been upgraded to recognition as the world record.

A remarkable aspect of Noor's and Citation's 1950 season was that this was but one of four world

Nearing the wire in the San Juan Capistrano, Noor and Citation appear inseparable.

records they set. Noor was to go on to two more victories over the once invincible star, and in each he set an additional world mark. On consecutive Saturdays in June, Noor won the nine-furlong Forty-Niners Handicap in an unprecedented 1:46⅘ and the Golden Gate Handicap in 1:58⅕ for a new world mark at ten furlongs. (Owner Howard had suffered a fatal heart attack in early June, and the Estate of C.S. Howard was listed as owner for subsequent victories.)

To be fair to Noor, it should be noted that the one-two finish order of the two horses remained the same, even as the weight spread in Noor's favor decreased. In the Forty-Niners, Noor (123) got but

five pounds from Citation and beat him a neck in another struggle. Then, in the Golden Gate, the pendulum had swung to the other side, and Noor, carrying 127, actually gave Citation a pound and beat him three lengths.

Between the Santa Anita and Golden Gate race meetings, Citation had put in a world mark of his own, getting a mile in 1:33⅗ in the Golden Gate Mile Handicap.

Noor later went East, where he failed in several races, but after being returned to the West late in the same season, he beat the eventual Horse of the Year, Hill Prince, while carrying 130 pounds in the Hollywood Gold Cup. Champions Next Move and

Assault were in the beaten field. In defeating Citation and the aging Assault (in the Gold Cup and an allowance in his last previous start), Noor had thus become the first horse to defeat two Triple Crown winners. (This airy status was matched in a single afternoon in 1978, when Exceller won the Jockey Club Gold Cup over a field including Triple Crown winners Seattle Slew and Affirmed.) It is also worth a note that Noor defeated three Horses of the Year in Citation, Assault, and Hill Prince. He won seven of twelve races in 1950 and was voted the champion older horse. Noor was retired with a lifetime record of twelve victories, six seconds, and six thirds in thirty-one starts.

Citation, who had lost only twice in his first two years, lost seven of nine races at five in 1950, but he finished second in all of his defeats. His owner's desire that he become the first horse to earn one million dollars was so much a sentimental motivation that, although Wright had died late in 1950, his widow and the Jones father-son team brought the horse back at six. He was raced into splendid form yet again, and he went over the goal in winning the Hollywood Gold Cup as a six-year-old. Citation was retired then with a career record of thirty-two wins in forty-five starts and earnings of $1,085,760.

San Juan Capistrano Handicap
Purse: $50,000 Added

7th Race Santa Anita - March 4, 1950

Purse $50,000 added. Three-year-olds and upward. 1 3-4 Miles. Main Track (Out of chute). Track: Fast. Gross value, $64,000. Net value to winner $40,400; second, $10,000; third, $7,500; fourth, $5,000.

P#	Horse	A	Wgt	Med	Eqp	Odds	PP	St	1/2	1m	1½	Str	Fin	Jockey
4	Noor	5	117		wb	3.40	4	7	7^{3}	$6^{\frac{1}{2}}$	2^{8}	2^{10}	1^{n}	J Longden
8	Citation	5	130		w	.60	8	2	4^{3}	2^{2}	1^{h}	1^{h}	$2^{12\frac{1}{2}}$	S Brooks
2	Mocopo	4	107		w	a-8.80	2	6	$6^{1\frac{1}{2}}$	$5^{1\frac{1}{2}}$	$5^{1\frac{1}{2}}$	$5^{\frac{1}{2}}$	3^{h}	G Lasswell
1	Old Rockport	4	108		wb	a-8.80	1	4	2^{2}	1^{h}	4^{3}	4^{1}	4^{h}	G Glisson
3	Hedgewood	4	105		wb	32.25	3	8	8	8	8	8	5^{1}	W Boland
6	Rose Beam	5	104		wb	10.50	6	3	3^{h}	7^{3}	6^{2}	$6^{4\frac{1}{2}}$	6^{8}	W Shoemaker
7	Safe Arrival	5	106		wb	29.40	7	5	$5^{1\frac{1}{2}}$	$4^{\frac{1}{2}}$	7^{4}	7^{3}	7^{2}	W Litz'erg
5	Moonrush	4	105		wb	19.50	5	1	$1^{1\frac{1}{2}}$	$3^{\frac{1}{2}}$	3^{2}	$3^{1\frac{1}{2}}$	8	N Wall

a - Coupled, Mocopo and Old Rockport.

Off Time: 5:12 Pacific Standard Time **Time Of Race:** :24 :47⅘ 1:12⅖ 1:38 2:02⅗ 2:27⅕ 2:52⅘ (New American record and track record)
Start: Good For All but Hedgewood **Track:** Fast
Equipment: w for whip; b for blinkers

Mutuel Payoffs

4	**Noor**	**$8.80**	**$3.00**	**$2.50**
8	**Citation**		**2.30**	**2.10**
2	**Mocopo (a-entry)**			**2.60**

Winner: Noor, br. h. by Nasrullah (Eng)—Queen of Baghdad, by Bahram (Trained by B. Parke).
Bred by H. H. Aga Khan (Ireland).

Start good from stall gate for all but Hedgewood. Won driving; second and third the same.
NOOR, hard held through the early running, was eased to the outside after the first mile, moved up with a bold rush to engage CITATION at the half-mile ground, raced head and head with that one thereafter and under a sustained drive, was up in the final stride. CITATION was never far back, raced on the outside for the first mile where he displaced OLD ROCKPORT and came to the inside, rallied gamely when challenged by the winner and under a very stiff drive just failed to last, although easily best of the others. MOCOPO passed only tired horses. OLD ROCKPORT showed early foot and weakened in the drive. MOONRUSH showed good speed for the first mile then gave way steadily. ROSE BEAM could not keep up. SAFE ARRIVAL was through early. HEDGEWOOD attempted to wheel at the start and trailed his field thereafter.
Overweight—Mocopo, 3 pounds; Hedgewood, 2; Safe Arrival, 2.

Owners: (4) C S Howard; (8) Calumet Farm; (2) C Mooers; (1) C Mooers; (3) E Lasker (6) Foxcatcher Farm; (7) Foster & Collins; (5) King & Luellwitz

©DAILY RACING FORM/EQUIBASE

Swaps confirming his Derby form in the Californian.

- CHAPTER 11 -

Duel of Derby Winners

The Kentucky Derby looks down from such exalted singularity on the American Turf that any meeting of winners of the event takes on a special significance. Meetings of Derby winners are not totally unheard of, but neither are they commonplace.

One of the most intriguing events in racing lore found not two, but three Derby winners, facing off. This was the 1917 Brooklyn Handicap. Regret, who would reign for sixty-five years as the only filly to have won the Derby, ran against two other Kentucky Derby winners, Old Rosebud and Omar Khayyam. The powerful field also included the fine handicappers Roamer, Stromboli, and Borrow. Alas, all three Derby winners were beaten by Regret's nine-year-old stablemate Borrow. The winner's rider was expected to defer to the female if he could, but kicked his old mount into high gear when it appeared that Old Rosebud might be a menace. Borrow won by a nose over Regret, who saved second after all. This gave owner Harry Payne Whitney a one-two finish, but such was the sportsman's affection for Regret

that it was said he was near tears.

Of the other pairings of Derby winners, a couple had unique twists: when Citation ran against Ponder, it was a matter of Calumet Farm flaunting two of its Derby winners; when Affirmed met Seattle Slew, it was not just two Derby winners, but two Triple Crown winners facing each other!

Also among the memorable Derby pairings were the duels of Ferdinand and Alysheba in the 1987 Breeders' Cup Classic and 1988 Santa Anita Handicap. The four-year-old Ferdinand held off the younger colt in the first meeting to clinch Horse of the Year, but Alysheba triumphed in their second meeting to help launch his own Horse-of-the-Year campaign. Either of the Ferdinand-Alysheba meetings could certainly represent the meeting of Derby winners in such a volume as this one. We have chosen another race to represent that scenario, however, in part because the 1955 Californian came earlier in the season than most meetings of three-year-olds and older horses. Indeed, the younger of the two rose-bedecked protagonists, Swaps, had won his Derby only two races before.

The Californian brought the fresh young Swaps head and head against the weathered and noble Determine, who had won the Derby in 1954.

Both horses were based in California and joined Calumet Farm's Hill Gail as the third Santa Anita Derby winner in four years to proceed to Churchill Downs and land the big prize. Nevertheless, some holdover scars remained along the Western psyche from the 1950 disappointment of California-based Your Host, so considerable state pride was generated as a result of Determine's and Swaps' consecutive Derby triumphs. While Determine was a Kentucky-bred adopted by the West, Swaps was a Californian from foaling and eventually would be hailed as the state's greatest racehorse of all time.

Determine was a gray son of Alibhai—Koubis, by Mahmoud, bred by Dr. Eslie Asbury and purchased by Californian Andy Crevolin for $12,000 at Keeneland as a yearling of 1952. He was tiny, said to weigh just less than nine-hundred pounds as a three-year-old, and his size and coat color helped to endear him to his fans. William Molter trained the horse and asked him to exhibit much of the ruggedness and durability Molter would ask a few years later of Round Table.

Determine won a pair of stakes from four victories in fourteen starts at two. Then, at three, he raced fifteen times, getting ten victories, all in stakes, despite having interruptions due to an abscessed jaw, a fever, and the hint of splint trouble. He defeated Hasty Road in becoming the first gray to win the Derby and then was returned to the West, where he was still winning stakes, at Golden Gate, in December. (The second gray to win the Kentucky Derby would be Determine's son Decidedly, in 1962.) Turn-to, High Gun, and Hasty Road were regarded from time to time as the top of that class of three-year-olds. Their Eastern campaigns, which perhaps were looked upon as more important, probably fueled that perception, especially when compared to Determine's less fashionable California schedule. At any rate, no three-year-old of that crop was tougher than Determine.

The little gray's three-year-old season segued into his next campaign, and he made his first start at four on the first day of 1955. He won only four of fifteen that year, but seemed always in the battle against the best, often carrying top weight. When an injury stopped him and he was galloped in a farewell ceremony at Del Mar later that summer, the crowd rose to greet him. Wrote *The Blood-Horse*'s Joe Estes, "In California he was among the most popular horses in history. The racing fans there might have admitted that they had seen better horses — a very few better horses — but virtually none of them would have admitted that they had seen a horse with greater courage."

Determine won eighteen races from forty-four starts and earned $573,360.

In addressing Swaps, we have the luxury of using the G word without reservation or condition. He was a Great horse. While this was not yet proven in June of his three-year-old year, it was beginning to be clear that he was something quite special, and quite marvelous. By the end of his four-year-old campaign, Californians had little reason even to wonder if they had seen a better horse, and many undoubtedly made the case that no one else had either.

Swaps was a California foal bred by Rex Ellsworth and was a son of Khaled, the Hyperion stallion

Determine with trainer William Molter and owner Andy Crevolin (right) in the winner's circle after the 1954 Kentucky Derby.

Ellsworth had purchased from the Aga Khan. The dam of Swaps was Iron Reward, a Beau Pere mare whose own dam, Iron Maiden, also became the dam of a Kentucky Derby winner, Iron Liege. Ellsworth and his trainer and friend, Mesh Tenney, were transplanted Arizona Mormons who would eventually rise to the top, as Ellsworth spent two seasons as both leading breeder and owner. (Sadly, many years later he was accused of failing to feed a number of horses adequately, but his and Tenney's prolonged success from happier times earned Tenney a place in racing's Hall of Fame.)

At the time Swaps emerged, Ellsworth and Tenney were not especially well known outside California. Their cowboy brand of horsemanship was seen as unusual by many Easterners, but it certainly

THE LOUISVILLE COURIER-JOURNAL

A California conquest: Swaps in the Kentucky Derby winner's circle in 1955 with trainer Mesh Tenney (at horse's head) and owner Rex Ellsworth. Bill Shoemaker is aboard.

proved effective. Not the sort to call on veterinarians and blacksmiths very often, Tenney worked adroitly and expertly with an infection in one of Swaps' somewhat shelly feet. His efforts included protecting the injury with a pad and leather, such as was used for soles of women's tennis shoes, and also packing the troublesome spot with lanolin and a sulfa drug. Even so, there were times when Swaps could not even be taken out of the stall and

walked, and it came down to a bit of savvy and intuition to get him to the post for the Kentucky Derby. A few days before the race, Tenney feared he was losing control of the ever-present problem, but he removed the shoe and filed the hoof to a different angle, thus easing the pressure on the aggravated area.

Swaps had been a nice stakes winner at two. Then, when he won the Santa Anita Derby the next winter,

Californians began to emote. Moreover, he was so impressive in his sprint prep at Churchill Downs a week before the Derby that as the betting was churning along, he seemed likely for a time to go to the post as the favorite. This happened in spite of his facing the immensely popular and imposing Eastern colt, Nashua.

Bill Shoemaker put Swaps on the lead early in the Derby, and they turned back everything the post-time favorite, Nashua, and Eddie Arcaro tried on them. Swaps sailed home by one and a half lengths, and then sailed home again, in a manner of speaking. Like Determine, he was returned to California, foregoing any effort to seek the Triple Crown. Nashua would go on to win the other two legs. (Tenney, who had slept in a stall nightly prior to the Derby, gave himself the luxury of sleeping instead in a car the night after the race.)

The pattern of Western stables leaving the Preakness and Belmont to others after winning the Derby was followed again the next time a California-based horse won at Churchill Downs. This was Tomy Lee, the 1959 winner. Most subsequent Derby winners from the West — and they have been frequent — have gone on to the Preakness as the Triple Crown's magnetism increased over the years. In fact, since Tomy Lee, only two Derby winners have missed the Preakness for reasons other than soundness. One was Gato Del Sol, the 1982 Derby hero whose connections simply thought the race and length of recovery time did not suit him and stuck by their convictions. The other was 1985 Derby winner Spend a Buck, whose owners were lured to the Jersey Derby to cash in on a rich bonus for an overlapping series of races.

Swaps' first start after the Derby came three weeks later in the Will Rogers Stakes at the Hollywood Park meeting. The returning conqueror won by a dozen lengths, getting a mile in 1:35.

The ordinary scenario for three-year-olds challenging their elders is for such meetings to come in the autumn, or in the case of Eastern horses, a race at Saratoga. Exceptions abound, of course, including Stagehand's Santa Anita Handicap victory over the older Seabiscuit and Citation's winter romps against his elders. Then, too, Elliott Burch and Woody Stephens successfully used the one-mile Metropolitan Handicap for three-year-olds heading into the Belmont Stakes. By and large, however, three-year-olds tend to challenge their elders in autumn weight-for-age races.

In contrast, Swaps faced a fine field of older horses as early as June 11, or five weeks after the Derby. The Californian had been added the previous year to the calendar, joining the Hollywood Gold Cup and Sunset Handicap as major targets during the Hollywood Park meeting. It was run at a mile and a sixteenth and offered a purse of $100,000-added, at that time a figure still close to the maximum of any purse. Both Kentucky Derby winners carried scale weight for the month and distance, 126 pounds on the older Determine and 115 on Swaps, that being the spread believed to compensate for the relative difference in strength and maturity between three-year-olds and older horses at that time of the year. The others were in receipt of weight from Swaps according to the scale, the older Mister Gus, Novarullah, and Travertine each in at 117, and the highly accomplished Rejected at 120.

Shoemaker was serving a suspension for careless riding, and Tenney and Ellsworth called Dave Erb in from Chicago. Erb had had some successes for them in the past.

The reputation of jockey John Longden for cleverness at controlling the pace of races from the front end, along with the proven ability of a colt named Mister Gus, had Ellsworth worried.

"We respected Determine and others in the race, but the horse that really worried us was Mister Gus," Ellsworth said. "He was the key to the whole race as far as we were concerned."

Robert Hebert's report of the race in *The Blood-Horse* recalled that the morning Erb arrived, he went to the barn for a strategy session with Tenney. The trainer warned Erb that Londgen might set a rapid pace of twenty-two or twenty-one seconds in the first quarter-mile and then slow it down and save plenty for the stretch. "I was afraid Longden might 'twenty-one' it out of the gate for the first quarter-mile or so, then gradually sneak back and slow up the field without others being aware of it, then gradually sneak off again," said Tenney. The specificity of that scenario was such that Tenney need not have added that Longden had "done it before." He was clearly speaking from memory.

Controlling a race from the front was something of Longden's stock in trade. Among many examples was the 1951 Santa Anita Handicap, when Longden gunned the 10-1 Moonrush through early fractions of :22⅗ and :46⅗ on a holding track, then eased off and had just enough left to defeat Next Move in the stretch. Even the *Racing Form* chart editorialized that Moonrush was "perfectly rated."

"It's good riding," Tenney said of such tactics, "but we didn't want it to happen to us. I cautioned Erb to watch out for that, then told him not to take back enough to make Swaps shake his head."

The crowd of more than 51,000 read the race's

form the same way and made Mister Gus a slight second choice at 9-2 over the revered Determine. Their new darling, Swaps, was favored at 3-5.

Erb found that his mount was so quick that he was in front out of the gate, and as he tried to rein in Swaps early, the big chestnut was so anxious to run that he threw his head up in resistance before relenting to the strategy. "Longden lulled Erb into thinking he was setting a blistering pace only for the first quarter, which was a slow :23⅕," Hebert noted.

Liz Whitney-Tippet's Mister Gus, from Charlie Whittingham's stable, led through a half-mile in :46 and six furlongs in 1:10. Erb knew the score and kept Swaps a couple of lengths off, but comfortably and menacingly. The sleek colt began to move up on the turn in response to hand riding and a couple of casual taps of the down-turned whip along the shoulder. Meanwhile, Ray York had Determine about four lengths off the pace and was aware of the need to keep in touch. He began urging his little star for more on the far turn.

Swaps had no trouble getting to Mister Gus, although the front-runner held on gamely for a while. As the crowd cheered Swaps on, he opened a daylight lead without coming under pressure to do so. He completed a mile in 1:34, and although his fellow Derby winner edged ever closer as they neared the wire, Erb looked back and knew he had total control. The new wonder flashed under the wire with a one and a quarter-length lead. Courage was one thing you could rely on Determine to demonstrate, and he was not found wanting. But his prolonged effort in the stretch got him only a strenuous half-length on Mister Gus for second. Determine was runner-up in the race for the second time, having been beaten by a speedy stablemate, Imbros, in the 1954 inaugural.

The time was 1:40⅖, a world record "achieved almost casually," noted Estes. "World record" would become almost synonymous with the name of Swaps in the future and of the Californian. Estes wrote admiringly that "the parallel of this performance — a 3-year-old in June beating a top-class field of older horses without a weight advantage — was beyond memory in American racing."

Tenney discounted the age difference: "I don't know where the idea originated that a young horse can be knocked out, or his heart broken, by running him against older horses. A horse does not know if the animal next to him is younger, older, or the same age. The only thing that will knock a horse out, or break his heart, is asking him to do something when he is not in the physical shape to do it."

Swaps continued winning, in California and Chicago, until he lost his summer match race with Nashua, a defeat his fans were quick to attribute to another flare-up of soreness. The following year he toured through major victories, most in record times, winning eight of ten, and was voted Horse of the Year. He had won nineteen of twenty-five races and earned $848,900. At the end of the century, he was rated twentieth in *The Blood-Horse*'s *Thoroughbred Champions: Top 100 Racehorses of the 20th Century*, and that seems hardly to flatter him.

Californian Stakes
Purse: $100,000 Added

7th Race Hollywood Park - June 11, 1955
Purse $100,000 added. Three-year-olds and upward. 1 1-16 Miles. Main Track. Track: Fast.
Gross value, $109,800. Net value to winner $63,700; second, $20,000; third, $15,000; fourth, $10,000. Mutuel pool $478,245.

P#	Horse	A	Wgt	Med	Eqp	Odds	PP	St	1/4	1/2	3/4	Str	Fin	Jockey
1	Swaps	3	115		w	.65	1	1	2^{3}	2^{2}	2^{2}	1^{1}	$1^{1\frac{1}{4}}$	D Erb
4	Determine	4	126		wb	5.30	4	4	3^{h}	3^{3}	3^{4}	3^{4}	$2^{\frac{1}{2}}$	R York
5	Mister Gus	4	117		wb	4.50	5	2	1^{2}	1^{2}	1^{1}	2^{3}	3^{3}	J Longden
2	Rejected	5	120		wb	5.55	2	6	6	6	5^{2}	4^{h}	4^{1}	I Valenzuela
3	Novarullah	5	117		w	17.90	3	3	4^{3}	4^{3}	4^{h}	5^{7}	5^{6}	G Glisson
6	Travertine	4	117		wb	66.00	6	5	5^{3}	5^{2}	6	6	6	M Volzke

Off Time: 5:21 Pacific Daylight Time **Time Of Race:** :23⅕ :46 1:10 1:34 1:40⅖ (new world record)
Start: Good For All **Track:** Fast
Equipment: w for whip; b for blinkers

Mutuel Payoffs

1	**Swaps**	**$3.30**	**$2.60**	**$2.10**
4	**Determine**		**3.90**	**2.50**
5	**Mister Gus**			**2.40**

Winner: Swaps, ch. c. by Khaled—Iron Reward, by Beau Pere (Trained by M. A. Tenney).
Bred by Mr. R. C. Ellsworth in Calif.

Start good. Won easily; second and third driving. SWAPS followed the pace under strong restraint, took command when ready without need of urging and held his advantage while still under restraint. DETERMINE was in hand to the second turn, was called upon, was put to increased pressure after reaching the final straightaway and finished with fine courage. MISTER GUS made the pace under good rating, saved ground, readily gave way to the winner and held on gamely. REJECTED was not persevered with when outrun, was called upon on the second turn, and could not get to the leaders. NOVARULLAH failed to rally when called upon. TRAVERTINE never threatened.

Owners: (1) R C Ellsworth; (4) A J Crevolin; (5) Llangollen Farm; (2) KIng Ranch; (3) N S McCarthy; (6) Mr & Mrs T M Kerr

©DAILY RACING FORM/EQUIBASE

*The best of one of the great foal crops
met in the Trenton Handicap, and
Bold Ruler prevailed.*

- CHAPTER 12 -

The Law of Rule

When crops of American three-year-olds are savored in aftermath, the mighty triumvirate of 1957 is always poured a considerable draught of respect. Bold Ruler, Gallant Man, and Round Table were all voted as being among the top three-dozen horses of the twentieth century by *The Blood-Horse*.

Underscoring the status of this group, the 1957 Kentucky Derby, which had them all, is often regarded as the best field in the race's history. (As it turned out, the sprite in the make-up of the racing gods had arranged for this great Derby field to coincide with one of the event's most bizarre outcomes — and none of the three top stars won the race!) At year's end they reassembled for their only other tripartite conference, in the Trenton Handicap. As a horse race, it was one of those that may fairly be regarded as anticlimactic — at least in two of the three camps. Weather conspired to compromise the form and handed a boost to the front-running Bold Ruler. However, as a race with legitimate pre-event excitement, importance to championship voting,

and sheer abundance of Thoroughbred radiance, the 1957 Trenton was "grade A" — as jockey Eddie Arcaro said of the winner.

Round Table and Bold Ruler had a shared destiny from birth. They were foaled on the same spring night, April 6 of 1954, at the same farm, the historic Claiborne Farm, where the Hancock family has fostered a three-generation fiefdom of the highest order. They were sons of two of Claiborne's best stallions, Nasrullah (Bold Ruler) and Princequillo (Round Table), and would eventually both return to Claiborne as stallions themselves.

Gallant Man was bred by another of the great operations, that of the Aga Khan II, and was foaled in Ireland. He was by the Prix de l'Arc de Triomphe winner Migoli and out of the Mahmoud mare Majideh, and was one of nine yearlings purchased privately from the Aga Khan by Humphrey S. Finney. The latter was acting on behalf of Ralph Lowe of Midland, Texas, and reports of the deal placed the package anywhere between $200,000 and

$300,000. Gallant Man was said to have been evaluated well off the top among the colts.

Bold Ruler (Nasrullah—Miss Disco, by Discovery) was the lone member of the three star colts to race for his breeder. He was a product of the well-established Wheatley Stable of Mrs. Henry Carnegie Phipps. Round Table (Princequillo—Knight's Daughter, by Sir Cosmo) raced in the silks

SKEETS MEADORS

Bold Ruler and Sunny Jim Fitzsimmons. The late Whitney Tower, who covered racing for* Sports Illustrated, *is behind Fitzsimmons.

of Oklahoma oilman Travis M. Kerr, who had purchased controlling interest from the breeder, A.B. (Bull) Hancock Jr. of Claiborne Farm, for $145,000 early in the colt's three-year-old season.

There were contrasts among the trainers. Bold Ruler was trained by the venerated old horseman Sunny Jim Fitzsimmons; Round Table by the West Coast-based Willie Molter, who also had topped the trainer standings; and Gallant Man was under the care of John Nerud, a future Hall of Famer but at the time a somewhat brash newcomer to the scene of top stakes success.

———⊱─⊷─◦─⊶─⊰———

Amazingly, there might have been another three-year-old of 1957 who, had he stayed sound, could have emerged as the champion over Bold Ruler, Gallant Man, and Round Table. This was Calumet Farm's Gen. Duke. In the winter of 1957, Gen. Duke and Bold Ruler swapped wins in the Bahamas, Everglades, and Flamingo. Bold Ruler won the first and the third, but Gen. Duke seemed to be getting the better of his rival by Florida Derby time. His mile and an eighth in 1:46⅗ in that race matched the world record, whereas Bold Ruler's 1:47 in the Flamingo had been "merely" a track record. The power of Gen. Duke's stretch drive elevated him to the status of Derby favorite. Alas, he fell lame and had to be withdrawn. (Gen. Duke's passage from heroic to tragic figure was swift, for he developed wobbler syndrome and died the following year.)

After the Florida Derby, Bold Ruler and Gallant Man put on a wonderful display in the Wood Memorial, coming to the wire together with Bold Ruler getting a nose win in 1:48⅘. That sent the winner into the Kentucky Derby as the favorite. Bold Ruler was the only member of the top three to have been a star at two. Indeed, after his early stakes victories had led to a triumph in the Futurity, he had seemed assured juvenile championship honors, but late season defeats at a mile and one-sixteenth denied him the crown and introduced doubts as to his stamina. The championship went to yet another Calumet colt, a sort of one-race wonder named Barbizon, who won the rich Garden State Stakes.

Gallant Man had come along well enough to win

the six-furlong Hibiscus Stakes early in 1957, and his effort in the Wood Memorial proved he was ready to challenge the best. Round Table had failed in his prime Western target, the Santa Anita Derby, but went into the Run for the Roses off a scintillating six-length victory in Keeneland's Blue Grass Stakes. Illustrative of the quality these colts were demonstrating is that the times for the Flamingo, Florida Derby, Wood Memorial, and Blue Grass had all been new track records.

Eddie Arcaro long afterward regretted trying to rate the front-running, free wheeling Bold Ruler in the 1957 Derby. He was gagging the colt back to stay out of a speed duel with a fleet colt named Federal Hill, who that year was responsible for some notable race times — and many a fatigued rival. Bold Ruler flattened out and could not challenge as Gen. Duke's less-regarded stablemate, Iron Liege, raced in front through the stretch. It was then that the 1957 Derby took on an enduring stamp of the weird. Bill Shoemaker had Gallant Man boiling up from seventh and seemed to have dead aim on Bill Hartack and Iron Liege. Then one of the greatest of all riders made one of the greatest of all gaffs. Mistaking the sixteenth pole for the finish line, Shoe rose in his stirrups. The mistake occupied a millisecond — and the rest of Shoemaker's career. Whether it cost Gallant Man

even an erg of momentum or speed is debatable, but he failed by a nose to catch Iron Liege. Round Table was third and Bold Ruler fourth.

The result of the Derby, then, could be seen to cast doubt on whether this had been such a great field after all. Subsequent form ratified that Bold Ruler, Gallant Man, and Round Table were even better than they had indicated prior to the first Saturday in May.

By the time they met again six months later, Bold Ruler had dominated the Preakness and added the Jerome, Vosburgh, and two other stakes, carrying up to 136 pounds victoriously.

Gallant Man had set an American record while whomping Bold Ruler in the mile and a half Belmont Stakes, added the Travers, defeated older horses, and won the two-mile Jockey Club Gold Cup.

Round Table had strung together eleven consec-

Round Table and Willie Molter (on lead pony).

93

utive wins, traveling about the country to take such races as the Hollywood Gold Cup, Westerner, American Derby, United Nations Handicap, and Hawthorne Gold Cup; he had switched adroitly from dirt to turf and back; beaten older horses; and won under 130 pounds.

Gallant Man and Bold Ruler already had met in an autumn showdown of quality, and there was no disgrace in their second- and third-place finishes, re-

Gallant Man and John Nerud.

spectively, behind the eventual older champion Dedicate in the Woodward Stakes.

The Trenton Handicap meeting came together rapidly after the trainers of Dedicate, Round Table, and Gallant Man considered and then declined invitations to run a mile and a half on grass in the Washington, D.C., International on November 11. The Trenton had never been one of the autumn's great championship stages, but it offered a nice purse of $75,000-added and was to be run November 9.

Garden State Park racing secretary Ty Shea assigned Dedicate top weight of 128 pounds, but the older horse seemed to be in need of freshening. The weights for the three-year-old cracks were 124 for Gallant Man and Round Table, 122 for Bold Ruler. Magically, all appeared, and no others challenged.

A crowd of 39,077 had trouble guessing who was the best. Gallant Man was a slight choice at 1.40-1 over Bold Ruler at 1.60-1, and Round Table the "outsider" at 1.70-1.

There was still no proof that Bold Ruler was effective in top company going a mile and a quarter, and he was not the soundest of horses. To help warm him out of a touch of arthritis, he was not walked to the paddock as most horses are before a race, but was jogged over from the backstretch with an exercise rider up.

Distance doubt or not, Arcaro had learned not to try to rate Bold Ruler. The big, dark Nasrullah colt sprang into the lead, evoking Arcaro's comparison to "a big cat," and established a clear margin early. Bold Ruler being in front was the presumption all along. Round Table figured to stalk the pace, but Round Table's one weakness was difficulty in handling off going. Rain had made the track wet, and it was still sticky, officially termed "good," at post time. Bill Harmatz nudged Round Table along in second, five lengths clear of the stretch-running Gallant Man, but Round Table could not stay in touch with Bold Ruler. Arcaro had the leader off sailing, and he increased the lead to eight lengths with six furlongs in 1:11⅖. That was it.

Gallant Man inexorably came to Round Table and drew off as the latter struggled with the going. Shoemaker and Gallant Man closed a good deal of ground, but never seemed to make a race of it, and

Bold Ruler flashed on home, winning by two and a quarter lengths. Gallant Man was second, Round Table eight and a half lengths farther back. The time was 2:01⅗, just three-fifths of a second outside the track record.

>—⟡—○—⟡—⟡—<

The Trenton tilted the balance of voting toward Bold Ruler. He was the three-year-old champion on both the *Daily Racing Form* and Thoroughbred Racing Associations polls and Horse of the Year on the *Form* poll as well. The TRA gave Horse of the Year to Dedicate. Round Table, while beaten in the showdown, had excelled enough on grass to salvage the first of his championships in that division.

The big three never gathered again, although each went on to sustained glory. Bold Ruler and Gallant Man swapped wins in the Carter Handicap and Metropolitan Mile, respectively, the next year in the only other meetings involving any two of the three. Both proved major winners at a mile and a quarter or more under heavy weights. Round Table reigned as Horse of the Year at four and extended his three years as grass course champion through his five-year-old season. He retired as racing's leading money winner, with forty-three wins in sixty-six starts and earnings of $1,749,869. Bold Ruler won twenty-three of thirty-three and earned $764,204, and Gallant Man won fourteen of twenty-six and earned $510,355.

All three were exceptional stallions, but even so, in that context Bold Ruler ran off (leading the list eight times) — just as he had done in the 1957 Trenton.

Trenton Handicap
Purse: $75,000 Added

7th Race Garden State Park - November 9, 1957
Purse $75,000 added. Three-year-olds and upward. 1 1-4 Miles. Main Track (Out of chute). Track: Good.
Gross value, $82,350. Net to winner $54,736.25; second, $17,705.25; third, $9,058.50. Mutuel pool $267,737.

P#	Horse	A	Wgt	Med	Eqp	Odds	PP	St	1/2	3/4	1m	Str	Fin	Jockey
1	Bold Ruler	3	122		wb	1.60	1	1	1³½	1⁸	1³½	1³	1²¼	E Arcaro
3	Gallant Man	3	124		w	1.40	3	3	3	3	2ʰ	2²	2⁸½	W Shoemaker
2	Round Table	3	124		wb	1.70	2	2	2⁵	2²¼	3	3	3	W Harmatz

Off Time: 4:10 Eastern Standard Time		**Time Of Race:**	:23⅗ :47⅕ 1:11⅕ 1:36⅖ 1:49⅗ 2:01⅗	
Start: Good For All	**Track:** Good			
Equipment: w for whip; b for blinkers				

Mutuel Payoffs

1	Bold Ruler	$5.20	$2.40	.....
3	Gallant Man		2.60	.....
	No Show Mutuels Sold.			

Winner: Bold Ruler, dk. b. c. by Nasrullah—Miss Disco, by Discovery (Trained by J. Fitzsimmons).
Bred by Wheatley Stable in Ky.

Start good. Won ridden out; second and third driving.
BOLD RULER was jogged to the paddock with exercise rider up. He quickly established a clear lead leaving the gate with Arcaro having a snug hold and steering out for the best footing. After pacing along evenly under steadying restraint, BOLD RULER slowed down slightly on the final turn, then willingly responded to hand pressure and, being occasionally "shown" the whip through the final three-sixteenths, and continued strongly to the end. GALLANT MAN was allowed to set his own speed through the initial quarter-mile, was very lightly roused through the next sixteenth, then was rated entering the first turn and until approaching the half-mile pole. Shoemaker steered GALLANT MAN inside of ROUND TABLE, rapidly making up ground on the final turn, failed to gain appreciably from the last furlong pole and into the final sixteenth, but was gaining slightly in the concluding yards. ROUND TABLE dropped his head at the start and swerved out slightly, recovered without effort and was restrained closest to the pace. Through the backstretch he appeared to dislike the footing, but responded to the challenge from GALLANT MAN and stayed with that rival for about three-sixteenths of a mile, then flattened noticeably in the last furlong.
Scratched—Wise Margin, 115; Beam Rider, 110.

Owners: (1) Wheatley Stable; (3) R Lowe; (2) Kerr Stable
©DAILY RACING FORM/EQUIBASE

*Early in the race, Tudor Era leads
Australia's Sailor's Guide, with Europe's
best and "the Russians" toiling behind.*

- CHAPTER 13 -

The Cold War Olympics

Over much of Thoroughbred racing's history, the difficulty of travel severely limited international competition. While no great waterways separated all continental European countries, there was the Channel between England and France, and there also was that bit of sea between Ireland and England. Inasmuch as it was those three countries that came to the fore in a racing sense, any competition between and among the greatest stars of each land required considerable adventure.

Luckily, adventure is likely to be lodged within the spirit of anyone game enough to breed and race horses. A portion of any owner's self-esteem also lies in the success of these beasts. In 1865, French pride received a considerable boost when the French horse Gladiateur lowered the colors of the Motherland of the Thoroughbred by winning both the Two Thousand Guineas at Newmarket and the English Derby at Epsom. His breeder and owner, Comte de Lagrange, the son of one of Napoleon's generals, had won the English Oaks

the year before with Fille de l'Air. One report, perhaps hysterical, in a French paper, had it that the crossness of the English at the thought of a French horse winning their Derby necessitated six hundred pugilists being employed to protect Gladiateur as the moment approached.

After the Derby, Gladiateur crossed the channel to allow his countrymen to celebrate his, and their, new celebrity by winning the Grand Prix de Paris. He then was returned to England to complete the Triple Crown by winning the St. Leger, further assuring the longevity of his nickname as "the Avenger of Waterloo." He also made further cross-channel journeys.

International competition between England and the United States required a major ocean voyage. Pierre Lorillard's Iroquois crossed the Atlantic to win the Derby of 1881, and there were some other successful encampments by American runners in England. Still, a quick hop across the Atlantic for a specific event remained for the future. A break-

CHAPTER **13**

through in trans-Atlantic competition came in 1923, when the Epsom Derby winner Papyrus was sent abroad to face an American three-year-old at Belmont Park. After some controversy, the organizers settled on Kentucky Derby winner Zev as the home entrant. Transatlantic horse flights would hardly have been a gleam in the eye of even a Charles Lindbergh, so Papyrus steamed across aboard the *Aquitania*. The trip took seven days, and a storm early on put Papyrus slightly off his feed for several days.

America greeted the adventurous English colt with such enthusiasm that some 60,000 turned out. They made him no worse than 5-4, although the wet going and his trainer's decision to eschew the American custom of replacing smooth shoes with stickers in such circumstances was widely questioned by insiders. The English Turf community seemed to view the match between the two countries' Derby winners as an unseemly bit of promotion and was disgruntled to learn that cinema rights had been contracted!

Harry Sinclair's Zev did the expected, beating Ben Irish's Papyrus handily as the English colt struggled over unfamiliar going with all-too-familiar plates. Nonetheless, the debacle on the racetrack had been accompanied by the logistical success of bringing the pair together. A few months later, the Chanel perfume entrepreneur Pierre Wertheimer traveled from France and signed an agreement to point his colt Epinard for three special international events in New York and Kentucky. Epinard, while a French colt, had received acclaim as well in England, where he had finished second in the Cambridgeshire. Epinard stayed sound and good and ran in all three, but, alas, was

second each time. Wertheimer's grandsons, Alain and Gerard, owners of 1993 North American Horse of the Year Kotashaan, tell of a blown-up duplicate of an American newspaper adorning a wall at their family home, an illustration of what big news such an event was in 1924.

With all manner of flight technologies thrust forward by World War II, air shipment of horses began in 1945. By the end off 1946, four horses had made an eight-thousand-mile flight from Buenos Aires, Argentina, to Newark, New Jersey, with some stops along the way, and the first horse flight across the Atlantic also had staked out new territory. The latter involved six horses on an American Airlines DC-4 that took off from Shannon, Ireland, one night and arrived in Newark the next morning.

James Butler, the entrepreneur who ran the Empire City track in New York, moved quickly to take advantage of the new mobility. He announced a $100,000 race of a mile and five-eighths with the intent of attracting horses from both sides of the Atlantic. He was unable to get any European horses to the gate for the first Empire City Gold Cup in 1947, and the South Americans Endeavour II and Ensueno provided modest international flavor. These finished unplaced behind a splendid American foursome of Stymie, Natchez, Assault, and Phalanx.

The next year, Butler called the race the International Gold Cup. He succeeded in attracting the Aga Khan's Irish Derby winner Nathoo and the Belgian horse Bayeux, who were flown over for the race. The reward for their wandering, however, was to fall quickly into the distant supporting roles that most were assigned when facing Citation. The Triple Crown winner and obvious Horse of the Year won easily over Phalanx. The Empire City race, which was run at Belmont Park those first two years, quickly faded from the scene.

In 1952, however, international racing received a boost that would eventually transform racing rarities into proliferation with a major addition to the sporting world. This was the Washington, D.C., International, the brainchild of John D. Schapiro, head of Laurel Park in the countryside of Maryland outside the Capitol City. Laurel had a long history of important races, but in concocting his grandiose international scheme, Schapiro sought to put it — and himself — on the map in a theretofore unprecedented way. It was an audacious plan. Not unexpectedly, it was received with condescension in the European racing capitals nearly three decades after the English had sniffed at Papyrus' voyage.

If the International were looked upon as unlikely to succeed, such a race was at least no longer a logistical impossibility. To those invited to participate in his new autumn event, Schapiro offered to pay the air freight, as well as pay for adequate staff. To assuage the various ways in which the Europeans were at a disadvantage, Schapiro prescribed that his race would be run on Laurel's turf course and that it would use a walk-up start — European racing being some years from conversion to starting gates.

In an outcome that many no doubt would have described as against all odds, the first International came off, and in a way that justified its concept; the English

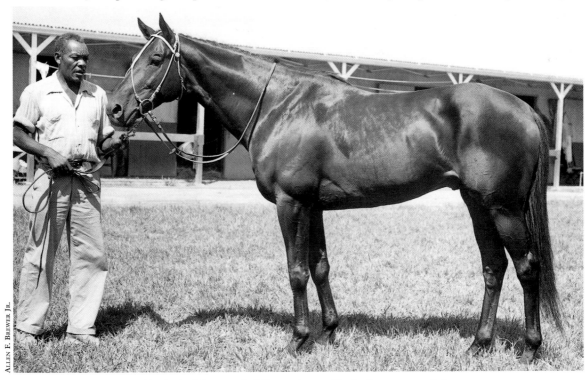

ALLEN F. BREWER JR.

Sailor's Guide traveled from Australia by boat to participate.

colt Wilwyn, owned by Robert Boucher, won the mile and a half race over the American Ruhe, with another European, Zucchero, finishing third.

Schapiro and his assistant and brother-in-law, the gregarious former baseball player Joe Cascarella, approached the annual International renewals as a personal crusade. Dapper and self-confident, in plush overcoats and homburgs, they traveled through Europe, enticing owners to prolong their season and ship to Laurel for what originally was a Veteran's Day event. A handsome trophy with a global motif was struck; portraits of the race's winners were commissioned. Schapiro became a familiar face abroad, hosting luncheon parties at the Ritz in Paris, approaching and cajoling the top owners and their representatives.

During the first few years of the Washington, D.C., International, the results fell into line as the organizers must have wished. After the English Wilwyn, another shipper, France's Worden II, won in 1953. Then an American got into the act when Fisherman won in 1954, and next a Venezuelan, El Chama, put in a blow for the South American contingent.

Moreover, during those first few years, Queen Elizabeth II and Sir Winston Churchill both had starters, adding more prestige to the event. Schapiro was able to finesse elegant International-eve receptions at a rotating lineup of embassies in Washington, D.C., and the youthful magazine *Sports Illustrated* devoted several pages of color — far from routine in the mid-1950s — to the social glitter of ancillary events in a feature entitled "The Elite at Laurel."

Then, in 1958, a series of events fell into place to create a race probably unequaled historically in its political connections, certification of importance, and sheer tumult.

By 1958 a dozen years had elapsed since British Prime Minister Churchill had coined the phrase "Iron Curtain." The American president was World War II hero Dwight Eisenhower, and the threat of

Ballymoss was the first Prix de l'Arc de Triomphe winner to race in Laurel's International.

nuclear conflict with the Soviet Union loomed large in American thought. Sputnik's launch had set this nation's confidence back, as the Soviets got the jump on us in a more telling way than Wilwyn. Four years would pass before the Cuban Missile Crisis, but the Cold War was nightly news and a constant presence in 1958. In the midst of this consuming reality, the dreaded, mysterious Soviets announced they would be sending a horse to contest the Washington, D.C., International. In fact, while they were at it, they would send two.

This exotic ingredient coincided with a fillip previously missing from the event. While good horses had been shipped over, the best of Europe had not yet given it a go. In 1958, however, the best horse in Europe happened to be owned by an American. John McShain's Ballymoss, trained by Vincent O'Brien, had toured through a campaign that included victory in England's somewhat new midsummer day's dream, the King George VI and Queen Elizabeth Stakes, and France's glamorous, climactic Prix de l'Arc de Triomphe. The American was game to test his champion on his own personal home soil.

One last element, almost too delicious to believe, was that McShain's construction firm had built the Pentagon. Thus, in a sporting way, a horse race mirrored the concept of current events — the Pentagon aligned against the Soviets! The precedence of friendly competition that might promote personal relationships was shadowed by the fear of an international incident that heightened tensions, and it was hard to tell which way it would go. The event attracted 40,276, at that time the largest crowd ever to see a race in Maryland. In a few short years, Schapiro thus had created a larger draw even than the state's beloved Preakness.

Strictly as an athletic contest, the 1958 Washington, D.C., International would hardly qualify as a great moment of the average week, much less a century. To many minds, the wrong horse won — twice. There was confusion at the start, accusations made and recanted, and the messiness of a disqualification while the best horse in Europe was defeated. Charlie Hatton of *Daily Racing Form* quipped that "if there ever is another exhibit of Laurel in Art, we shall not be surprised to find Picasso's *Guernica* depicting the '58 International."

As the field roiled about prior to the start of the mile and a half test, Lester Piggott's mount, Orsini II, was so disruptive, lashing out at other horses, that he was ordered to the outside of the others. Piggott tried several times to sneak back toward the rails. Starter Eddie Blind was shouting instructions to jockey Kovalev, aboard the Russian Zaryad, but the relay via on-site interpreter was not notably successful. Zaryad tried to break off prematurely at least twice, and at length a handler took hold of his reins. When the start was finally ordered, Zaryad dwelt. Favored Ballymoss was battered about at the start and lost substantial ground later when Orsini II bounded off the hedge into him and forced Ballymoss into the American Clem, who never recovered.

An English horse named Tudor Era led from the start, representing the American owner Mrs. Herbert Herff. The Australian hope Sailor's Guide raced along in second. Nearing the stretch the final time, Tudor Era cut off Sailor's Guide and then widened his lead to hit the wire three and a half lengths in front. Ballymoss closed well enough to be third, only a head behind Sailor's Guide. The champion of Europe had been defeated.

As it turned out, that defeat was a narrow one, for

CHAPTER 13

Howard Grant on Sailor's Guide claimed foul against Bill Harmatz on Tudor Era. After more than twenty minutes, the stewards finally took down the apparent winner. Sailor's Guide moved up to first, so that Ballymoss officially was second and had come within a head of winning.

The Russian Garnir finished sixth, satisfying his camp that the Russians could be competitive. Zaryad was last, and jockey Kovalev claimed the assistant starter held the reins too long. When films showed that not to have been the case, the Soviets denied that the complaint ever had been made — one of the options one has when dealing through interpreters.

Zev winning an early international match against England's Papyrus.

In contrast to the state-of-the-art transport that had begun bringing some of the Laurel contestants, Sailor's Guide had come the old-fashioned way — by boat. On a three-week voyage from Australia that August, racing journalist and bloodstock adviser Jim Shannon and his wife, Nancy, attended Sailor's Guide. Shannon years later became general manager of the far-flung racing operation of Nelson Bunker Hunt. Sailor's Guide was trained in this country by J. Bowes Bond and raced in the colors of A.C. and Keith Dibb. The son of Lighthouse II had won the Victoria Derby and the V.R.C. and A.J.C. St. Legers.

The 1958 introduction of Soviet horses to American audiences led to a rather pleasant underscoring of the principles of sportsmanship. The Russians came back several times. Their Zabeg was third in 1960, and the champion Soviet horse Aniline was third and then second in later runnings.

The appearance of Ballymoss in a sense ratified the race's importance but probably discouraged owners of succeeding European champions to risk their horses' prestige. The next several decades did see a number of brilliant classic winners come from abroad, however. Also, the great American Kelso lost three splendid runnings of the International before finally defeating Gun Bow in a memorable running; Bald Eagle won back-to-back runnings; and ten years after the Ballymoss race, Raymond Guest's Epsom Derby winner Sir Ivor punctuated his career with a luminous rally at Laurel.

For some time, Schapiro's race held sway as the singular spectacle of such internationalism on these shores. Eventually, though, pioneers face imitators, and the Man o' War and Turf Classic in New York and the Canadian International at Woodbine in time reached similar status. The most amazing internationalist of all, All Along, earned North America's Horse of the Year title in 1983, making three transAtlantic flights to win the Turf Classic, the Rothmans (Canadian) International, and the Washington, D.C., International after already having won the Arc.

Somewhat tellingly, though, when All Along returned the next autumn, it was to run instead in the first Breeders' Cup Turf.

At two-million dollars and as part of the incomparable institution of the Breeders' Cup itself, that Turf race was something neither the Laurel race nor other American grass events could equal. Schapiro's successors as heads of Laurel, the late Frank De Francis and then his son Joe, accepted reality and tried several different distances and placements on the calendar to find a new niche for the International. It was still a fine event into the 1990s, buoyed by sponsorship from Budweiser, but it would not sustain itself. The original did not survive, but the trend it created remains one of racing's most important strengths a half-century later.

Washington, D.C., International
Purse: $100,000

7th Race Laurel Race Course - November 11, 1958
Purse $100,000. Three-year-olds and upward. By invitation only. Weight for age. About 1 1-2 Miles. Turf Course. Track: Firm.
Gross value, $100,000. Net to winner $70,000; second, $15,000; third, $10,000; fourth, $5,000. Mutuel pool $490,539.

P#	Horse	A	Wgt	Med	Eqp	Odds	PP	1/4	1/2	1m	1¼	Str	Fin	Jockey
9	Tudor Era [D]	5	126		w	6.50	9	1^2	1^1	1^1	1^1	1^4	$1^{3/2}$	W Harmatz
5	Sailor's Guide	6	126		w	8.30	5	$4^{1/2}$	$3^{1/2}$	$2^{1/2}$	$2^{1/2}$	$2^{1/2}$	2^h	H Grant
7	Ballymoss	4	126		w	1.10	7	7^1	$7^{1/2}$	6^4	5^3	3^2	$3^{4/2}$	A Breasley
4	Tharp	3	122		w	15.30	4	2^1	2^h	$3^{1/2}$	$4^{1/2}$	$5^{1/2}$	4^h	E Arcaro
2	zOrsini II	4	126		w	12.20	2	8^2	6^2	$4^{1/2}$	3^1	4^3	$5^{1/2}$	L Piggott
10	Garnir	3	122		w	a-18.50	10	6^h	$4^{1/2}$	5^1	6^2	$6^{1/2}$	6^{nk}	N Nasimov
3	Escribano	4	126		w	38.50	3	$3^{1/2}$	8^2	9^2	7^4	7^8	7^6	N Camac'ro
8	Clem	4	126		w	4.20	8	5^h	5^1	10	10	9^1	8^3	W Shoemaker
6	Revoque	3	122		w	42.00	6	9^{10}	9^6	$7^{1/2}$	9^4	10	9^2	I Valenzuela
1	Zaryad	3	122		w	a-18.50	1	10	10	8^h	$8^{1/2}$	8^1	10	V Kovalev

[D]-Disqualified and placed second. a-Coupled, Garnir and Zaryad. z-Placed on extreme outside at start.

Off Time: 3:55½ Eastern Standard Time   **Time Of Race:**   2:33⅕
Start: Good For All but Zaryad   **Track:** Firm
Equipment: w for whip

Mutuel Payoffs

5	Sailor's Guide	$18.60	$8.00	$4.00
9	Tudor Era		7.60	4.00
7	Ballymoss			2.40

Winner: Sailor's Guide, br. h. by Lighthouse II—Jehane, by Legend of France (Trained by J. B. Bond).
Bred by M. V. Point (Australia).

Start good from flag for all but ZARYAD. Won ridden out.
TUDOR ERA broke alertly, was taken under stout restraint, set the pace under excellent rating and, after dropping in on SAILOR'S GUIDE entering the stretch the final time, drew clear under intermittent urging. He was disqualified for interfering with SAILOR'S GUIDE and was placed second. SAILOR'S GUIDE was in a rather precarious position along the hedge during the race, was taken up sharply entering the stretch while endeavoring to move through on the leader, then gave way gradually. Grant's claim of foul against the winner for interference was allowed. BALLYMOSS raced in contention, was bothered when ORSINI II hit him just before completing a turn of the course, recovered well to remain a factor until nearing the stretch, then drifted wide and failed to respond. THARP appeared full of run while under rating early but lacked the needed response when set down. ORSINI II was placed on the outside after kicking repeatedly at the starting point, improved his position steadily until hitting the hedge after about seven furlongs, recovered to be prominent until the final quarter and faltered. GARNIR weakened after having been prominent. ESCRIBANO was crowded after seven furlongs. CLEM failed to recover after BALLYMOSS was knocked into him at the clubhouse turn. REVOQUE showed nothing. ZARYAD broke far behind the field and was outrun. The start was delayed for considerable time, largely to ZARYAD breaking through.

Owners: (9) Mrs H Herff; (5) A C & K Dibb; (7) J McShain; (4) C H Palmer; (2) Baron H Thyssen; (10) U S S R; (3) A Lechin; (8) Mrs Adele L Rand; (6) Dr E J Wasserman; (1) U S S R

©DAILY RACING FORM/EQUIBASE

*Sword Dancer perseveres on the rail to
defeat his elders in the Woodward.*

- CHAPTER 14 -

The Sword of the Big A

The first major project of the New York Racing Association was replacing the old Aqueduct with a new one. The efficient, modern version quickly established itself in racing parlance as "the Big A." Opened September 14, 1959, the track's first great race followed twelve days later. The $100,000-added Woodward Stakes brought out three established stars of the season. These were the older Round Table, defending Horse of the Year, and Hillsdale, one of the best developments of the season, against the flashy little three-year-old Sword Dancer.

Sword Dancer had already participated in one of the most exciting races in the history of the Kentucky Derby. He had been the unwitting foil of the talented Bill Shoemaker on Tomy Lee in a breathtaking stretch run marred somewhat by a bit of rough stuff attributable to both contestants. Now, months later, Sword Dancer had wrested status as leading three-year-old and was facing off against some tough older fighters of proven depth.

Sword Dancer was a chestnut with a good deal of white. He was by Sunglow—Highland Fling, by By Jimminy, no fashion statement insofar as mid-century pedigrees go. But he was a homebred from the historic Brookmeade Stable. Isabel Dodge Sloane was the grande dame of Brookmeade, and runners in its white silks with blue cross sashes had twenty-five years earlier made her the country's first woman owner of the leading racing stable. This was in 1934, when her Cavalcade won the Kentucky Derby and High Quest won the Preakness. Ethel V. Mars, Mrs. Payne Whitney, Elizabeth Arden Graham, and Lucille Parker Markey later joined that society of Turf queens, and Mrs. Sloane repeated the feat of a win in a Triple Crown race in 1951.

The 1951 Preakness victory of Brookmeade's Bold had been but one of many fine moments shared with the distinguished trainer Preston Burch. By 1959 Burch's son Elliott had taken over Brookmeade. It was he who guided Sword Dancer through a campaign that spoke to the soul of all traditional Eastern owners and their followers.

A late-developing but busy sort at two, Sword Dancer had won three of fourteen starts, including the Mayflower Stakes. In Florida in the winter of 1959, he had proven not quite able to beat the best. But by the time he and jockey Bill Boland rallied around a bunch of horses into the stretch of the Kentucky Derby on May 2, he was ready. Shoemaker, already one of the most accomplished of American riders, shouted encouragement to Boland, something like "Go on! You can win it."

Indeed most observers would have concurred that Shoemaker's mount, the delicate English colt Tomy Lee, although right there at the moment, seemed unlikely to gut out the closing quarter-mile of the Derby. Instead of folding when Sword Dancer laid down the challenge, though, Tomy Lee retained his composure and will to win. In one of the greatest rides in a career of wonderful achievement, Shoemaker pushed and urged Tomy Lee, tight as he was along the rail. The two colts buffeted one another, but neither conceded. In the final strides, Tomy Lee surged just enough to win by a nose.

Boland was distraught, and he claimed foul.

Hillsdale, an Indiana-bred.

Burch was not overly pleased at the prospect of a Brookmeade horse claiming foul in order to win a classic, but no harm was done. After seventeen minutes, the stewards let the original finish stand.

While Tomy Lee went back West to rest, Sword Dancer demonstrated a constitution perhaps not immediately associated with his three white stockings and modest size. He was second in the Preakness and then won the one-mile Metropolitan Handicap against older horses. The rigors of the Triple Crown notwithstanding, Burch made a practice of slipping in a run in the Met before they went on to win the Belmont Stakes.

Sword Dancer took the Metropolitan and then won the classic Belmont at one and a half miles. Between the Belmont and the showdown of the Woodward, he added another victory over older horses, in the mile and a quarter Monmouth Handicap; was second to Babu in the Brooklyn; and then won the good old Travers at Saratoga.

Five more weeks passed before the Woodward. After the Derby, Shoemaker had become Sword Dancer's regular rider, but he had been partnered with Round Table during three seasons and stuck with the older horse. Far from panicked, Burch tapped "The Master," Eddie Arcaro.

><+>+O+<+>+<

Travis Kerr's Round Table (see chapter on 1957 Trenton Handicap) was already a champion, tried and true. No distance on either dirt or turf intimidated him, and he carried 130 pounds or more with frequency. In fact, only a week before the Woodward, this ironclad and steel-hearted five-year-old carried 136 pounds to victory in the United Nations Handicap on turf. His only weakness was off going, and that was no concern in the Woodward.

The Blood-Horse

Round Table and Bill Molter.

Round Table, like Sword Dancer, was the product of an historic operation. He was bred by Claiborne Farm and was by Princequillo—Knight's Daughter, by Sir Cosmo. Travis Kerr had purchased controlling interest when the horse was three.

In contrast was the remaining member of the Big Three at the Big A that day. This was Hillsdale, bred by Murlogg Farm in Indiana, a state that is something of an outpost in Thoroughbred breeding. Hillsdale brought no blue-ribbon pedigree to his craft. He was by Take Away—Johann, by Johnstown. It is true that he shared a broodmare sire with Nashua and that Johnstown had been a Derby-Belmont winner. Take away Hillsdale from Take Away's sire record, though, and you would have taken away the only stakes winner.

Former football player C.W. "Catfish" Smith had purchased Hillsdale from Murlogg owner Helen Kellogg. The colt was trained by Marty Fallon and ridden by Tommy Barrow, and he was the apogee in the racing careers of all concerned. At three, Hillsdale came along to win five stakes spanning the coasts. At four, he perhaps benefited in California from Round Table's being on the shelf for a while and then racing in Chicago, but Hillsdale proved a horse of high order. He won nine major stakes, from January to September, from seven furlongs to one and a quarter miles. This included some key names on the West Coast, such as the San Fernando, Santa Anita Maturity, Californian, and Hollywood Gold Cup. He was beating the likes of Terrang, Find, Seaneen, Fleet Nasrullah, and Amerigo. In the two races Hillsdale lost, he was second, once forcing the grand filly Bug Brush to a world record for one and an eighth miles in the San Antonio Handicap.

For a horse entering the glitter of top quality stakes in New York, Hillsdale had an unusual lead-up. Fallon trained him for a time at Charles Town in West Virginia and at Detroit Race Course in the two months between the Hollywood Gold Cup and his Aqueduct debut. Once in the Big Apple, he won a handicap at Belmont Park and then took up 132 pounds to defeat Cain Hoy Stable's Bald Eagle in the Aqueduct Handicap on the official opening of the ultra-modern Big A. Hillsdale was the goods, no longer a poor relation in any significant sense.

><+>+O+<+><

The crowd for the one and a quarter-mile Woodward was 53,290, the largest for a New York race in five years. They made Round Table the 7-10 favorite, although he had never won in his few earlier tries in New York. Hillsdale was second choice at nearly 5-2, Sword Dancer off at nearly 3-1, and the only remaining starter, Inside Tract, was the outsider at 22-1.

When it was over, Arcaro was celebrated as he had been so often in the last thirty years. "One More Moment For The Master" was *Sports Illustrated*'s take on the race, but, in fact, Arcaro had almost muffed it, twice. First he misjudged Sword Dancer. The trainer Sunny Jim Fitzsimmons, for whom Arcaro had ridden Nashua and Bold Ruler within the last decade, gave him some encouragement, but Arcaro apparently had little faith that a smallish three-year-old could handle Round Table and Hillsdale. Then, in the heat of battle, Arcaro admitted he for-

got Inside Tract was in the race and, at a critical moment, it was that long shot who loomed up to scuttle Arcaro's anticipated outside bid.

There was no natural front-runner in the race, but Barrow was wise enough to allow Hillsdale to take the lead when the fractions were moderate. Hillsdale led by a length or less most of the way, as Shoemaker on Round Table tracked him comfortably through cautious splits of :24⅖, :49⅕, 1:14⅖, and 1:40. Sword Dancer trailed along in third, never more than four lengths off the pace. Ray Broussard allowed Inside Tract to drop several lengths behind Sword Dancer, but this was not a bad horse. In fact, Inside Tract had won the Jockey Club Gold Cup the previous year and had placed in numerous stakes.

As Inside Tract made his move to the outside, Sword Dancer suddenly was in a blind switch — a "jackpot" as Arcaro put it. This led to what The Master termed "my idiotic move." The veteran rider was less than four months past a horrifying spill. Black Hills had snapped a leg and gone down with him in the Belmont, resulting in sprains and bruises that kept Arcaro out of the saddle for nearly a month. Nonetheless, faced with a desperate situation, with a $100,000 race and more than a bit of prestige on the line, Arcaro reacted instinctively. Barrow on Hillsdale had figured — known — that Arcaro would have to be coming on the outside if he came at all. He had let his big bomber drift ever so slightly off the rail rather than make him cut the corner tighter than necessary as he still rocked along with Round Table poised beside him. In a

Trainer Elliott Burch and champion Sword Dancer.

flash, Arcaro jerked Sword Dancer across Hillsdale's heels and suddenly was challenging, not on the right, but along the rail to Hillsdale's left.

Hillsdale put away Round Table, but not the little tiger to his left. Arcaro had no room to whip right-handed, so he slapped the little colt on the left. Sword Dancer surged; Hillsdale resisted. Sword Dancer surged; Hillsdale resisted. Sword Dancer surged yet again, and with strides as magical as they were determined, got to the wire a head in front!

The *Bloodstock Breeders' Review*, caught up in the scene, suggested that the race was concluded "amid probably the greatest ovation ever heard at a New York track." Such matters do not lend themselves to quantification, but the fact that it would even be stated helps put the 1959 Woodward into perspective.

For the record, Hillsdale had one and three-quarter lengths over Round Table, whose team thought he might have suffered from the arduous task of his previous week. Inside Tract, having fired, fell back, finishing five lengths behind Round Table. The time of 2:04⅖ indicated a sprightly, and testing, final quarter-mile in :24⅖ — racehorses turning in a racehorse stretch drive.

Hillsdale called it a year. Round Table the rugged came back two weeks later to break his New York "maiden," winning the Manhattan over Bald Eagle. When he and Sword Dancer met again October 31 in the two-mile Jockey Club Gold Cup, however, Arcaro and the little three-year-old drew off to win by seven lengths. Brookmeade and Burch had the Horse of the Year, ratifying what was foretold in the Woodward.

Woodward Stakes
Purse: $100,000 Added

7th Race Aqueduct - September 26, 1959

Purse $100,000 added. Three-year-olds and upward. Weight for age. 1 1-4 Miles. Main Track. Track: Fast.
Gross value, $109,800. Net to winner $70,170; second, $21,960; third, $10,980; fourth, $5,490. Mutuel pool $489,381.

P#	Horse	A	Wgt	Med	Eqp	Odds	PP	1/4	1/2	3/4	1m	Str	Fin	Jockey
4	Sword Dancer	3	120		b	2.90	4	3^{5}	3^{4}	$3^{2\frac{1}{2}}$	$3^{1\frac{1}{2}}$	$2^{1\frac{1}{2}}$	1^{h}	E Arcaro
2	Hillsdale	4	126			2.40	2	1^{1}	$1^{\frac{1}{2}}$	$1^{\frac{1}{2}}$	1^{h}	1^{h}	$2^{1\frac{3}{4}}$	T Barrow
3	Round Table	5	126		b	.70	3	$2^{1\frac{1}{2}}$	$2^{2\frac{1}{2}}$	2^{2}	2^{1}	3^{3}	3^{5}	W Shoemaker
1	Inside Tract	5	126		b	22.25	1	4	4	4	4	4	4	R Broussard

Off Time: 4:48 Eastern Daylight Time **Time Of Race:** :24⅖ :49⅕ 1:14⅕ 1:40 2:04⅖
Start: Good For All **Track:** Fast
Equipment: b for blinkers

Mutuel Payoffs

4	**Sword Dancer**	**$7.80**	**$4.00**	.....
2	**Hillsdale**		**3.70**	.....

No Show Mutuels Sold.

Winner: Sword Dancer, ch. c. by Sunglow—Highland Fling, by By Jimminy (Trained by J. E. Burch). Bred by Brookmeade Stables in Va.

Start good. Won driving.
SWORD DANCER, away alertly, was taken in hand soon after the start and saved ground until near the stretch, was steadied momentarily at the final turn and moving to the inside of HILLSDALE for the drive, wore down the latter in the last seventy yards. HILLSDALE went to the front before reaching the first turn and made the pace to the mile while engaging ROUND TABLE, raced the latter into defeat in the upper stretch and continued gamely but was unable to withstand SWORD DANCER. ROUND TABLE, well placed within striking distance of HILLSDALE to the stretch, gave way during the drive and had no excuse. INSIDE TRACT began sluggishly and, after making a mild bid at the mile, tired.
Scratched—Babu, Ozark, Anisado, Find.

Owners: (4) Brookmeade Stable; (2) C W Smith; (3) Kerr Stable; (1) D-M Stable

©DAILY RACING FORM/EQUIBASE

*Locked together throughout, Jaipur
(blinkers) and Ridan fought to the wire.*

- CHAPTER 15 -

"Closer Than the Paint on the Fence"

The three-year-olds of 1962 were a high-class group, and what was most remarkable about their season was the number of great stretch duels they orchestrated. Well before Saratoga's August congress, there had been at least five races of which one might logically have said as each unfolded: "That must be the race of the year."

Yet awaiting, in the weathered form of the old Travers Stakes, was a race that instantly was seen to have nudged its way into timelessness. Describing it for *The Blood-Horse*, the eloquent Dave Alexander began:

"I have seen a lot of races over a lot of years, and up to now I've always held that the most thrilling event I ever saw was Seabiscuit's score in the Santa Anita Handicap 22 years ago. That is no longer true. The most thrilling race I ever saw at any time at any track was last Saturday's Travers Stakes at Saratoga."

To add even more luster to the performances of Jaipur and Ridan, the noble protagonists that day, was the fact that for each it was the third of those

gripping, grinding, searching contests that distinguished the entire 1962 season.

⤞⟶◇⟵⤝

Ridan and Jaipur both had stood out early in the foal crop of 1959. Ridan showed first. He was a strapping, quick-maturing bay with a dashing white blaze. He was a son of Nantallah—Rough Shod II, by Gold Bridge, a mating that in time was to be repeated with such compelling results as Horse of the Year Moccasin, stakes winner Lt. Stevens, and Thong, a female forebear of both Nureyev and Sadler's Wells. At the time Rough Shod II produced the first of her foals by the young Nasrullah stallion Nantallah, she was owned by Thomas Girdler, retired president of Republic Steel. Girdler's health was failing, so he sold his bloodstock. The Nantallah colt went for $11,000 as a yearling to a partnership of Mrs. Moody Jolley, Ernest Woods, and John L. Greer. Mrs. Jolley's husband was a successful, well-established trainer, but the colt was sent to the care of their young son,

LeRoy Jolley, then a sapling of promise and an eventual Hall of Famer. The rakish colt was seen to resemble the Nasrullah colt Nadir, whom the elder Jolley had trained to win the Garden State Stakes for Claiborne Farm, so the name was reversed, hence Ridan.

Ridan was one of those precocious two-year-olds that burst out of the starting gate at Hialeah for a three-furlong victory in the winter of his juvenile season and never did anything to flatter the disapproving attitudes of those against two-year-old racing. He swept spectacularly through seven races winter, spring, and summer before developing an enlarged splint bone in a foreleg and being rested. Ridan shared juvenile championship honors with Crimson Satan. The latter emerged late in the year, by which time Sir Gaylord and Jaipur had taken turns suggesting championship form of their own. All four were back for a tumultuous second round at three.

The first of the great battles in top level races in the winter of 1962 involved the most spectacular of the young colts, Ridan, and the rugged little champion among the fillies, Cicada. Going a mile and an eighth in the Florida Derby, Cicada met his challenge at the furlong pole and, instead of gradually giving way, she fought back along the rail. Ridan was forced for the first of many times to reach for the depths of his awesome talent. It was male over female, but barely, a snorting nose over a demure one.

That spring, another of the major three-year-old preps produced an even closer finish, originally, when Admiral's Voyage and Sunrise County finished in a dead heat in the Wood Memorial. Moreover, Admiral's Voyage already was the veteran of a great battle in a lesser race, having won the Louisiana Derby by a nose over Roman Line. Sunrise County was a quirky sort who had already been disqualified from an apparent victory over Ridan for taking the other horse wide in the Flamingo. Now, in the Wood Memorial, he was guilty of bumping and his number was taken down again.

The Kentucky Derby was one race with an emphatic margin as Decidedly won by two and one-quarter lengths in record time. Roman Line was second, with Ridan a neck behind him. The Preakness, though, found Decidedly wrung out and also found Ridan ready for another heated battle. This time the camera went against Ridan, as Greek Money got home by a nose. The brazen Manuel Ycaza, riding Ridan, stuck an elbow out at his opponent near the finish, a moment caught in a head-on photograph, but it was he who claimed foul against Greek Money. The stewards, not amused, left Greek Money's number up and suspended Ycaza.

The next throbbing finish of a major race among 1962's three-year-olds introduced Jaipur into the motif. Jaipur's owner, George D. Widener, was not comfortable with racing a three-year-old one and a quarter miles early in May, so he had not aimed his colt for the Derby. Jaipur ran in the Preakness but was not really yet in prime shape, having had but a pair of mile races at three, and he trailed home tenth. (Ordinarily the phrase "classic prep" means a race leading toward a classic; Jaipur's Preakness could be read as using one "classic" as a "prep" for another, Widener having a lifelong ambition to win the Belmont Stakes.)

Jaipur was a son of Nasrullah—Rare Perfume, by

Jaipur got into full swing in the late spring of his three-year-old season.

Eight Thirty, and he had the bull-headedness often associated with his sire. Nasrullah, nevertheless, was a great stallion and led the sire list five times. Jaipur was looked upon as perhaps his swan song when he came out at two to win the Hopeful and Cowdin. As it turned out, however, Nasrullah had one more champion, as Never Bend emerged from the last crop the stallion conceived before his death in the spring of 1959.

Eleven days after the Preakness Jaipur appeared in the Jersey Derby, a mile and an eighth event tucked in amongst the Triple Crown races, ten days before the Belmont Stakes. Jaipur led early and then in the stretch was challenged by the iron-tough Admiral's Voyage as well as Crimson Satan. The latter had a tendency to lug in, and he leaned over to his left, spoiling a superb event by nudging Admiral's Voyage into Jaipur. The three seemed to hit the wire together, but the camera spotted Crimson Satan in front. The film also spotted his misdemeanor, and

113

he was moved back to third. Jaipur had a nose on Admiral's Voyage for the original second place and inherited the victory.

In the upper stretch of the mile and a half Belmont Stakes, the Jersey Derby scenario was unfolding again, except Admiral's Voyage that time had the rail. Manuel Ycaza had replaced Larry Gilligan on Crimson Satan, and while he was more successful in combating the colt's tendency to lug in, that internecine skirmish cost Crimson Satan focus and momentum. He gradually fell back in the decisive final furlong. The great Bill Shoemaker had replaced Larry Adams on Jaipur and got him home a nose ahead of Braulio Baeza and Admiral's Voyage. The longest of the Triple Crown races had results in the shortest of margins.

Admiral's Voyage's owner, Fred W. Hooper, had been in the game nearly twenty years. Jaipur's breeder and owner, George D. Widener, had been in the game nearly fifty. Eventually, Hooper would pass the centenarian mark and be the grand old gentleman that had the Turf's sentiment on his side. In June of 1962, however, it was Widener, the patrician chairman of The Jockey Club, whose victory was greeted with satisfaction. The Philadelphian was of the ilk of Eastern sportsmen who placed the Belmont above all other races, and, now, at last, he had won it.

> ⭑◆⭑○⭑◆⭑

After the Belmont Jaipur turned so sour that he refused on occasion to train. Veteran trainer Bert Mulholland got the message and freshened him. When he returned nearly two months later, Jaipur had no trouble handling Crimson Satan in the Choice Stakes. The Travers came up next, two and a half weeks after the Choice.

Ridan was also pointed for the Travers, it being his camp's ambition to quiet any thought that one and a quarter miles was beyond his effective tether. Moreover, his splint had kept him from any of the climactic New York races the previous year, so he had yet to prove himself on that circuit. Following the Preakness, Ridan had returned to the scene of his biggest wins at two, Chicago. He won off by seven lengths in the Arlington Classic but was upset by Black Sheep in the American Derby two weeks before the Travers.

Seven lined up for the ninety-third Travers, which in recent years had been revived to the sort of prestige it had enjoyed over most of its history. The filly Cicada was back to try again, under 118 pounds to 126 on Ridan and Jaipur. The knowledge rather than guess that Jaipur could handle the distance was in part responsible for his being a strong choice of the 26,000-plus, at only slightly more than 3-5. Ridan went off at a little over 5-2.

Ridan broke from the inside, Jaipur right beside him. They quickly distanced themselves from the others. Thus commenced a two-horse race in a seven-horse field, although 23-1 Military Plume came along under his 114 pounds to get to within a length in third — and become the answer to a trivia question.

As *The Blood-Horse*'s Alexander described it:

"It was a two-horse duel from the moment that Jaipur and Ridan, two of the handsomest Thoroughbreds of our time, came plunging out the stalls side by side. They were side by side and well in front of the others for all of the mile and a quarter, and they were nose to nose at the finish…

"The duel was clean and true. Neither had an excuse nor needed one…There never was more than a neck, a head, a nose between them. Willie Shoemaker was trying desperately to rate Jaipur, but his horse was hell-bent-for-running on this afternoon and even so great a reinsman as The Shoe had trouble restraining him.

"Ridan (Ycaza up) never quit. It seemed to me

Hatton, described a slightly different, although compatible, impression: "At about the eighth pole, Jaipur seemed finally to have Ridan in trouble and may have been a short neck in front, but we had seen Ridan do that before. He was only 'shifting gears.' In a trice, he was back at Jaipur's muzzle again. Both

Ridan and trainer LeRoy Jolley.

that he came to the lead again 20 yards from the finish, and it was here that Jaipur, which had kept his lead in front from the quarter-pole, proved his greatness and that Shoemaker demonstrated his remarkable qualities as a stretch rider. Jaipur came again to take the hair's-breadth decision."

Daily Racing Form's maestro of words, Charlie

Shoemaker and Ycaza were driving for all they were worth now, while the finish pole came up to meet them. And both colts were drawing up all their resources for one last mighty effort.

"They finished right together, closer than the paint on the fence. A long silence ensued and in that interval most of the crowed seemed to think

Ridan had won…"

Back to Alexander: "I happened to call Jaipur, but this may have been more prejudice than keen eyesight, for he's my favorite horse and to my mind

to the last inch of ground."

While debate went on before the official finish was posted, Shoemaker was thinking he had gotten it right at the wire. Young Jolley was even more

Ridan eventually got the better of Jaipur, in the Palm Beach Handicap of 1963.

one of the most brilliant performers the Turf has seen in decades. Ridan's race in the Travers was (also) magnificent, one of the greatest any horse has run this year. LeRoy Jolley said he was hoping to prove Ridan could go more than a mile. After the race, Moody Jolley said Ridan had proved it. He was eminently correct. The big colt ran straight and true, showed no tendency to bear out, and fought

certain what his fate was, commenting "I knew Jaipur beat us. I saw The Shoe drop his head down right at the finish."

Finally the order was posted: Jaipur by a nose in a race that the length of the battle, the endurance of the competitors, and the lack of rough running placed the Travers as even better than the earlier duels of that remarkable season.

The five quarter-mile segments of the Travers were recorded as follows — :23⅘, :23⅗, :23⅗, :24⅖, and :26⅕. This made for six furlongs in 1:11, a mile in 1:35⅖, and ten furlongs in 2:01⅗. The final time matched the track record set in 1946 by the older Lucky Draw under five fewer pounds. It also bettered the Travers record of 2:01⅘ set many years before by none other than Man o' War, a record that had survived the Travers victories of such as Twenty Grand, Granville, Eight Thirty, Whirlaway, Native Dancer, Gallant Man, and Sword Dancer.

Alexander mused that horsemen "were still discussing it and arguing about it at the Lantern Lodge near the track at Sunday breakfast. They were discussing it in Saratoga bars and under Saratoga's elms. Folks who love racing will be discussing it a hundred years from now, I suspect, because it must go down in history books as one of the most thrilling contests the Turf has produced."

Hatton added the further compliment that neither colt after the race seemed distressed by the monumental effort. Jaipur, of course, had clinched the three-year-old championship. Nevertheless, each had two or three more starts that year, and neither won another race.

Then again, they had certainly done enough.

Travers Stakes
Purse: $75,000 Added

6th Race Saratoga - August 18, 1962
Purse $75,000 added. Three-year-olds. 1 1-4 Miles. Main Track. Track: Fast.
Value of race, $82,650. Value to winner $53,722.50; second, $16,530; third, $8,265; fourth, $4,132.50. Mutuel pool $269,335.

P#	Horse	A	Wgt	Med	Eqp	Odds	PP	1/4	1/2	3/4	1m	Str	Fin	Jockey
2	Jaipur	3	126		b	.65	2	2^{5}	2^{5}	2^{2}	1^{h}	1^{h}	1no	W Shoemaker
1	Ridan	3	126			2.65	1	$1^{1/2}$	1^{h}	1^{h}	$2^{1 1/2}$	2^{2}	2^{1}	M Ycaza
4	Military Plume	3	114		b	23.30	4	7	7	7	7	4^{h}	$3^{3/4}$	J Sellers
7	Smart	3	114			a-6.30	7	4^{1}	5^{1}	5^{h}	4^{h}	5^{2}	4^{2}	P J Bailey
3	Cyane	3	120			a-6.30	3	$3^{1/2}$	3^{h}	$3^{1/2}$	3^{2}	3^{h}	5^{2}	E Nelson
6	Flying Johnnie	3	114		b	27.15	6	6^{4}	6^{6}	6^{6}	6^{1}	7	6^{1}	C Burr
5	Cicada	3	118			10.05	5	5^{1}	4^{4}	4^{1}	5^{2}	$6^{1/2}$	7	R Ussery

a - Coupled, Smart and Cyane.

Off Time: 4:48 Eastern Daylight Time **Time Of Race:** :23⅘ :47⅖ 1:11 1:35⅖ 2:01⅗ (equals track record)
Start: Good For All **Track:** Fast
Equipment: b for blinkers

Mutuel Payoffs

2	**Jaipur**	**$3.30**	**$2.30**	**$2.20**
1	**Ridan**		**2.70**	**2.60**
4	**Military Plume**			**3.00**

Winner: Jaipur, dk. b. c. by Nasrullah—Rare Perfume, by Eight Thirty (Trained by W. F. Mulholland).
Bred by Erdenheim Farms Co. in Ky.

Start good. Won driving.
JAIPUR raced on even terms with RIDAN from the break and they continued as a team in a torrid duel. JAIPUR, on the outside of RIDAN, had a slight lead at the quarter pole and won narrowly in a race in which neither horse gave way. RIDAN, showing brilliant speed, was unable to shake off JAIPUR while saving ground throughout. He raced courageously to the end and was beaten narrowly in a thrilling duel. MILITARY PLUME was sharply impeded at the break when CICADA rammed into him. He dropped far out of it in the early stages, but came on strongly from the five-sixteenths pole to the wire, while racing in the middle of the track. SMART, unhurried early, was going well at the end, while racing between horses. CYANE, also impeded at the start, moved up early to follow the pacemakers, while racing on the rail. He changed course in the final eighth when RIDAN came in slightly, but was tiring at the time. FLYING JOHNNIE was outrun throughout. CICADA bore in sharply immediately following the break, impeding MILITARY PLUME and CYANE. She then failed to display any speed in the running.
Scratched—Zab.

Owners: (2) G D Widener; (1) Mrs M Jolley; (4) Mrs W M Jeffords; (7) Christiana Stable; (3) Christiana Stable; (6) Jopa Stable; (5) Meadow Stable

©DAILY RACING FORM/EQUIBASE

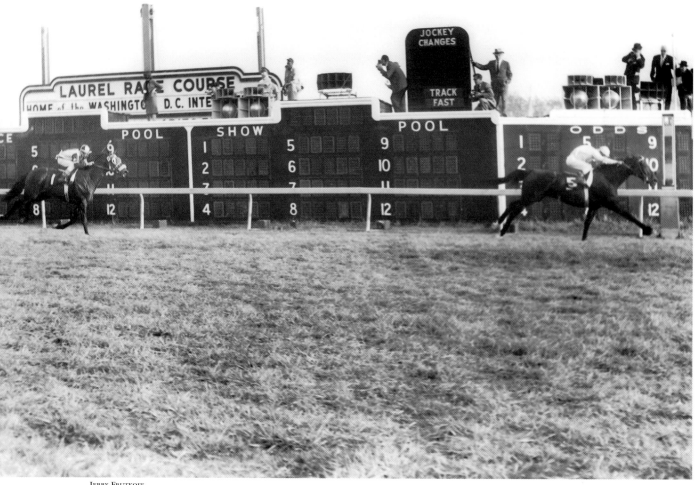

JERRY FRUTKOFF

Kelso exorcised two personal demons — Gun Bow
and three losses in the same race — winning
Laurel's International.

- CHAPTER 16 -

The King and the Prince

Chronicles of sport are replete with many a doleful coda. Great prizefighters enter the ring once, or twice, too often. Yesterday's football titans waffle in the line-up of unfamiliar teams, in the afterthought of their careers. Great horses litter past glories with unsightly dross.

There were moments in the summer of 1964 when such unseemliness appeared to hover over the career of even one of the grandest, Kelso.

An uninspired race here, a stunning loss there, left even the most barnacled fans wondering if, alas, greatness had slipped from the seven-year-old's sinews. Few sequences in racing, or any other sport, therefore, are as succulent in personal recall as a series of races in which the grizzled King forestalled the lustful Prince in two out of their final three jousts.

➤ ◆ ➤ ◇ ◆ ◀

Kelso's emergence as an idol and a king began late in his three-year-old form of 1960. Kelso was bred and raced by Mrs. Allaire du Pont, who owns Woodstock Farm in the pleasant countryside of Maryland and races in the name of Bohemia Stable. The horse was a son of Your Host, himself a mercurial customer who was injured so severely in a race that his very survival seemed a pipe dream. Veterinary devotion, and an admirable stance on the part of an equine insurer, transferred Your Host from a forlorn hope to an exemplar. He was never a great sire, but he was allowed his chance to survive, and when crossed with the Count Fleet mare Maid of Flight, Your Host became the unknowing co-conspirator of greatness as sire of Kelso. Maid of Flight's dam was sired by the heroic Man o' War. At the end of the twentieth century, Man o' War was reckoned the best of one hundred years, and Kelso was rated fourth — bloodlines of the equine gods.

Gelded as a two-year-old to counter an irascible nature, Kelso developed at three under trainer Carl Hanford. The most famous jockey of the time, Eddie Arcaro, signed on as Kelso's rider just as the gelding was getting good. Earlier that year, the three-year-old crop's leaders had been Bally Ache, Venetian Way, Celtic Ash, T. V. Lark, and Tompion; Arcaro had been pretty well shut out of the glamorous wins. In the rather plain-looking Kelso, however, he had found one of those pals who eventually made him less emphatic than he used to be in assessing Citation as the greatest mount of his career.

Arcaro took Kelso through five consecutive victories to end his 1960 campaign. The Jockey Club

Whisk Broom II in 1913 and Tom Fool in 1953 preceded Kelso in its domination in a single year. Like Tom Fool, Kelso completed his sweep by carrying 136 pounds in the Brooklyn.

More applicable to this narrative, Kelso in the autumn of 1961 faced contenders from the first of four three-year-old crops that would flaunt their youthful vigor with a view to bring him down. Over that and the next three seasons, he turned back, in suc-

Kelso edged away from Gun Bow in the Aqueduct (above), but later lost to him in the Woodward.

Gold Cup was among them, and Kelso was named Horse of the Year for what turned out to be merely the first of an unmatched five times. At four, Kelso swept the old New York Handicap Triple, comprising the Metropolitan, Suburban, and Brooklyn. Depending upon an observer/fan's age, this sweep is either a postscript to or one of the greatest achievements in history. At the time, the Handicap Triple was the ultimate for handicap horses, and only

cessive years, such worthy challengers as Derby-Preakness winner Carry Back, Belmont-Travers winner Jaipur, and the formidable Never Bend.

Bring on thy youthful pretenders, Kelso declared, and ye shall see them consigned into mine enduring shadow.

Then, in 1964, Kelso was seven and Gun Bow was not three, but four. Kelso had already had a disappointing adventure in California, so it was a time when youth seemed about to be served, but age, experience, and hardened greatness would prevail for one maximal autumn.

The dust-up began in the Brooklyn Handicap, in late July. Kelso lunged too early, banged his head on the gate, and was saved from slumping onto his haunches only by the efforts of a gate man. After the real break came, he ran as if dazed and finished fifth, beaten fourteen lengths. Perhaps more daz-

California state Senator Hugh M. Burns, Elizabeth Graham, Eddie Neloy, and jockey Manuel Ycaza in the winner's circle with Gun Bow.

ing than a bump on the head was the fastest mile and a quarter in the history of New York racing, which is what Gun Bow turned in at Aqueduct that day, leading throughout and drawing off by twelve lengths. The time of 1:59⅗ marked the first occasion in the proud history of New York that two minutes had been bettered for ten furlongs. Whisk Broom II had set the old record of 2:00 for New York tracks in 1913. The timing accuracy of methods that produced that mark was always doubted, but its officialdom had withstood many a great runner's efforts. It had been matched by Kelso himself in the 1961 Woodward at Belmont Park and again by Beau Purple in the Brooklyn Handicap at Aqueduct in 1962.

Gun Bow was an 11-1 shot in the Brooklyn, but he was already a star in American racing. He had been bred by a very prominent owner, Elizabeth Arden Graham, who had devoted part of the fortune earned from her cosmetics empire to establish Maine Chance Farm in Kentucky. Mrs. Graham,

who had won the Kentucky Derby with Jet Pilot in 1947, stood the modestly successful Hyperion horse Gun Shot. Gun Shot begot Gun Bow when crossed with the War Admiral mare Ribbons and Bows. The colt was purchased from Mrs. Graham after his three-year-old season, along with another Gun Shot colt, Gun Boat, for $125,000. The trainer, Eddie Neloy, had been one of the many trainers fired by Mrs. Graham. The originator of Elizabeth Arden cosmetics, Mrs. Graham was noted for her frequent changes in trainer, sometimes based on the poor fellow's refusal to utilize her creams and salves on the horses. Neloy delighted in telling how he once had felt compelled to hide behind the front seat of an automobile when he arrived with a client at Maine Chance to look at prospective purchases and realized that the lady of the manor was at large.

In helping the Gedney Farm of John T. Stanley and Mrs. Harry Albert acquire Gun Bow, Neloy was doing himself quite a favor. Prior to the colt's sensa-

121

tional Brooklyn Handicap victory, Gun Bow at four had won four major races. In California, he swept through a division of the San Fernando by five and a half lengths, the Charles H. Strub Stakes by twelve, and the San Antonio by four. After a couple of defeats, he then changed coasts and won the Gulf-

The Brooklyn gave Gun Bow a leg up in Horse-of-the-Year mentality, which took on an unusually emotional aura that year due to Kelso's four-year grip on the honor. Anyone who dislodged the grand one would be greeted with respect, but the cheers might be begrudgingly tendered.

Kelso, with trainer Carl Hanford.

stream Park Handicap in Florida. Gun Bow lost twice again, then was rested a couple of months, and, upon his return, was third in the Monmouth Handicap as Mongo defeated Kelso in one of those two champions' fine duels. Gun Bow carried 124 pounds to Kelso's 130 in the Monmouth, and in the Brooklyn he got in with two pounds less, whereas Kelso remained at 130.

After the Brooklyn, Gun Bow took up 130 pounds and demolished Mongo by ten lengths at even weights in the Whitney Handicap at Saratoga and shipped to Chicago to win the Washington Handicap under 132. Kelso, meanwhile, was freshened for a month, got his head cleared, and matched the world record for a mile and one-eighth in one of his few races on turf, this in an overnight race at

Saratoga. On September 7, during the Labor Day weekend, Kelso and Gun Bow met again, in the mile and one-eighth Aqueduct Stakes. Allowance condition of the event dictated 128 pounds for each.

Arcaro had retired after Kelso's second championship season, to be replaced by the seemingly obvious selection of Bill Shoemaker. Surprisingly, however, the partnership of America's greatest rider of the time and greatest horse of the time did not develop into a highly productive fit. After a number of races, Ismael (Milo) Valenzuela became Kelso's partner for the gelding's last twenty-five starts over portions of 1962, all of 1963, and then 1964. (Eventually, Valenzuela rode Kelso in thirty-five of his thirty-eight races commencing with an allowance race in August of his five-year-old season.) Walter Blum, who had hooked up with Gun Bow for his four previous races, was aboard again for the Aqueduct.

As the professional reporter and horse lover William H. Rudy recorded it for *The Blood-Horse*, "In the 53rd start of his amazing career, Kelso the Magnificent won the $100,000-added Aqueduct and left his owner, his trainer, his jockey, and most of the millions who saw him, live or on television, limp and breathless...Kelso

stalked Gun Bow, an odds-on favorite, and pressed the betting choice every step of the way. Under a drive for nine furlongs he had slowly, inch by inch, gotten to his rival, raced with him stride for stride, and then as relentlessly pulled away."

Trainer Hanford wanted Kelso to go with Gun Bow, but his charge just did not have the sheer speed to do it. Thus, Kelso was facing a five-length deficit at one point. Once Kelso had reduced it to a length, Gun Bow edged out again to a daylight spread. Never a horse to be discouraged, Kelso dug in again and finished the job, drawing even. "At the head of the

Allaire du Pont, leading in Kelso after victory.

stretch, Kelso had him," Rudy observed, "and everyone who knew Kelso felt that he would keep him."

The old champion could never draw clear, but he painstakingly achieved a three-quarter-length lead at the wire. The time of 1:48⅗ was only two-fifths of a second outside Cicada's record for the distance at the new (five-year-old) Aqueduct.

The crowd of 65,000 had relented to what it accepted as reality. Collectively, that assemblage had made Gun Bow 1-2 and Kelso more than 2-1, but the prolonged and profound cheering of the result indicated there would be a great many tickets discarded without rancor. This was New York, Kelso territory, and over five years an affair to remember had withstood the test of true love.

Rudy shared in that love, but he also understood nature. His report on the Aqueduct waxed both exultant and submissive: "Riders in the jockey room were excited and they pounded Ismael Valenzuela on the back. Trainers were excited, this race having been as good as they come." Then, a few paragraphs later, Rudy admitted that, "In fiction, the story can end with the old and bloody champ still the champion, but in reality the day comes when he has met his match. Happily, that day is not here yet, and when it does come, 65,066 people can say they saw Kelso win the 1964 Aqueduct and hold off the inevitable."

A month after the race "as good as they come," Kelso and Gun Bow put on a better one.

This was the mile and a quarter Woodward Stakes, run on October 3. The weight-for-age conditions of the Woodward put 126 on both Gun Bow and Kelso, and 121 on the three-year-old Quadrangle, winner of the Belmont Stakes and Travers. The field was small, only five showing up, but this was hardly an occasion when even the most gambling-oriented customer bewailed the limited wagering opportunities. Kelso was just a nickel under even money, Gun Bow a nickel under 3-2. Quadrangle was 11-2, and even the long shots were accomplished horses. The 11-1 Colorado King, from South Africa, had matched the world record for a mile and one-eighth in winning the American Handicap by eight lengths that summer, and had added the Hollywood Gold Cup by two and Sunset Handicap by seven. The 51-1 Guadalcanal, oddly, never won a stakes but was so reliable in placing in top company that he became one of the leading sons of the great Citation.

Walter Blum put Gun Bow on the lead early, but this time, Kelso was able to keep the margin from growing beyond one and a half lengths. At the head of the stretch, the veteran had come virtually to even terms again. Trainer Neloy had cut the holes in Gun Bow's blinkers a bit larger, and perhaps the Gedney Farm colt could see his slavering rival more clearly. Vengeance laid nearly a quarter-mile ahead, with combat inherent in every yard.

Again, Rudy rose to the timbre of his subject: "At the head of the stretch, Kelso and Gun Bow were heads apart and stride for stride. Through the gripping last quarter-mile there was contact three times as they strained for the lead. Neither faltered. In one sense, neither came again, for each came again, with each stride. Head up, he had a narrow lead; head down, his rival edged him. At the finish, no one could tell. The eye is not that quick, and in the days before the camera finish the decision of the three placing judges could have gone either way. Out of deference to two gallant horses, judges justifiably might have called it a dead heat.

"There was a delay of some minutes, Ismael Valenzuela and Walter Blum sitting their mounts near the winner's circle, eyes on the infield board. Eddie Neloy, Gun Bow's trainer, said later that his throat was so dry he could not speak.

"…A quick look at the official photo disclosed no margin. Only close examination showed that Gun

quire Gun Bow as a future stallion. The erudite Gaines came up with a comment that exhibited the depth of his respect for the runner-up: "Kelso is a transcendent horse. With all he has accomplished over several years, he is compared with Exterminator and Man o' War. For our horse, it's like comparing, let's say, Zero Mostel with Charlie Chaplin."

Gun Bow and trainer Eddie Neloy.

Bow, head up, had his nose on the line, while Kelso, head down and gathering himself for the next stride, lacked an inch, or maybe less than that."

John R. Gaines, whose Gainesway Farm was then relatively new as a force in the Kentucky breeding industry, had put together a million-dollar deal to ac-

(Mostel was currently topical as the star of "Fiddler on the Roof.")

So, the tiniest of pendulums had tick-tocked back in Gun Bow's favor. Yet, there was more to come.

The Jockey Club Gold Cup was still run at two miles, and Kelso had owned the race since 1960.

Neloy decided he wanted no part of that, and Kelso duly celebrated his fifth triumph in the event, winning by five and a half lengths over yet another set of three-year-olds in Roman Brother and Quadrangle. A week before, Neloy had allowed Gun Bow to test his legs on grass, and he had run very gamely although beaten three-quarters of a length by Turbo Jet II in the mile and five-eighths Man o' War Stakes.

When John Schapiro of Laurel Race Course in Maryland conceived his Washington, D.C., International early in the 1950s, he was dreaming of meetings of stars from many nations. As matters unfolded in 1964, the International was to be the deciding race for two domestic heroes. The calendar dictated that the Horse of the Year must be decided soon, and it was to Laurel that both Gun Bow and Kelso repaired, although grass was not the favored footing for either combatant.

If Kelso were human, he would have had license to look at the stolid Laurel grandstand and the luxuriant International Village amid the blazing autumn colors of Maryland and think, "Good God. Not this hellhole again." For Kelso had run three of his noblest races in Internationals past and had suffered three of his most galling defeats. First, in 1961, it was T. V. Lark that bested him. Then, in 1962, after

Brooklyn Handicap
Purse: $100,000 Added

7th Race Aqueduct - July 25, 1964
Purse $100,000 added. Three-year-olds and upward. 1 1-4 Miles. Main Track. Track: Fast.
Value of race, $110,000. Value to winner $71,500; second, $22,000; third, $11,000; fourth, $5,500. Mutuel pool $666,298.

P#	Horse	A	Wgt	Med	Eqp	Odds	PP	1/4	1/2	3/4	1m	Str	Fin	Jockey
3	Gun Bow	4	122		b	11.30	3	1^2	1^2	$1^{2\frac{1}{2}}$	1^2	1^4	1^{12}	W Blum
1	Olden Times	6	122		b	36.10	1	5^4	3^1	3^2	$2^{\frac{1}{2}}$	$2^{\frac{1}{2}}$	2no	H Moreno
2	Sunrise Flight	5	113		b	17.65	2	8	$7^{\frac{1}{2}}$	7^3	7^5	$5^{\frac{1}{2}}$	3^h	D Pierce
4	Iron Peg	4	118			2.55	4	$2^{\frac{1}{2}}$	2^1	$2^{\frac{1}{2}}$	3^3	3^5	4^2	W Shoemaker
5	Kelso	7	130			.85	5	6^4	6^6	6^6	$5^{\frac{1}{2}}$	6^6	$5^{1\frac{1}{2}}$	I Valenzuela
8	Malicious	3	110		b	5.35	8	4^h	4^1	4^3	4^3	4^h	6^8	J L Rotz
7	Garwol	6	112			109.65	7	$7^{1\frac{1}{2}}$	8	8	8	8	7^5	W Chambers
6	Dean Carl	4	115			21.80	6	$3^{\frac{1}{2}}$	5^4	5^2	6^2	7^1	8	R Ussery

Off Time: 4:50½ Eastern Daylight Time **Time Of Race:** :22⅗ :46½ 1:10⅕ 1:35 1:59⅗ (new track record) (against wind in backstretch).
Start: Good For All **Track:** Fast
Equipment: b for blinkers

Mutuel Payoffs
3	**Gun Bow**	$24.60	$10.60	$7.60
1	**Olden Times**		24.20	11.20
2	**Sunrise Flight**			9.50

Winner: Gun Bow, b. c. by Gun Shot—Ribbons and Bows, by War Admiral (Trained by E. A. Neloy).
Bred by Maine Chance Farm in Ky.

Start good. Won easily.
GUN BOW, away alertly, was superbly rated and saved ground while setting the pace to the mile, responded readily when flicked twice with the whip before reaching midstretch and drew clear without the need of further urging. OLDEN TIMES, forwardly placed from the start and saving ground, made a bold challenge at the stretch turn but was unable to reach GUN BOW and was placed under strong handling during the drive to retain the place by a short margin. SUNRISE FLIGHT, in hand until reaching the stretch, responded readily during the drive but could not overtake OLDEN TIMES for second, just missing. IRON PEG, prominent from the beginning made a game effort to reach GUN BOW after five-eighths mile and faltered during the stretch run. KELSO, rough at the post, fell inside the stall gate before the start, was outrun to the mile and could not threaten the leaders when set down in the drive. MALICIOUS, away fast, raced well until inside the stretch and tired. GARWOL, never close, had no mishap. DEAN CARL gave way after showing early speed.
Overweight—Sunrise Flight, 1 pound.

Owners: (3) Gedney Farms; (1) R C Ellsworth; (2) Little M Farm; (4) Cain Hoy Stable; (5) Bohemia Stable; (8) Greentree Stable; (7) Harbor View Farm;
(6) P Bongarzone
©DAILY RACING FORM/EQUIBASE

he had turned back American protagonists Carry Back and Beau Purple in a sizzling duel, France's Match II came along to defeat him in a race so courageous that Valenzuela was in virtual tears afterward as he praised the valor of his mount. In 1963, it was Mongo who out-dueled Kelso to win the International by a half-length.

So, to rest his case for retaining his Horse of the Year status on one and a half miles of grass in Laurel's International was hardly seen as bidding to Kelso's strong suit. On the other hand, as we have seen, Gun Bow had come up short in the only previous try on grass of his career. All in all, the International seemed ready-made for one of those deflating moments when an upstart dashes home while the supposed stars struggle in feckless anticlimax.

Instead, Kelso turned it into one of his many crowning moments.

The drought-parched turf course at Laurel that autumn was far from deep, lush, or holding, and Gun Bow and Kelso scudded along as if it were the best stuff they had ever trod upon. There were some nice other runners, six of them, from Russia, Europe, and Japan, but they were never much more than curious tourists. They joined the Veteran's Day crowd of nearly 38,000 in watching a two-horse duel, and their vantage point gradually worsened.

The crowd suspected as much, but not with true confidence. Kelso was favored, but only at 6-5, while Gun Bow was second choice at 3-2. Blum put Gun Bow on the lead early, and the pace was swift as Kelso tracked him three or four lengths behind

Aqueduct Handicap
Purse: $100,000 Added

7th Race Aqueduct - September 7, 1964
Purse $100,000 added. Three-year-olds and upward. 1 1-8 Miles. Main Track. Track: Fast.
Value of race, $107,700. Value to winner $70,005; second, $21,540; third, $10,770; fourth, $5,385. Mutuel pool $665,991.

P#	Horse	A	Wgt	Med	Eqp	Odds	PP	St	1/4	1/2	3/4	Str	Fin	Jockey
3	Kelso	7	128			2.20	3	2	2^2	2^4	2^3	$1^{1/2}$	$1^{3/4}$	I Valenzuela
5	Gun Bow	4	128		b	.55	5	1	1^4	1^5	$1^{1\frac{1}{2}}$	2^6	2^6	W Blum
2	Saidam	5	119			7.45	2	5	$4^{1/2}$	5	4^1	4^3	$3^{4\frac{1}{2}}$	B Baeza
1	Delta Judge	4	116			19.25	1	4	3^1	3^1	3^2	3^h	4^2	J L Rotz
4	Uppercut	5	116			13.10	4	3	5	$4^{1/2}$	5	5	5	J Sellers

Off Time: 4:51 Eastern Daylight Time **Time Of Race:** :23⅕ :46⅗ 1:10⅘ 1:35⅗ 1:48⅗ (with wind in backstretch).
Start: Good For All **Track:** Fast.
Equipment: b for blinkers

Mutuel Payoffs

3	**Kelso**	**$6.40**	**$2.60**	**$2.20**
5	**Gun Bow**		**2.20**	**2.10**
2	**Saidam**			**2.30**

Winner: Kelso, dk. b. or br. g. by Your Host—Maid of Flight, by Count Fleet (Trained by Carl Hanford).
Bred by Mrs. R. C. du Pont in Ky.

Start good. Won driving.
KELSO, away alertly, saved ground while under occasional urging and in closest attendance of GUN BOW, took command from the latter entering the stretch and, responding to strong handling during the drive, retained a safe advantage. GUN BOW began fast and moved to the inside when clear of the field at the initial turn, set the pace until reaching the stretch and continued courageously after losing command to KELSO, was unable to hold the latter but was easily best of the others. SAIDAM, outrun for three-quarters mile, could not threaten the leaders when set down through the stretch. DELTA JUDGE had no mishap but weakened during the stretch run. UPPERCUT, never close following the break, had no excuse.
Scratched—Decidedly.

Owners: (3) Bohemia Stable; (5) Gedney Farm; (2) Mrs J D Alexander; (1) Ada L Rice; (4) W L Harmonay
©DAILY RACING FORM/EQUIBASE

through six furlongs in 1:10⅖. Valenzuela then urged Kelso toward the leader, and he reached even terms at the half-mile pole. The first mile was run in a stunning 1:34⅘. Kelso brushed Gun Bow lightly, and it took another supreme effort to begin to draw away, his powerful haunches and graceful old legs carrying onward with unwavering speed.

The old fellow matched the exacting standard of 2:00 for a mile and a quarter again, but this time he still had two more furlongs to run. In that final stretch, he did something he had never done before — distance himself from Gun Bow. The margin and the cheers grew together, and at last Kelso had conquered the International. He hit the wire in 2:23⅘, a new course and American record for one and a half miles on grass. Gun Bow was beaten four and a half lengths, but had nine lengths on the Russian champion Aniline.

It had gone down to the last half-mile in a four-race combat totaling five and one-eighth miles, but Kelso had his fifth Horse of the Year crown. Mrs. du Pont and Hanford, not for the first time that autumn, found themselves saying that this had been the most exciting of all.

Amazingly, there was more glory ahead for

Woodward Stakes
Purse: $100,000 Added

7th Race Aqueduct - October 3, 1964
Purse $100,000 added. Three-year-olds and upward. Weight for age. 1 1-4 Miles. Main Track. Track: Good.
Value of race, $108,200. Value to winner $70,330; second, $21,640; third, $10,820; fourth, $5,410. Mutuel pool $583,934.

P#	Horse	A	Wgt	Med	Eqp	Odds	PP	1/4	1/2	3/4	1m	Str	Fin	Jockey
2	Gun Bow	4	126		b	1.45	2	1^{1}	$1^{1\frac{1}{2}}$	$1^{1\frac{1}{2}}$	1^{h}	$2^{1\frac{1}{2}}$	1no	W Blum
3	Kelso	7	126			.95	3	2^{4}	$2^{3\frac{1}{2}}$	2^{h}	2^{1}	1^{h}	2^{4}	I Valenzuela
4	Quadrangle	3	121			5.45	4	3^{3}	3^{5}	3^{12}	3^{20}	3^{25}	3^{25}	M Ycaza
5	Guadalcanal	6	126			51.45	5	5	5	5	4^{8}	4^{10}	4^{18}	J Ruane
1	Colorado King	5	126			11.00	1	4^{7}	4^{8}	4^{5}	5	5	5	W Hartack

Off Time: 4:50 Eastern Daylight Time **Time Of Race:** :23⅘ :48⅕ 1:12⅕ 1:37⅕ 2:02⅖ (no wind in backstretch)
Start: Good For All **Track:** Good.
Equipment: b for blinkers

Mutuel Payoffs

2	**Gun Bow**	**$4.90**	**$2.40**	**$2.10**
3	**Kelso**		**2.30**	**2.10**
4	**Quadrangle**			**2.10**

Winner: Gun Bow, b. c. by Gun Shot—Ribbons and Bows, by War Admiral (Trained by E. A Neloy).
Bred by Maine Chance Farm in Ky.

Start good. Won driving.
GUN BOW, taken in hand leaving the gate, saved ground drawing clear on the first turn and raced with neck bowed when taken under double wraps entering the backstretch. Jockey Blum gradually loosened restraint approaching the half-mile pole and had him under pressure rounding the stretch turn. He was headed briefly by KELSO at the three-sixteenths marker and was gradually forced in by that rival passing the furlong marker, where he regained a slight advantage which he maintained narrowly under extreme hand urging. KELSO, lightly hustled to show first away from the gate, was taken under restraint when joined by GUN BOW after the opening furlong and dropped back until clear on the first turn. He was then put to light pressure to remain close to GUN BOW, moved up strongly around that rival and QUADRANGLE on the stretch turn and gained a brief advantage, hung briefly when he bore in slightly on GUN BOW in midstretch and lost command, then resolutely came again under hand riding and just missed. QUADRANGLE was permitted to settle into comfortable stride, saved ground steadily moving to the top pair next to the rail through the backstretch and reached even terms with KELSO at the three-furlong marker but lacked the response to take advantage of an opening next to the rail inside GUN BOW after entering the stretch. The jockey had to stop driving for a couple of strides when the top pair drifted in front of him and closed the opening just inside the furlong marker, and he then weakened gradually. GUADALCANAL was outrun and weakened. COLORADO KING lost his action after six furlongs and was not ridden out.
Scratched—Decidedly.

Owners: (2) Gedney Farm; (3) Bohemia Stable; (4) Rokeby Stable; (5) R L Dotter; (1) R W Hawn
©DAILY RACING FORM/EQUIBASE

Kelso. His eight-year-old season did not produce a sixth Horse of the Year title, but it may not have been old legs and muscles that ended his reign. An eye infection of all things canceled most of his annual autumn schedule. Before that, however, he had put in another signature Kelso triumph when he outbattled Malicious to win the Whitney by a nose while giving him sixteen pounds at historic Saratoga. Then, in what turned out to be his final race before his New York congregation, he won the Stymie by eight lengths before the eye trouble stopped him. He made one start in Florida at nine, but the soundest of horses finally suffered an injury, a fracture in the right forefoot, and he was retired immediately.

Gun Bow won the Metropolitan Handicap in 1965, but had only two later races before his retirement, so he and Kelso did not meet again after their Laurel battle. They already had given the sport as many gifts as could be reasonably asked.

Washington, D.C., International
Purse: $150,000

7th Race Laurel Race Course - November 11, 1964
Purse $150,000. Three-year-olds and upward. By invitation only. Weight for age. 1 1-2 Miles. Turf Course. Track: Hard.
Value of race, $150,000. Value to winner $90,000; second, $25,000; third, $15,000; fourth, $10,000; fifth and sixth, $5,000 each.
Mutuel pool $482,555.

P#	Horse	A	Wgt	Med	Eqp	Odds	PP	1/4	1/2	1m	$1\frac{1}{4}$	Str	Fin	Jockey
5	Kelso	7	126			1.20	5	$2^{2\frac{1}{2}}$	$2^{1\frac{1}{2}}$	1^{h}	$1^{\frac{1}{2}}$	1^{3}	$1^{4\frac{1}{2}}$	I Valenzuela
1	Gun Bow	4	126		b	1.50	1	1^{3}	1^{4}	2^{3}	2^{8}	2^{10}	2^{9}	W Blum
7	Aniline	3	122			17.20	7	5^{h}	$6^{1\frac{1}{2}}$	$6^{\frac{1}{2}}$	4^{4}	3^{h}	$3^{3\frac{1}{2}}$	N Nasibov
3	Biscayne II	3	122			35.40	3	$3^{\frac{1}{2}}$	5^{2}	$5^{\frac{1}{2}}$	5^{3}	5^{2}	$4^{1\frac{1}{2}}$	W J Wil'm'n
4	Belle Sicambre	3	119			29.50	4	$4^{1\frac{1}{2}}$	3^{h}	3^{3}	3^{4}	4^{4}	$5^{2\frac{1}{2}}$	L Piggott
2	Primordial II	7	126			26.20	2	8	8	8	8	$6^{1\frac{1}{2}}$	6^{6}	L Pincay
6	Veronese II	4	126			5.20	6	7^{5}	7^{3}	7^{7}	7^{4}	7^{2}	$7^{3\frac{1}{2}}$	F Jovine
8	Ryu Forel	5	126			72.80	8	6^{3}	$4^{2\frac{1}{2}}$	4^{3}	6^{4}	8	8	I Miyamoto

Off Time: 3:51 Eastern Standard Time **Time Of Race:** :24 $:46\frac{4}{5}$ $1:10\frac{2}{5}$ $1:34\frac{4}{5}$ 2:00 $2:23\frac{4}{5}$ (new course and new American record)
Start: Good For All **Track:** Hard
Equipment: b for blinkers

Mutuel Payoffs

5	**Kelso**	**$4.40**	**$2.40**	**$2.40**
1	**Gun Bow**		**2.60**	**2.20**
7	**Aniline**			**3.80**

Winner: Kelso, dk. b. or br. g. by Your Host—Maid of Flight, by Count Fleet (Trained by Carl Hanford).
Bred by Mrs. R. C. du Pont in Ky.

Start good from tape. Won handily.
KELSO broke smoothly and alertly and easily came around BISCAYNE II to settle into closest pursuit of GUN BOW after the initial furlong. He moved rapidly on the second turn to be lapped outside GUN BOW settling away in the backstretch and gained a slight advantage completing the mile. On the stretch turn he was brushed very lightly by GUN BOW and came over slightly on that rival a few yards farther on when punished twice left-handed. Maintaining a straight course thereafter, he drew away under hand riding with complete authority. GUN BOW was away well and rushed up along the inside under alert handling to take a clear lead after the initial sixteenth mile. He jumped a slight path in the grass at the furlong marker and his action became high when the jockey attempted to take him under wraps passing the stands the first time. Running smoothly under pressure around the next turn and in the backstretch, he continued resolutely after being headed by KELSO, but bore out slightly and brushed that rival at the head of the homestretch. A few yards farther on he was crowded slightly for a couple of strides by KELSO and, attempting to bear out, was taken out sharply after dropping back clear, and could not keep up thereafter while under strong hand urging. An objection lodged by the rider on GUN BOW against KELSO for alleged interference in the upper stretch was not allowed. ANILINE failed to gain while racing next to the rail and under pressure, came out slightly to pass horses after a mile and finished strongly to be going away over the the others. BISCAYNE II began fastest but dropped off the pace early and performed evenly thereafter while besting tiring rivals. BELLE SICAMBRE was well placed behind the top pair but could not keep up with them under pressure in the backstretch and weakened. PRIMORDIAL II lacked speed. VERONESE II raced along the outside and was outrun. RYU FOREL raced wide early and tired badly after a mile and a furlong.

Owners: (5) Bohemia Stable; (1) Gedney Farm; (7) U S S R; (3) Mrs J Reid; (4) Mme Suzy Volterra; (2) Renato Fabris-S Ledwith; (6) Com A Perego-Dr M Perego; (8) T Miyoshi

©DAILY RACING FORM/EQUIBASE

*George Royal (No. 10) gets home by a
nose after one and three-quarter miles.*

- CHAPTER 17 -

John Longden's Last Ride

John Longden had a flair for the dramatic, or perhaps drama arrogated him as an accomplice. When Longden completed the Triple Crown of 1943 as the jockey of the great Count Fleet, he did it by taking the Belmont by twenty-five lengths and in stakes-record time. When he surpassed Sir Gordon Richards' record as the world's leading jockey in number of wins, Longden did so not in some otherwise pedestrian overnight race, but by getting Arrogate home by a nose in a major Labor Day stakes, the 1956 Del Mar Handicap — again in track-record time. After his retirement from riding, he slid immediately into the role of trainer, and at the 1966 Keeneland July sale outbid two others to purchase the first $200,000 yearling for his client. Finally, three years later, when he became the only Kentucky Derby-winning jockey to win the race again as a trainer, he did so with another record-priced yearling, a dazzling colt that was unbeaten at the time!

As glorious as those moments were, however, they do not quite match the magical mastery of how Longden handled his retirement as a jockey. That he was still riding at fifty-nine years of age strained credulity; that he was still competitive on the major Southern California circuit was even more amazing; that he won a race early on the card of his announced final day of racing was a sweet nicety. Then came the actual finale. He had won the San Juan Capistrano the year before on the haphazardly bred British Columbia hero George Royal, and he was riding him again in that demanding one and three-quarter-mile race so revered by the Arcadia (California) faithful. The horse had been troubled with a joint problem and on form did not seem likely to repeat. Moreover, he was in a field of major winners, and it may well have been more heart than handicapping that prompted 60,792 fans to tug his odds down to a respectful 13-2. And then, John Longden went out and won his final race — by a nose. Drama? Of course. That was the Longden way.

⊱—◆—○—◆—⊰

A native of Wakefield, England, Longden had

In the winner's circle for the last time on George Royal.

his only two rides on Stymie; three consecutive triumphs on T. V. Lark, culminating in a victory over Kelso in the Washington, D.C., International; and victories on such cross-country stars as Market Wise, Pavot, Berseem, Your Host, Porterhouse, St. Vincent, Real Good Deal, Fleet Nasrullah, El Drag, Moonrush, Bobby Brocato, and Swaps. These were days far removed from swapping victories with Don Meade in the Winnipeg Futurity, when it was worth $1,800 to the winner in the early 1930s.

Much of Longden's career was based on the West Coast, and he won multiples of the greatest races there: four Santa Anita Handicaps; five Santa Anita Derbys; five Santa Margaritas; four California Derbys; five Hollywood Derbys. His riding rhythm garnered the nickname "The Pumper," and the specialty assigned him by his fans was waiting, and staying, on the lead.

Eventually, though, it had to end.

Longden was to be guest of honor at a dinner in Pasadena, California, a circumstance with so many precedents that he probably had lost count. He had been thinking about retiring — after all, it was at least a dozen years since he had been asked about it in response to an injury. Then, "On the way to the dinner, I asked myself, why put it off any longer? This is it."

He announced his plans at dinner, and the end of an era was but days away.

Longden's partner in what was to be his last ride had some oblique similarities in background.

emigrated early, and he scuffled up to the top rungs of North American racing by way of the leaner circuits of middle Canada. He had been a jockey for nearly forty years when he announced in 1966 that he was ready to retire.

Longden had first led the nation's jockeys in races won in 1938, and he had repeated in 1947 and 1948. He had led all riders in earnings in Count Fleet's year, 1943, and had repeated in 1945. He had won his Kentucky Derby, as well as the entire Triple Crown, on Count Fleet, and had reigned for ten years as the world leader in wins. Along the way he had hooked up with some of the best.

Count Fleet was always Longden's favored mount, but there were those four wins over Citation on Noor; four wins on that troublesome darling Whirlaway as a two-year-old; the sequence of victories on Busher that made her the Horse of the Year as a three-year-old in 1945; a Saratoga Cup in one of

George Royal, too, had career origins in one of the more western provinces of Canada. At the time, only Northern Dancer had broken through as a world-class Canadian-bred, but he had been foaled in Ontario, the garden spot of that huge country insofar as racehorse production was concerned. While anyone in Canada might speak with pride of the "Canadian-bred Kentucky Derby winner," there was no sense abroad that just any place in Canada was relevant to this new success. To suggest otherwise would be similar to presuming that when Needles won the Derby as the first Florida-bred star in 1956, his prowess heightened the status of horses bred in Washington state, or Texas.

George Royal was bred in British Columbia, home to the picturesque ocean-side city of Vancouver and to a great many marvelous mountains and spectacular vistas. The province of B.C. had plenty of history in racing and in breeding a certain level of solid runner, but George Royal quickly assumed pride of place in the history of his birthplace. He was a son of the Alibhai stallion Dark Hawk and out of Polly Bashaw, by Pasha. (Pasha was imaginatively named, being by The Porter—Fatima II.)

George Royal was bred in the name of D.J.W. Dunn and was sold with another yearling, reportedly for three-thousand dollars, to Ernest C. Hammond and Robert W. Hall. He was trained for them by Don Richardson. At two and three, George Royal won seven stakes on the local British Columbia circuit centered in Vancouver, at what was then known as Exhibition Park.

At four he trod lightly up a number of rungs within the hierarchy of the North American Turf. With Longden aboard, he was third in the Santa Anita Handicap, behind bona fide California and national stars Hill Rise and Candy Spots, then won the San Juan Capistrano over Duel and Hill Rise. Late in the year, Longden and George Royal added Woodbine's Canadian International, which earned the horse a berth in the Washington, D.C., International at Laurel. In that international showdown, he finished fourth behind the French pair of Diatome and Carvin II and the Horse of the Year Roman Brother. George Royal was beaten by only about one and a half lengths.

The following winter, back in California, George Royal had his problems, as mentioned above. He and Longden finished eighth in that year's Santa Anita Handicap in a sterling race won by Kentucky Derby winner Lucky Debonair, with the likes of Native Diver, Hill Rise, and Bold Bidder scattered about in the finish order. Richardson read through the raw results and sensed that George Royal was coming back to his best form. In the San Juan Capistrano, George Royal was facing eight horses, and the top weight and favorite was the distinguished and versatile Hill Rise, assigned 126 to George Royal's 118. The others included Plaque, coming off a win in a one and a half-mile overnight race on grass and carrying 115. The high-class turf stakes winners Or et Argent, Cedar Key (the 1964 San Juan Capistrano winner), and Polar Sea, were also in the field, as was the stout distaffer Straight Deal.

Longden had only a few minutes of future as a jockey, but he had some good history with the marathon of the San Juan Capistrano. As was true of the other top races at Santa Anita, he had multiple wins in the race, dating to before its switch to the grass course. In 1950, there had been his dramatic photo finish victory on Noor over Citation (see chapter on the 1950 San Juan Capistrano), and then Longden had come back to win it again the next year on Be Fleet. His third win came in the 1955 San Juan on St. Vincent, and ten years later he had won his fourth on George Royal. A chance for a fifth, and last, lay just ahead.

Plaque opened a daylight lead in the early furlongs, as Longden allowed George Royal to race along in last place. It was a master tactician in a masterful, sneaky performance. Along the backstretch, Longden sent George Royal on a rapid rally, and one of those the horse wheeled by with alacrity was the noble Hill Rise. As they swept into the stretch, George Royal's momentum carried him to the front, and it seemed that he would draw away. What a commotion those 60,000-plus Longden lovers could have made as he sat motionless for a stroll through the stretch, tipping his cap, if only mentally.

Instead, this last stretch run was to be a struggle that reached down for the last ounce of strength and adrenaline. Bob Ussery, no novice himself, had saved plenty on Plaque, and the 7-1 shot dug in. He even regained the lead. Now the fifty-nine-year-old Longden could no longer rely on savvy. He had to be "the Pumper," for sure, and against a younger man. Through the final furlong the charge continued. Longden of the era of Noor was back on the firing line, and in a moment unique in his life, and in the annals of racing. Would it be a storybook finish or a deflating "not-quite"? The answer would come quickly and would last forever.

"I thought that other horse would never give up," said Longden, and Plaque indeed never did. George Royal, directed by a master of so many miles of pushing and driving, did not give up either, and he lunged back into the lead. They flashed under the wire, and the camera caught George Royal's nose as the one in front. Tom Cat came charging along to be third, beaten barely a half-length.

Longden returned, drained, to the winner's circle, where an old friend, Joe Burnham, somehow managed to hold his movie camera steady enough to film the last dismount. The camera was about the only thing steady at the moment, for Longden clunked down out of the saddle, managing to appear rubber-legged and stiff at the same time, and with plenty of justification.

John Longden had won a horse race for the 6,032nd time. He had already reigned for a decade as the most successful individual in winning horse races in

Majestic Prince, the Kentucky Derby winner trained by a Kentucky Derby winner.

THE BLOOD-HORSE

history. Now he had one last trophy. No one else had ever done what John Longden had done.

Four years later, Bill Shoemaker would pass the total wins mark, but by then, Longden had moved on to new distinctions. In 1967, he and longtime friend Frank McMahon had set a record of another different sort, in bidding on yearlings, taking a sparkling young Raise a Native colt out of the Keeneland sale for $250,000. In the winter and spring of 1969, Longden the great rider segued into Longden the astute trainer — and exercise rider. On the first Saturday in May 1969, with a sitting presi-

dent of the United States (Richard Nixon) present at a horse race for the first time in living souls' memory, an Adonis of a colt by the name of Majestic Prince went under the wire as an undefeated winner of the Kentucky Derby. Of course, it had to be dramatic — a neck margin over Arts and Letters after a prolonged stretch duel, a fifth win for jockey Bill Hartack as he matched the Derby-winning record number of Longden's contemporary, Eddie Arcaro.

A Derby-winning jockey had become a Derby-winning trainer. No one else has ever done what John Longden has done.

San Juan Capistrano Handicap
Purse: $125,000

8th Race   Santa Anita - March 12, 1966
Purse $125,000 invitational handicap. Three-year-olds and upward. By invitation. About 1 3-4 Miles. Turf Course. Track: Firm.
Value to winner $75,000; second, $25,000; third, $15,000; fourth, $10,000. Mutuel pool $776,538.

P#	Horse	A	Wgt	Med	Eqp	Odds	PP	1/4	1/2	1m	1½	Str	Fin	Jockey
9	George Royal	5	118			6.50	9	9	9	7$^{\frac{1}{2}}$	5$^{\frac{1}{2}}$	1^h	1no	J Longden
4	Plaque	5	115			7.10	4	1^2	1^2	1^h	1^1	2^2	2$^{\frac{1}{2}}$	R Ussery
1	Tom Cat	6	114			5.60	1	4$^{\frac{1}{2}}$	5^2	8^2	8^3	4^1	3$^{1\frac{1}{2}}$	W Mahorn'y
7	Hill Rise	5	126			2.00	7	7^2	7^2	6$^{1\frac{1}{2}}$	4^h	3$^{\frac{1}{2}}$	4^2	M Ycaza
6	Tudor Fame	4	115		b	19.20	6	6^2	6$^{\frac{1}{2}}$	9	9	8^2	5^4	J Lambert
3	Straight Deal	4	116		b	17.80	3	5^3	4^1	5^1	7^4	7^1	6^{nk}	H Gustines
5	Or et Argent	5	120			12.00	5	2$^{\frac{1}{2}}$	3$^{1\frac{1}{2}}$	3^2	3$^{\frac{1}{2}}$	6$^{\frac{1}{2}}$	7$^{1\frac{1}{2}}$	W Blum
8	Cedar Key	6	124		b	4.10	8	8^2	8^3	4$^{\frac{1}{2}}$	6$^{\frac{1}{2}}$	9	8^2	W Shoemaker
2	Polar Sea	6	118		b	16.00	2	3$^{\frac{1}{2}}$	2$^{3\frac{1}{2}}$	2^4	2^1	5^h	9	W Hartack

Off Time: 4:48 Pacific Standard Time   **Time Of Race:**   2:48⅗
Start: Good For All.   **Track:** Firm
Equipment: b for blinkers

Mutuel Payoffs

9	**George Royal**	$15.00	$8.20	$4.80
4	**Plaque**		7.40	4.80
1	**Tom Cat**			4.00

Winner: George Royal, b. h. by Dark Hawk—Polly Bashaw, by Pasha. (Trained by D. Richardson).
Bred by D. J. W. Dunn in Canada.

Start good. Won driving.
GEORGE ROYAL, without early speed, raced on his own courage to the far turn, began to move up while on the extreme outside, shook off HILL RISE on the stretch turn to wear down PLAQUE and, after a long, hard stretch duel, won gamely under clever tactics. PLAQUE broke in stride, took a good early lead without need of urging and loafed along until joined by POLAR SEA, put that one away and, when challenged by the winner, held on tenaciously while saving ground, losing the advantage in the final strides. TOM CAT, unhurried to midstretch, saved ground, swung out for a clear path and finished fastest of all. HILL RISE made his bid on the far turn and moved closer, then hung in the drive. TUDOR FAME came to the stretch wide and weakened. STRAIGHT DEAL raced well early and tired. OR ET ARGENT was done when the real test came. CEDAR KEY saved ground, was well placed around the final turn, then suddenly had to take up on the stretch turn and gave way. POLAR SEA forced the pace through the intermediate stages and fell back.
Scratched—Going Abroad, O'Hara.
Overweight—Plaque, 1 pound.

Owners: (9) Hammond-Hall; (4) High Tide Stable; (1) C V Whitney; (7) El Peco Ranch; (6) Silver Creek Ranch; (3) Ethel D Jacobs; (5) C Campbell; (8) J Basta;
(2) E-H Seltzer

©DAILY RACING FORM/EQUIBASE

Damascus rocketed to victory in the Woodward, leaving Buckpasser and Dr. Fager in his wake.

- CHAPTER 18 -

The Road of Damascus

The perfect match up is elusive in any sport. In college basketball, the long-awaited championship game between two behemoths can be scuttled by a poor-shooting night or a bit of defensive genius. College football lives in the angst of contriving an annual climactic showdown between the "real" No. 1 and No. 2, but true young men or untrue bounces of the ball often confound the scriptwriters. Wimbledon and the Masters present every opportunity for the best in the world to square off in their respective finals, but weeks, or days, of fierce competition do not always funnel the desired names to the top of the last-round list.

To the exigencies inherent in competition, Thoroughbred racing brings fragility of the competitors and a specific difficulty in deciding in advance that one, two, or three champions will be produced at concert pitch on an appointed date. Few races have come as close to perfection as the 1967 Woodward, wherein three consecutive Horses of the Year — Buckpasser (1966), Damascus (1967), and Dr.

Fager (1968) — went to the post. As it turned out, even here there were imperfections. Dr. Fager was goaded into a sort of self-destructive rite that played upon his savage competitiveness, and, to be fair, it became difficult to accept that the noble Buckpasser's effort was a true reflection of his ultimate quality.

There were three decades-plus of the twentieth century yet to bring on their Triple Crown winners and Foregos and John Henrys and Cigars, but at the conclusion of the century, when *The Blood-Horse* published a poll of the entire one hundred years, Dr. Fager, Buckpasser, and Damascus all made the top twenty. Now, that is a field of racehorses.

So it was a heady experience for those who gathered at Aqueduct on September 30, 1967. There were 55,259 of them, which was some 12,000 fewer than had shown up on Labor Day to see two of the titans, Damascus and Buckpasser, square off for the Aqueduct Stakes, only to be let down. The four-year-old Buckpasser, with a history of quarter cracks, etc., which had kept him out of his spring classics, developed some heat in an ankle and was scratched.

After all three Hall of Famers were long since retired, it was Dr. Fager who was voted sixth-best in

The Woodward would be Buckpasser's final start.

the aforementioned poll, to Buckpasser's fourteenth and Damascus' sixteenth. If polled immediately after the Woodward, the 55,259 present might have had trouble foretelling this result. The crowd had had trouble deciding on a favorite, eventually falling back on the adage that a great older horse should beat great three-year-olds. It seems unlikely

that many could have concocted a notion that any of the three would win off by many lengths.

Buckpasser, Damascus, and Dr. Fager collectively and individually had compelling past performances. They had won forty-eight of fifty-eight prior starts.

Buckpasser was a surpassingly handsome son of 1953 Horse of the Year Tom Fool and out of Suburban Handicap winner Busanda, a daughter of the great War Admiral. Ogden Phipps bred Buckpasser and introduced him into a stable full of star colts and fillies by Bold Ruler. Phipps' mother, Mrs. Henry Carnegie Phipps, had bred and raced Bold Ruler, and in the early 1960s that young stallion was emerging as dominant. Yet, here was arguably the best horse either of the Phippses had ever bred, and he was a Tom Fool.

Trainer Bill Winfrey brought Buckpasser out at two in 1965, and the colt was a stakes winner by early summer and a champion by year's end. At three, Eddie Neloy took over as Winfrey retired. A quarter crack caused Buckpasser to miss all the Triple Crown races, but he came back better than his two-year-old form had suggested and by the end of 1966 had wrested Horse of the Year from the other three-year-olds and the older

THE BLOOD-HORSE

horses. At four, he had his soundness problems again, but his two-season winning streak reached fifteen races.

An experiment of running him on grass with a view toward a French adventure ended the winning streak, but Buckpasser had bounced back to win the historic Suburban Handicap under 133 pounds. He lost to Handsome Boy in the Brooklyn under 136 and then had the problem that caused him to miss the Aqueduct. When he lined up for the Woodward, he had not raced for two months and a week. All the same, he and stablemate Great Power were 1.60-1. It marked the first time since the Sapling Stakes, in the summer of his two-year-old season, that Buckpasser was not odds-on!

Damascus was the reigning three-year-old pro tem at the time, although Dr. Fager had beaten him in their only meeting. A medium-sized son of champion Sword Dancer out of unraced Kerala, by My Babu, Damascus had been bred by Mrs. Thomas Bancroft in partnership with her mother, Mrs. William Woodward Sr.

William Woodward had founded the massively successful Belair Stud, which late in his life had produced the great Nashua. William Jr. inherited that colt, but after his own death in 1955, the Belair horses had been dispersed. Mrs. Bancroft, determined to establish her own breeding and racing operation, purchased Kerala from another of the great sporting families, John Hay Whitney and Mrs. C.S. Payson of Greentree Stud. Mrs. Bancroft employed the historic Belair colors, white with red polka dots and a red cap, but she was an invalid by the time Damascus emerged to place her beside her own father as the breeder of a champion.

Trainer Frank Whiteley had brought Damascus

along slowly, winning the Remsen among only four starts at two. At three, he had lost early to Dr. Fager at a mile in the Gotham, but Dr. Fager's trainer, John Nerud, chose not to push his headstrong soldier into the classics. Damascus won the Wood Memorial, was upset in the Kentucky Derby, but then won the Preakness and Belmont. Since then, he had seemed to be even better, his summer including a seven-length victory in the American Derby and an astounding twenty-two-length triumph in the Travers Stakes! In his first foray against older horses, he had won the Aqueduct by two lengths while giving six pounds of actual weight to the Widener Handicap winner, Ring Twice.

Damascus owned the more prestigious list of trophies, but the big, lengthy Dr. Fager was seen as an extraordinary three-year-old as well. In time, he like the others would be seen to represent an Establishment breeding operation, but at the time, W.L. McKnight's Tartan Farms was a newcomer at the top ranks. Moreover, Dr. Fager was a Florida-bred and was by Rough'n Tumble, the first nationally prominent stallion to stand in that rising state. Dr. Fager was out of Aspidistra, a Better Self mare whom McKnight's 3-M Company staff had acquired for him as a birthday present.

At two Dr. Fager had burst onto the scene with a twelve-length score in the World's Playground Stakes, and but for a headstrong dash that weakened him to Successor's advantage in the Champagne, would likely have been the champion two-year-old. After defeating Damascus at a mile in the Gotham the next spring, Dr. Fager continued merrily along a non-classic path. His aggressiveness got him taken down after a runaway win in the Jersey Derby, but he soared without official reprimand in the Withers, the Arlington Classic (by ten lengths), the Rockingham Special, and New Hampshire Sweepstakes Classic.

Just as Buckpasser had been routinely a short-priced favorite for two years, Damascus had been odds-on for his last seven races, Dr. Fager for his last five. Of the three trainers (all destined for the Hall

Nerud turned to Bill Boland. It had been seventeen years since Boland won the Kentucky Derby as an apprentice on Middleground. Boland had been cast as a stand-in before. The great rider Eddie Arcaro had faced a question of which champion to ride prior to the 1955 Sysonby Stakes. He took one of his regulars, Nashua, over another of his regulars,

Damascus was the clear choice for 1967 Horse of the Year.

of Fame, by the way), only Nerud had a rider problem. Braulio Baeza had ridden Dr. Fager in most of his races at three, but he also had ridden Buckpasser in twenty-seven of his thirty career races. Baeza stuck with Buckpasser. Shoemaker had ridden Damascus in all but two of his seventeen starts, and was aboard again.

High Gun. Boland got the mount — and the win — on High Gun.

In the 1967 Woodward, however, Boland was the silent lamb upon a sacrifice. For years, pacemakers have been used to help orchestrate a certain result, but for the Woodward the word "rabbit" was popularized to describe not one, but two, pacemakers.

Neloy put the speedy Great Power in as Buckpasser's stablemate, to make sure Dr. Fager raced his head off early. Whiteley put Hedevar in as Damascus' stablemate, to make sure Dr. Fager raced his head off early.

Nerud, Dr. Fager's trainer, might have seethed, but he had little wiggle room insofar as decrying the sportsmanship of the tactic. An even ten years before, Nerud had employed Bold Nero in a similar role to race Bold Ruler off his feet and allow Gallant Man to come along and win the Belmont Stakes. It worked for the biggest win of Nerud's career to that point. Gallant Man won in record time by eight lengths, while Bold Ruler struggled home third. For Nerud, the Woodward was a matter of the rabbits coming home to roost — to use a slightly ill-fitting expression.

So, they went to the gate for the Woodward, the three-year-olds under 120 pounds, the older horses under 126, for a purse of $100,000-added, going one and a quarter miles, passing the stands twice. The pacemakers went dashing out, their riders screaming in Kamikaze unison. Great Power and Hedevar yapped Dr. Fager through a quarter-mile in :22⅖. Great Power called it a day, or a quarter-mile. Hedevar continued to harangue Dr. Fager, who rushed a half-mile in :45⅕ and six furlongs in 1:09⅕, at that point holding a one and a half-length lead.

Baeza on Buckpasser and Bill Shoemaker on Damascus contentedly allowed this assisted suicide to play out in front of them. Dr. Fager had won

the macho game and lost the war. Damascus was about nine lengths back after six furlongs, and a length ahead of Buckpasser. The two moved to challenge, but it was Damascus, whose eruptive rallies had impressed before, who dashed away from the older horse. Within a quarter-mile Damascus had taken over from the fatigued but determined Dr. Fager, and he sped through the arc of the turn. Buckpasser's progress was inexorable, Damascus' rocket-like. By mid-stretch, Damascus had a five-length lead and, amazingly, he doubled it, winning by ten.

Despite the wounds of his own making, Dr. Fager struggled on, and it was only in the final twenty yards that Buckpasser got by him, taking second by

Dr. Fager was known for his blazing speed.

a half-length. (Had Damascus been absent, and all other things as they were, this would have gone down as an epic example of an older warrior refusing to let a younger one get home first. And if Buckpasser had won by a half-length over Dr. Fager, who among us would have entertained any thought that,

track record set by Gun Bow when he dashed Kelso in the 1964 Brooklyn Handicap. (Aqueduct's new track had opened in 1959.)

"He's light on his feet," Shoemaker said of Damascus. "He's got good balance, that horse. He's quick as a cat."

Damascus, alone on the rail and heading for home in the Woodward.

"You know, if Damascus had been in there, he'd a beat 'em both by ten lengths.")

Handsome Boy finished fourth, thirteen lengths behind Dr. Fager and twenty lengths ahead of Hedevar, who, in turn, had six lengths on Great Power. The mile had been run in 1:35⅗, and the final time of 2:00⅖ was only a second outside the

Two days after the dream race that the Woodward had almost been, Buckpasser's retirement was announced. The ankle was active again.

Dr. Fager bounced back to win the Hawthorne Gold Cup and the Vosburgh before the year was out.

Damascus went on to another sweeping rally and

victory in the two-mile Jockey Club Gold Cup, but in his first try on grass failed to overtake Fort Marcy in a wrenching stretch run in the Washington, D.C., International. Nevertheless, he had won twelve of sixteen at three and earned a one-year record of $817,941. He was the clear choice as Horse of the Year for 1967.

As mentioned earlier, Dr. Fager eventually would be rated above the two others. Buckpasser raced no more after the 1967 Woodward, but his three-year-old adversaries came back at four. Dr. Fager and Damascus split their two additional meetings, and the motif continued: When Hedevar was in the race as pacemaker, or rabbit, Damascus won; otherwise Dr. Fager won. Dr. Fager supplanted Buckpasser as holder of the world record for a mile; won at various distances on dirt and grass; and wound up as Horse of the Year, handicap champion, grass champion, and sprint champion of 1968. He had a career record of eighteen wins in twenty-two starts and earnings of $1,002,642. Damascus had a very good year at four, too, and wound up with a career mark of twenty-one wins in thirty-two starts and $1,176,781. Buckpasser had retired with twenty-five wins in thirty-one starts and earnings of $1,462,014.

Three great horses they were, and one day in 1967 they met in a race that, if not perfect, was nonetheless a race to conjure up dreams, and memories.

Woodward Stakes
Purse: $100,000 Added

7th Race Aqueduct - September 30, 1967
Purse $100,000 added. Three-year-olds and upward. Weight for age. 1 1-4 Miles. Main Track. Track: Fast.
Value of race, $107,800. Value to winner $70,070; second, $21,560; third, $10,780; fourth, $5,390. Mutuel pool $648,902.

P#	Horse	A	Wgt	Med	Eqp	Odds	PP	1/4	1/2	3/4	1m	Str	Fin	Jockey
5	Damascus	3	120			a-1.80	5	5^{1}	$5^{1\frac{1}{4}}$	4^{1}	$1^{\frac{1}{2}}$	1^{5}	1^{10}	W Shoemaker
6	Buckpasser	4	126		b	b-1.60	6	6	6	5^{3}	3^{4}	3^{6}	$2^{\frac{1}{2}}$	B Baeza
2	Dr. Fager	3	120			1.80	2	$1^{\frac{1}{2}}$	1^{h}	$1^{1\frac{1}{2}}$	2^{3}	2^{3}	3^{13}	W Boland
4	Handsome Boy	4	126		b	10.50	4	4^{5}	4^{5}	3^{1}	4^{3}	4^{12}	4^{20}	E Belmonte
1	Hedevar	5	126			a-1.80	1	2^{1}	2^{5}	2^{6}	5^{8}	5^{3}	5^{6}	R Turcotte
3	Great Power	3	120		b	b-1.60	3	3^{3}	3^{2}	6	6	6	6	R Ussery

a-Coupled: Damascus and Hedevar; b-Buckpasser and Great Power

Off Time: 4:50 Eastern Daylight Time **Time Of Race:** :22⅖ :45⅕ 1:09⅕ 1:35⅗ 2:00⅗ (with wind in backstretch)
Start: Good For All **Track:** Fast
Equipment: b for blinkers

Mutuel Payoffs

5	**Damascus (a-Entry)**	**$5.60**	**$2.60**
6	**Buckpasser (b-Entry)**		**2.80**
	No Show Mutuels Sold.		

Winner: Damascus, b. c. by Sword Dancer—Kerala, by My Babu (Trained by F. Y. Whiteley, Jr.).
Bred by Mrs. T. Bancroft in Ky.

Start good. Won easily.
DAMASCUS, steadied after beginning alertly, saved ground while in hand for three-quarters, moved up determinedly thereafter and, taking command from DR. FAGER near the stretch turn, drew clear without the need of urging. BUCKPASSER, outrun until near the stretch turn but saving ground, responded readily during the drive but was no match for DAMASCUS and was under brisk handling to best DR. FAGER for the place. The latter went to the front before a quarter, was much used racing HEDEVAR into defeat and faltered when challenged by DAMASCUS. HANDSOME BOY tired before entering the stretch. HEDEVAR, away alertly, engaged DR. FAGER for three-quarters and had nothing left. GREAT POWER was finished early.

Owners: (5) Edith W Bancroft; (6) O Phipps; (2) Tartan Stable; (4) Hobeau Farm; (1) Edith W. Bancroft; (3) Wheatley Stable

©DAILY RACING FORM/EQUIBASE

The thrilling stretch battle of the 1970 San Juan Capistrano — Quicken Tree (No. 3) pulling even with Fiddle Isle, with Fort Marcy (shadow roll) only a nose back.

- CHAPTER 19 -

"A Thundering Duel"

In a verdant way, racing returned to its roots during the 1930s when glamorous Hialeah's infield grass course began making turf racing a popular "novelty." That it could be so described is ironic, since formalized racing began on the heaths of England. It was in 1821 that the Union Course in New York was "skinned" of its natural thatching, and American racing eventually followed that new custom of horses running on dirt ovals.

The effects of this dirt preference trend was in part responsible for the most marked difference in the conduct of racing in North America and that in Mother England and the Continent. To wit, the dirt tracks could withstand sustained racing, whereas a grass course must be pampered. Thus, American tracks could have meetings extending hundreds of days, whereas European racing has remained a charming gypsy game of three or four days here, and then on to the next meeting.

As infield grass courses sprouted at racetracks across North America, the American racehorse theoretically was given an opportunity to prove a versatility denied many of the world's runners. He could show his prowess on distinctly different footing, and his trainer and owner had more options. In practice, however, very few horses have excelled at the highest levels on both dirt and grass. The richness of stakes programs on both surfaces gave rise to largely separated populations of dirt and grass runners. By 1953, *Daily Racing Form* had created a separate grass division for its championship balloting, and, eventually, the division was split into male and female categories. Trainers tended to race disappointing horses, or foreign ones, on grass, and when an animal found a home there it frequently remained. Meanwhile, horsemen debated what made a good turf foot — a broad, flat one that doesn't sink in, or a nifty little one that cuts through.

Among the most remarkable exceptions, horses that did switch adroitly back and forth, was the late-1950s champion Round Table. This iron horse apparently liked any surface, so long as it was not

CHAPTER 19

San Juan Capistrano International into one of the most gripping, and gritty, stretch battles in history. At the conclusion of one and three-quarter miles on grass, one of the longest races in America, Quicken Tree and Fiddle Isle were adjudged to be in a dead heat for first, while Fort Marcy was beaten only a nose and Hitchcock only another neck.

Of the winners, Quicken Tree was the more versatile. His career was not of the status of Round Table's or John Henry's, but he was in their league in terms of how he could switch. He had been winning races on grass and dirt for a couple of years, and his dis-

Quicken Tree was at home on both turf and dirt.

overly wet. In the 1980s the gelding John Henry consistently displayed a similar versatility of footing, while champions who were regulars on one surface but achieved at least one major score on the other included Kelso, Dr. Fager, and Secretariat.

An unusual measure of versatility was demonstrated by three of the four runners that turned the 1970

tance capacity seemed unlimited as well. Two years before the epic San Juan Capistrano, he had won the two-mile Jockey Club Gold Cup on dirt back East. In 1970, a month before he won Santa Anita's biggest grass race, Quicken Tree had won the track's most important dirt race, the storied Santa Anita Handicap.

Fiddle Isle, the other co-winner of the San Juan,

showed such good form that the great rider Bill Shoemaker was ready to compare him with the best horses he had ever ridden. He never won a major race on dirt, but he was second to Quicken Tree in the self-same Santa Anita Handicap.

Hitchcock, fourth in the San Juan, was a German-bred who had been a stakes winner over grass in his native country and in France. In his first full year of racing in this country, the four-year-old Hitchcock was on the most familiar footing available, that is to say grass, and prior to the San Juan he had pushed Fiddle Isle to a photo finish in a division of the San Luis Rey Handicap. Hitchcock switched courses and coasts, winning the historic Suburban Handicap, two runnings of the Gallant Fox, and a rendition of the Display — all on dirt — while racing through age six.

The reader may have noticed that, in reviewing the varied nature of the contestants in the 1970 San Juan, nothing has been said about the versatility of third-placed Fort Marcy. There is good reason. At three, Fort Marcy was so modest in his achievements, primarily on the main track, that his owner, Paul Mellon, and trainer, Elliott Burch, concluded that putting him in a sale and letting someone else deal with him was a smart move. Burch, however, was not willing to let him go when the bidding stalled at $76,000, so at $77,000 his representative rescued the gelding. Switched to grass a second time, Fort Marcy found a home, and this time he rarely strayed back to the dirt track. By year's end, he had defeated Damascus in the Washington, D.C., International, en route to the first of his three grass-course championships.

If Fort Marcy was persnickety about racing on grass alone, he was certainly not particular about where that grass might be growing. He had a versatility of another kind. Burch observed that the horse seemed actually to like flying, perhaps perceiving the grass to be greener on the other side of a flight pattern. Over four seasons, Fort Marcy crisscrossed the country, winning sixteen major grass stakes in New York, California, Illinois, New Jersey, Florida, and Maryland. While many Eastern-based horses have come a cropper when sent to California, Fort Marcy had no problems reproducing his best form along the Pacific. In the two summers before the race in question here, he had traveled West to land the one and a half-mile Sunset Handicap one year and the Hollywood Park Invitational at the same distance the next.

That 1968 Sunset had brought the first fierce scrum involving Fort Marcy, Quicken Tree, and Fiddle Isle. Fort Marcy was forced to a course record to hold Quicken Tree off to win by a nose under matched weights of 122 pounds, while the three-year-old Fiddle Isle closed to within a half-length under 108. One and a half miles of combat were not sufficient, and the stewards were called in to verify the result amid a flurry of foul claims by the riders of the second and third finishers.

So, two years later, these accomplished campaigners met in a field of eleven for the San Juan Capistrano. Quicken Tree was by then age seven, Fort Marcy six, and Fiddle Isle five. (Fort Marcy had finished second in the previous year's running to Petrone.) The weight differences were negligible, Fiddle Isle in with 125, Quicken Tree and Fort Marcy even at 124. The Hialeah Turf Cup winner Vent du Nord was actually the top weight, however, at 126. Hitchcock carried 119, and the weights for the others ranged down to 112.

What was destined to form the first quartet had distinguished connections. Three of the trainers and three of the jockeys eventually were elected into racing's Hall of Fame:

• Quicken Tree, a gelding by Preakness winner Royal Orbit, was bred by Lou Rowan, who owned him in partnership with Wheelock Whitney. He was trained by W.T. Canney and ridden by Fernando Alvarez.

• Fiddle Isle, a homebred by Bagdad, was owned by Howard B. Keck and trained and ridden by Hall of Famers Charlie Whittingham and Bill Shoemaker, respectively.

• Fort Marcy was an Amerigo gelding, a homebred from Mellon's Rokeby Farm; he was trained by Hall of Famer Elliott Burch and ridden by Hall of Famer Jorge Velasquez.

• Hitchcock, by Waidmannsheil, had been purchased by Sigmund Sommer. He was trained by Hall of Famer Pancho Martin and ridden by Hall of Famer Laffit Pincay Jr., the only participant in this scene still prominent in his profession in 2001, or thirty-one years later.

⋗—⊶—◇—⊷—⋖

While the Santa Anita Handicap is revered by the handsome California track's faithful, the San Juan sends a special message to their love of beauty, elegance, and the Thoroughbred. The race was begun in 1935, and its historic moments include Noor's upstart upset of Citation in 1950. It was a dirt race then, but in 1954 the San Juan found its special identity when moved to the grass. Known as El Camino Real — "The King's Highway" — the Santa Anita turf course offers a unique and voluptuous design. The start of the San Juan lures the eye from the stands off into the distance. The majestic San Gabriel Mountains vie for attention as the field is released down a hillside that leads to a graceful curve, eventually crossing the dirt course at the stretch turn and consigning the combatants to more than a loop of the tighter turns of the infield turf course.

In the 1970 creation of this jewel, the 75-1 long shot Off was allowed his moments in that meld of slanting sunlight and yawning shadow which celebrates a late afternoon at Santa Anita. He led by five lengths on the graceful descent, and his merry pranks carried him in front 'til after they had run a mile. He thereafter relented and retreated, to tenth. In the final furlongs, there was enough race riding going on that *Daily Racing Form* charts applied a "steadied" or "squeezed through" to three of the eventual battlers of the front rank. Fort Marcy and Hitchcock were fourth and sixth early, while Fiddle Idle and Quicken Tree were next-to-last and last.

Robert Hebert described the race for *The Blood-Horse*:

"As they went into the far turn, Quilche was in front, but Vent du Nord, Hitchcock, and Fort Marcy all were on the move for strong challenges. At the three-eighths turn, Vent du Nord came in a bit sharply, putting both Fort Marcy and Hitchcock in close quarters for several strides.

"At that moment, Shoemaker decided it was time to move with Fiddle Isle, and the chestnut fairly flew around the leaders on the turn. Quicken Tree was right at his heels. (That pair had made up about a dozen lengths since completing a mile.)

"As they swept around the last turn into the stretch, Fiddle Isle was five horses wide, with Quicken Tree right behind him. For a few strides, as the field straightened out at the top of the stretch, Vend du Nord had the lead, but Fiddle Isle's momentum swept him past the French invader. When Vent du Nord weakened and dropped back in the torrid drive, it became a thundering duel between Hitchcock on the rail, Fort Marcy just outside him, and Fiddle Isle and Quicken Tree out in the middle of the course.

"In midstretch, Fiddle Isle began lugging in, as is his habit. He appeared to crowd Fort Marcy, which was floated over onto Hitchcock. Had Fiddle Isle run straight and true through the stretch, he probably would have won it alone."

Shoemaker told Hebert that he had Fiddle Isle's head turned sideways through the stretch, attempting to counter the horse's tendency, but that he was getting bumped as well as doing some bumping.

" 'At the head of the stretch, I looked to the inside, figuring that if I could get him on the rail he would not lug in,' Shoemaker said, 'but the field was jammed up there, so I had to stay on the outside.' "

Alvarez, on Quicken Tree, knew his horse. Per-

haps more importantly, he also knew Shoemaker's horse. " 'I knew that he (Fiddle Isle) would lug in and give me room, so I stayed right behind him,' " Alvarez said.

"Thus, when Fiddle Isle began lugging in

Fiddle Isle and trainer Charlie Whittingham.

through the stretch, Quicken Tree was the only one with a clear path," Hebert continued. "Velasquez said Fort Marcy was bothered a bit leaving the half-mile pole when Vent du Nord came in and was bothered again by Fiddle Isle. Pincay said Hitchcock was bothered by Vent du Nord approaching the three-eighths pole and again near the finish," adding that his mount "got a little tired."

As they battled to the wire, so many furlongs

Handicap dead heat of Brownie, Wait a Bit, and Bossuet. Hitchcock was a noble fourth, lapped on the front three.

The drama, as had happened in the Sunset, did not end. Pincay on Hitchcock claimed foul against

Fort Marcy (rail) besting his San Juan Capistrano rivals in an earlier match.

THE BLOOD-HORSE

since the picturesque break, Fiddle Isle straightened out enough to match Quicken Tree, and they swept under the wire as one. Fort Marcy was but a nose from making it the second three-horse dead heat in the history of major American stakes, which would have joined the race with the 1944 Carter

both Fiddle Isle and Fort Marcy, while Velasquez on Fort Marcy claimed against Fiddle Isle.

"After a long look at the films, stewards decided that the trouble began at the top of the stretch, when Fort Marcy forced Fiddle Isle a bit wide," Hebert explained. "There, they said, Fiddle Isle drifted in approaching the finish. Stewards ruled that Hitchcock was already in fourth place when his rider had to steady."

The original result was made to stand — two winners, a narrow loser or two, and no one disgraced.

By the end of the year, it was Fort Marcy who had climbed back to the top. He not only was voted grass course champion again, but shared Horse of the Year honors with Personality, becoming the first grass-course specialist to achieve that specific acclaim. His later victories that year included triumphs over Fiddle Isle when the latter went East twice for the United Nations Handicap and Washington, D.C., International. Quicken Tree failed to win another stakes.

On April 4 they had formed a sprightly trio of equine Musketeers. In the case of these Musketeers, however, their virtual unity was an affront to the intentions of each.

San Juan Capistrano Invitational Handicap
Purse: $125,000

8th Race Santa Anita - April 4, 1970

Purse $125,000. Three-year-olds and upward. By invitation. About 1 3-4 Miles. Turf Course. Track: Firm.
Value to winners $50,000 each; third, $15,000; fourth, $7,500; fifth, $2,500. Mutuel pool $755,709.

P#	Horse	A	Wgt	Med	Eqp	Odds	PP	1/4	1/2	1m	1½	Str	Fin	Jockey
8	Fiddle Isle DH	5	125		b	a-4.00	8	10^{6}	10^{3}	$10^{2\frac{1}{2}}$	4^{h}	4^{2}	1	W Shoemaker
2	Quicken Tree DH	7	124		b	4.60	2	11	11	11	$6^{1\frac{1}{2}}$	5^{5}	1no	F Alvarez
3	Fort Marcy	6	124		b	8.50	3	4^{1}	4^{1}	5^{1}	$5^{2\frac{1}{2}}$	3^{h}	3^{nk}	J Velasquez
4	Hitchcock	4	119			2.60	4	$5^{\frac{1}{2}}$	6^{4}	6^{4}	$3^{\frac{1}{2}}$	$2^{\frac{1}{2}}$	$4^{2\frac{3}{4}}$	L Pincay Jr.
6	Vent du Nord	5	126			3.50	6	$6^{2\frac{1}{2}}$	$5^{\frac{1}{2}}$	$4^{\frac{1}{2}}$	2^{1}	1^{h}	5^{8}	R Turcotte
10	Royal Dynasty	4	114		b	30.60	10	$8^{\frac{1}{2}}$	9^{6}	$8^{\frac{1}{2}}$	$8^{1\frac{1}{2}}$	7^{2}	$6^{\frac{3}{4}}$	J Tejeira
9	Quilche	6	118			12.70	9	$3^{\frac{1}{2}}$	$3^{1\frac{1}{2}}$	$2^{\frac{1}{2}}$	$1^{1\frac{1}{2}}$	6^{1}	7^{h}	J Lambert
1	Jay Ray	4	116		b	46.50	1	7^{1}	$8^{\frac{1}{2}}$	$9^{2\frac{1}{2}}$	$10^{1\frac{1}{2}}$	8^{h}	$8^{\frac{1}{2}}$	W Mahorney
5	Makor	4	112		b	a-4.00	5	$9^{1\frac{1}{2}}$	7^{h}	$7^{2\frac{1}{2}}$	$9^{1\frac{1}{2}}$	9^{2}	9^{4}	R Rosales
11	Off	6	112		b	75.00	11	1^{2}	1^{5}	1^{h}	7^{h}	10^{5}	10^{7}	F Toro
7	Figonero	5	120			18.50	7	2^{1}	2^{h}	3^{1}	11	11	11	A Pineda

a-Coupled, Fiddle Isle and Makor; DH-Dead-heat.

Off Time: 4:51 Pacific Standard Time **Time Of Race:** :23⅘ :47⅕ 1:10 1:34⅖ 2:00⅕ 2:24 2:46⅖
Start: Good For All. **Track:** Firm
Equipment: b for blinkers

Mutuel Payoffs

8	**Fiddle Isle (a-entry) DH**	**$5.00**	**$4.60**	**$3.60**
2	**Quicken Tree DH**	**5.40**	**5.80**	**4.40**
3	**Fort Marcy**			**6.20**

Winners: Fiddle Isle, ch. h. by Bagdad—Nascania, by Nasrullah (Trained by C. Whittingham); bred by H. B. Keck in Ky.
Quicken Tree, ch. g. by Royal Orbit—Mother Wit, by Counterpoint (Trained by W. T. Canney); bred by L. Rowan in Calif.

Start good. Won driving.

FIDDLE ISLE was taken in hand at the start, dropped far off the early pace, caught his best stride on the far turn, rallied wide to join the pacemakers midway in the drive and steadied briefly while lugging in, responded in the final strides and held to finish on even terms with QUICKEN TREE. The latter broke clearly, fell back lagged to the far turn, rallied wide, had a clear path when straightened for the drive, accelerated late and finished fastest to deadlock. FORT MARCY raced close up early while in hand, took up approaching the far turn when blocked in close quarters, rallied in the drive and was squeezed through the late stages to finish gamely. HITCHCOCK raced on his own courage early, moved nearer midway, positioned himself along the rail for the drive and steadied when put in tight quarters late in the drive. VENT DU NORD was hard held early, moved nearer steadily midway while being kept wide, had his best bid on the stretch turn to be first in the stretch and weakened. QUILCHE forced much of the pace and faltered. OFF stopped. FIGONERO was an early factor and gave out in the drive. The rider on HITCHCOCK and the rider on FORT MARCY both claimed foul against FIDDLE ISLE. The stewards ruled that the crowding in no way affected the order of finish and disallowed the claims.

Owners: (8) H B Keck; (2) Rowan-Whitney; (3) Rokeby Stable; (4) S Sommer; (6) E Mittman; (10) G K Collins; (9) Kerr Stable; (1) Claiborne Farm; (5) Mrs H B Keck; (11) Siteen Ton Stable; (7) C L Hirsch

©DAILY RACING FORM/EQUIBASE

Secretariat's Belmont — a moment for the ages.

- CHAPTER 20 -

Perfection on the Run

Restraint need not be a consideration in addressing the 1973 Belmont Stakes. Indeed, conveying the feelings it engendered to anyone not fortunate enough to have seen the event is probably beyond reality. "Superb," "astounding," "spectacular," "unprecedented" are generally rather strong adjectives, but when applied to the 1973 Belmont of Secretariat they seem as banal and ineffective as mentioning that the peak of Mount Everest is "pretty high."

Secretariat won the Belmont that day by thirty-one lengths, in record time. It was the longest margin in the history of the American Triple Crown races, eclipsing the twenty-five lengths by which Count Fleet had won the same event thirty years before. Secretariat's maximum moment was hailed immediately by racing men of many years' experience:

"I think it was the greatest exhibition of speed and stamina that I have ever seen," said the crusty but wise old Greentree Stable trainer John Gaver. He then reiterated, "It was an exhibition. There was no race to it."

"I never saw a performance like that," said a fellow Hall of Fame trainer, Allen Jerkens.

"I guess Secretariat is the best horse I have ever seen," added another, Buddy Hirsch. "I thought Citation was, until Saturday. Now I will have to say Secretariat is a better horse than Citation."

Yet another Hall of Famer, Woody Stephens, concurred: "I just don't think I have ever seen any better."

Until Bill Nack had completed his definitive volume on Secretariat, *Big Red of Meadow Stable*, much of the most eloquent and persistent chorus heralding the horse's greatness in print had sprung from the typewriter of *Daily Racing Form* columnist Charlie Hatton. Whereas there were a number of horsemen around who had seen Citation, most living racetrackers by that time had only heard of Man o' War. Hatton had seen them both.

"Impressions of long standing tend to become fixed, and assume a prescriptive right not to be questioned," Hatton observed in the *American Racing Manual*, "but Secretariat is the most capable horse we ever saw, and geriatrics defeat any thought of seeing his like again."

Nearly thirty years later, during a confluence of centuries, various polls of the greatest racehorses reverted to Man o' War as supreme, with Secretariat second over Citation. Perhaps the "prescriptive right" of the impressions of longest standing had something to do with those results. Then again, Secretariat did lose two of his remaining six races after that startling zenith of Belmont Day, so we are not quick to cast any doubt on the intellectual integrity of the rankings.

While Secretariat's Belmont was powerful in its physical playing out, it cannot be addressed adequately without recognition of the emotional Vesuvius it unleashed. This had to do with many other horses, their promises and failings, and with the mythical importance of a three-race series known as the Triple Crown.

The Triple Crown might be described as the masterpiece of American racing except for the circumstance that there is no "master" to laud. The importance of the Kentucky Derby, Preakness, and Belmont Stakes, and their inseparable, shared identities, is not to be put down as owing much to the brilliance of any one racetrack management. Indeed, the races coalesced in the distant aftermath of attempts to create a similar prestige for other series.

Just why Americans, including horsemen, have spent a great deal of their history selecting aspects of English culture to imitate and others to mock is a morass of social psychology to which we personally give a wide berth. Suffice it to say that, on occasion, tracks in New York and Kentucky had made con-

scious efforts to replicate the trio of English three-year-old races that also became recognized as a Triple Crown. These were the Two Thousand Guineas, Epsom Derby, and St. Leger, and the races spanned much of the season and a range of distances from one mile to one and three-quarter miles. The structure had logic in its timing and presented a thorough test of versatility, stamina, durability, and class.

The New York and Kentucky models were meticulous in their imitation of this design, but neither caught on.

Instead, a series of disconnected races in three states — two with no fixed relationship as to which came first in any given year — took on, willy-nilly, the signature status that the local threesomes had envisioned. These were, of course, the Kentucky Derby at Churchill Downs, the Preakness Stakes at Pimlico in Baltimore, Maryland, and the Belmont Stakes at Belmont Park on Long Island.

As tests of the gallant, these three races were certainly admirable, but they were imperfect as progressive steps in distances, for they require action at one and a quarter miles, one and three-sixteenths miles, and one and a half miles. As well-thought-out season-long tests, they whirl away from the British model, being crammed into a space of five or six weeks. Yet, as history has transpired on both sides of the Atlantic, the English Triple Crown, and its nearly identical counterparts in Ireland and France, have virtually passed from consideration. Often the Guineas is won by a colt with neither pedigree nor ambition geared toward the Derby, while the St. Legers of today are often the purview of second-tier colts lacking the speed to satisfy modern fashion. Indeed, the Irish and French threw up their hands and

Secretariat and jockey Ron Turcotte led in by Penny Chenery.

opened their St. Legers to older horses. This nullifies their status as "classics," at least to the extent that their importance was based on their being cast on the original model in England.

In 1919, when Sir Barton won America's Derby, Preakness, and Belmont, these races were not yet identified as the Triple Crown. By the conclusion of the 1930s, when Gallant Fox, Omaha, and War Admiral swept the three, the races had become identi-

fied with each other. Then, in the 1940s, the frequency of Triple Crown winners continued, with Whirlaway, Count Fleet, Assault, and Citation bringing the total to eight Triple victors. Here was a series that was supposed to separate the great runners from the mere champions — a category to which horses are anointed every year. Perversely, however, the series was being won so often that it almost suggested a weak crop whenever a spring did not produce a Triple Crown winner.

Prolonged deprivation changed all that.

Indeed, by the time there was another Triple Crown winner, the many years without one had caused weak spines among the Turf cognoscenti to suggest the series somehow should be made less arduous. In the interim, the Thoroughbred Racing Associations had further solidified the relationship of the three races by producing a tri-cornered tro-

a little of its vitality to the rarity of a Triple Crown winner.

Yet, how discouraging did those years become.

It was not until a decade after Citation's 1948 waltz through the Triple Crown that another colt arrived at Belmont Park with a chance to become the ninth to wear the crown. This was Tim Tam, like Whirlaway and Citation a product of the vaunted Calumet Farm. Tim Tam broke sesamoids in the

In an era of Vietnam and Watergate, Secretariat was cathartic.

phy to present winners of the sweep and, in more recent years, the three tracks involved have further deepened the partnership to include joint nomination, cooperative marketing, etc.

The years without a Triple Crown winner made the hunger for one all the stronger. The condensed magic of public enthusiasm that became invested in the sport for a number of weeks each year owed not

stretch and was well beaten by Cavan, and then was immediately forced into retirement by his injuries.

Three years later, an unlikely candidate for stardom appeared in Carry Back, the son of a mare taken over by the breeder in lieu of a board bill who was sired by an obscure horse with the unpromising name of Saggy. Interestingly, it was none other than Saggy who had handed Citation his lone defeat at three. Carry Back had become beloved as "the people's horse." A lowly pedigree was far from their minds as his fans cheered his amazing rallies in the stretch, and his cluster of wins carried through the Derby and Preakness. Then, at 1-2 and with former President Dwight Eisenhower in attendance, Carry Back finished seventh behind the 65-1 Sherluck in the Belmont. A second dream scenario had been built only to be dashed.

In 1964 the jaunty little Canadian Northern Dancer captured the throne and the mace, but could not achieve the crown. Trainer Horatio Luro was suspect of the colt's ability to get the distance, and jockey Bill Hartack tried to hold him back early. The little colt had little left and finished third behind Quadrangle. Two years later Kauai King arrived at Belmont with a chance. Even though he was perhaps viewed as a pretender — since the sterling colts Graustark and Buckpasser had been injured — it was still yet another letdown when he finished fourth behind Amberoid.

In 1968 a situation developed that left many fans hoping the Triple Crown would not be consummated, lest an unsightly asterisk accompany a winner's name into eternity. Forward Pass had been named tentatively the Derby winner because Dancer's Image had been disqualified from victory after testing positive for Butazolidin, an anti-inflammatory drug that at the time was not allowed in Kentucky. Forward Pass then won the Preakness without question. Obviously, a great deal of courtroom time was ahead, so a victory by Forward Pass would have produced a situation of being a Triple Crown winner or not, according to future adjudication. Fortunately, Greentree Stable's Stage Door Johnny came through to win the hundreth Bel-

mont. Thus, when Forward Pass eventually was certified as the Derby winner, it did not create a meek addition to the roll of Triple Crown winners.

One of the most glamorous horses in racing history was the next to tease hopes for Triple Crown glory. This was the aptly named Majestic Prince, the record-priced yearling of his time and the first horse to win the Derby while undefeated since Morvich in 1922. Surely, this breathtakingly handsome chestnut would not let us down. Alas, talk was bandied about that trainer John Longden knew the Prince needed a rest and should skip the Belmont Stakes, but had been overruled by the owner, Frank McMahon. Again, Hartack was the rider and again he was on a princeling with too little left in the stretch, and Derby-Preakness runner-up Arts and Letters drew away. Majestic Prince would not race again.

It had now been more than two decades since Triple Crown nectar had been sipped. The next colt to send hearts soaring, though, was a colt whose background bespoke a stunning romance. Surely, finally…

This latest hopeful presented stark contrasts to the handsomeness and royalty of Majestic Prince. While the latter had commanded a record price as a yearling, Canonero II had sold for $1,200 as a Kentucky yearling. A crooked front leg held more attention than other, attractive, aspects of his breeding and conformation. Raced in Venezuela by an owner in reduced financial status and trained by an intense Venezuelan named Juan Arias, Canonero II burst back upon the American scene with a startling stretch run from far back to win the Derby. His odds would have been astronomical but for his being grouped in the mutuel field, and he paid "only" $19.40. He was ridden by a Venezuelan hero, Gustavo Avila, and when he added the Preakness in record time, Canonero II became the darling by association of the vast Hispanic population in New York City. His fans swelled the Belmont Stakes Day crowd to a record 82,694, and they waved their national banners and chanted "Canyonero, Canyonero," as he went to the post. The caprice of Dame Fortune grants no ethnic waivers, however, and before the race it had been learned that Canonero II's handlers had been trying to deal with an outbreak of thrush, a foul-smelling infection, in the frog of a hoof. The mercurial colt was dull, and he brought the celebrations to a halt with a thud. Canonero II, hailed in headline and song, finished fourth. Pass Catcher won.

Thus, when Secretariat was three, a full quarter-century had passed agonizingly. Seven times had the Derby and Preakness been won by the same horse, and seven times that horse's Triple Crown had been scuttled in the sweep of Belmont's turns and the length and dust of her stretch. In addition, there were no fewer than eight others who wound up winning two-thirds of the Triple Crown series in some other combination, again reminding us how close, and yet how elusive, was this idol we had placed before our best young racehorses. This other roll of winners of two of the three was also impressive: Capot, Middleground, Native Dancer, Nashua, Needles, Chateaugay, Damascus, and Riva Ridge. A lessened bit of traffic here, a change of track condition there, might have added another Triple Crown winner to the ranks of this singular club, as might a less arduous workout or a more sanguine response to an uproarious crowd.

The most recent of these heart-wrenching two-out-of-threes had occurred only a year before Secre-

tariat was called upon the stage. In 1972 his very stablemate, Riva Ridge, had warmed many a heart as he won the Kentucky Derby to soothe past losses for the family of Christopher T. Chenery. An entrepreneur and sportsman of high ilk, Chenery had won many important races, but the Derby had eluded him. In 1950 Chenery's Hill Prince had been the post-time Derby favorite, but had finished second to Middleground. In 1962 Chenery's Sir Gaylord was expected to be favorite, or nearly so, but he turned up lame and was unable to participate. To make the situation even more nettlesome, the scratching of Sir Gaylord came barely too late for the stable to change the plans for its wonderful filly, Cicada, and run her in the Derby instead of the Kentucky Oaks the day before.

Now, in 1972, Chenery was in the final year of his life, in a nursing home, and one of his daughters, Helen (Penny) Chenery, was heading the stable's management. Riva Ridge, champion two-year-old of 1971, toured around the Churchill Downs oval in splendid isolation. Hill Prince and Sir Gaylord had been avenged.

Then, a muddy track proved Riva Ridge's undoing in the Preakness, so old hurts were revisited, although he then salved a portion of them by winning the Belmont Stakes. If ever a stable shared intimately the racing public's understanding of the uncertainties of the Triple Crown, it was the Meadow Stable of the Chenery clan.

The years 1972 and 1973 were an emotional vortex for the family. There was the irony of the father's dreams coming true, but his being unable to participate fully in the long-sought glory. On the racetrack — a different level of emotion, to be sure, but not one to be minimized — Riva Ridge continued the up-and-down pattern and by the end of 1972 was not even voted champion three-year-old, Derby and Belmont wins notwithstanding. By then, however, a more extravagant hero had come to the fore in the burly chestnut shape of the two-year-old Secretariat. So compelling were his rallies on the turn to convert competitions into show time, so wonderfully handsome was he, and so forceful were his victories that Secretariat became the first two-year-

and Seth had a large responsibility of helping run the farm thrust upon him. The Hancocks and Chenerys had had a long association, and Hill Prince had been a stallion at Claiborne many years before.

In the end the various leading cast members of this post-modern Greek drama all proved their worth: Penny Chenery emerged as the queen of the Turf, young Seth quickly showed his mettle by arranging a syndication of Secretariat for a record at

Announcer Chic Anderson marveled that Secretariat was "moving like a tremendous machine."

old to be voted Horse of the Year on any poll since Moccasin in 1965.

The sad continued to mingle with the uplifting. Mr. Chenery died, and estate matters meant it was logical to syndicate Secretariat. Young Seth Hancock of Claiborne Farm and his family had been dealing with their own sorrows. His father, A.B. (Bull) Hancock Jr., had died in September of 1972,

the time of more than six-million dollars, and his brother, Arthur III, extricated himself from the complications of inheritance by establishing his own successful farm. Meanwhile, trainer Lucien Laurin and jockey Ron Turcotte proved equal to dealing with the pressures of having a Riva Ridge one year and a Secretariat the next. The horses did their part, too, both winning division championships in 1973,

Secretariat as three-year-old and again Horse of the Year and Riva Ridge as champion older horse.

Riva Ridge was a champion Thoroughbred, and Secretariat was something above even that exalted designation. He was a Virginia-bred son of the great stallion Bold Ruler and the Chenerys' distinguished Princequillo mare Somethingroyal, also dam of Sir Gaylord, as well as other major stakes winners First Family and Syrian Sea. So popular had Bold Ruler become that the Phipps family, who owned him, had asked Bull Hancock, as stallion manager, to develop a plan whereby services to the horse were offered on a two-foal basis, the owner of a mare to get one foal and the Phippses to get the other. A coin toss would decide who got the first foal. No stud fee would be involved. The Phipps family thus could reach out for fresh blood from among the best of other broodmare bands, and the owners of such mares could have access to the (eventual) eight-time leading sire. Somethingroyal had produced the stakes-winning Bold Ruler filly Syrian Sea before that special arrangement was offered, so she was a natural to go back to the stallion. Ogden Phipps got the first foal, a filly named The Bride. As matters turned out, The Bridesmaid might have been a better name, for the second foal, retained by the Chenerys, was Secretariat.

By the time of the Belmont Stakes of 1973, Secretariat had transcended sports. In those days the Vietnam War and Watergate scandal had long meant that national and world news headlines were virtually always laced with shame, violence, and sorrow. Secretariat's appearance on the covers of *Time* and *Newsweek*, as well as *Sports Illustrated* and other sports press, was a break, a balm eagerly accepted. Here were power, beauty, style — in a word, perfection.

After a blip when he ran third in the Wood Memorial, Secretariat powered from behind to win the Kentucky Derby in 1:59⅖, breaking Northern Dancer's record of 2:00 for the most famous of American horse races. In the Preakness, jockey Turcotte was taken on a rapid blast-off from last to first, while looping the turn into the backstretch, and then Secretariat continued to race away to win again. Only a mix-up in the official time denied him official recognition for having set a record in that race, too — and, as we later would see, in all the Triple Crown events. (Secretariat's official Preakness time was 1:54⅖, although *Daily Racing Form* caught him in a stakes-record 1:53⅖.)

Such were the magnitude and magnetism of Secretariat by Preakness Day that young men and women in the infield broke through the restraining barrier and perched along the rail — not to disrupt as young crowds so often had in that era, but to feel, close up, the pulse of heroism.

Television ratings soared.

Now, only the final act remained: the Belmont Stakes. Surely, where we had been so often denied, a Triple Crown at last awaited. Didn't it?

We were privileged to be there, and remember very well how the impression of invincibility in this one massive horse sparred with the senses of reality borne of the past; how the crowd noise swelled as the 1-20 choice left the paddock and minutes later addressed the starting gate in front of the stand; how we were stunned to see the stretch runner take the lead from the start.

A very good colt named Sham, a dark and racy lancer, had finished second in both the Derby and Preakness, and now he was back to try once more. On the broad and lengthy strip of land that is Bel-

Secretariat — in a word, perfection.

mont's curve toward and onto the backstretch, Sham, too, tried new tactics. He had not withstood the withering stretch runs of "Big Red"— a nickname for Secretariat popularly reprised from Man o' War's Day. So, we remember, Sham tried forceful early tactics, too. He dared put his head in front — then the length of his neck.

We remember how the shocking alacrity of the early markers spawned fears of doom for both — a half-mile in :46⅕, with a mile yet to run! The challenge, though, was brief, and Secretariat began to edge away. Yet, the pace was still frightful — six furlongs in 1:09⅘. Many a great sprint has been won at Belmont in slower time. What was Turcotte thinking?

And then, we remember, came the beginnings of confidence, or at least hope, as Secretariat's margin began to swell, while none of the others seemed ready to come out of the pack. After a mile in 1:34⅕, he was in front by seven, but the last four Metropolitan Handicaps had been won in slower time — and that was a one-mile race around only one turn. There was still a grinding half-mile remaining, the final phases of the final test of champions, still time for the big horse in the blue and white blinkers to become rubber legged and relent to the grip of reality.

We remember how, as always, Turcotte seemed to be virtually pulled forward out of the saddle, so massive was the beast and so lengthy his stride. Most horses of greatness and stamina present a picture of doing their masterful work with little effort, but Secretariat seemed always striving, as if he were determined that the next stride would be swifter than the last.

Then, we recall, it began to seem that Turcotte had not confused the longest classic with the six-furlong Toboggan Handicap, after all. Secretariat's lead was lengthening with enthralling speed. Announcer Chic Anderson watched in amazement and improvised a memorable phrase. Secretariat, he marveled, was "moving like a tremendous machine."

They turned for home, or rather he turned for home. The mile and a quarter were completed in 1:59 — faster than his Kentucky Derby record for heaven's sake! There were still two furlongs facing him, and those specific furlongs had a certified history for heartbreak. On and on he came, over and over the pistons of his haunches and the rapiers of his forelegs repeated their thrilling cadences; quickly the brown earth flowed beneath his feet. Farther back a small field of horses toiled in his wake. There were nobly bred Thoroughbreds in that field, but their names became Feckless and Futile.

We remember how Secretariat gave us the luxury of knowing well in advance that we were seeing what we longed to see. A Triple Crown was finally in the offing, and with a greatness to be recognized, not merely in retrospect, but in the very moment of its coming. Secretariat swept under the wire so very, very far in front. Turcotte, with his own sense of history, glanced to his left at the teletimer, a message board whose news was 2:24, a new American record for one and a half miles and more than two seconds under the old record.

We remember the senses — amazement and thanksgiving — and knew already that they could ever be summoned anew in recollection of that pungent sequence.

The official margin was thirty-one lengths over Twice a Prince. Sham retreated to last. We remember that a few weeks later, it was announced that Sham had been injured in a workout, but we have always suspected that the mischief began on the backstretch on Belmont Day.

Penny Chenery — she was married to John Tweedy at the time and was famed as Penny Tweedy — was at her best as a sporting owner. She was not speechless, although she would have been excused had she been, but neither did she feign any less awe than the rest of us. She waved happily to the crowd who gazed up to cheer her at the rail of the clubhouse, and then she floated down the stairs to join this dauntless nobleman of Nature.

Turcotte and Laurin at times had a prickly relationship, and even in this ultimate moment there was a point of disagreement. Laurin kept pushing Turcotte that surely he had urged on the colt at some point. "No," said the jockey. "I never pushed him. Listen, tell you one thing: This is the best horse I ever saw." No dissenters stepped forward.

⋗―⇢―⊙―⇠―⋖

Not even Secretariat could be immune to life's eddy, however, nor could those around him. Ahead lay a couple of stunning defeats, amidst additional, magnificent victories, including a world record when he defeated intramural champion Riva Ridge in the first Marlboro Cup. His racing days ended in glorious solitude as he brightened the stretch at Woodbine on a dark and rainy autumn day to win the Canadian International by six and a half lengths. Secretariat had won sixteen of twenty-one races and earned $1,316,808.

For Mrs. Tweedy, the ensuing years would bring divorce and dissolution of the family stable, but also a lasting talent for life and for enjoying and sharing the experience of Secretariat. Trainer Laurin retired later and lived until the age of eighty-eight, passing away on June 25, 2000.

Turcotte had engendered sympathy when a suspension caused him to miss that one last ride on Secretariat at Woodbine. (Eddie Maple had the mount that day.) An outpouring of sympathy over that circumstance would come to seem almost a sinful frivolity when, some years later, Turcotte went down in a racing spill; he has been consigned ever since to a wheelchair.

Secretariat entered stud in 1974 at Claiborne. He overcame a brief concern about his fertility and went on to a worthy stallion career, although begetting such champions as Lady's Secret and Risen Star might not have satisfied all that was hoped for him. He died at nineteen, of laminitis, and the Grayson-Jockey Club Research Foundation still receives contributions in his honor for research into that dreaded malady. Secretariat is seen today as an enduring influence as a broodmare sire.

No, Secretariat was not supernatural. He just seemed to be, never more so than on a long-ago June Day at Belmont Park. We remember — how we remember! — and the sun has never set upon that day.

Belmont Stakes
Purse: $125,000 Added

8th Race Belmont Park - June 9, 1973

Purse $125,000 added. Three-year-olds. 1 1-4 Miles. Main Track. Track: Fast.

Value of race, $150,200. Value to winner $90,120; second, $33,044; third, $18,024; fourth, $9,012. Mutuel pool $519,689. Off-track betting $688,460.

P#	Horse	A	Wgt	Med	Eqp	Odds	PP	1/4	1/2	1m	1¼	Str	Fin	Jockey
1	Secretariat	3	126		b	.10	1	1^h	1^h	1^7	1^{20}	1^{28}	1^{31}	R Turcotte
4	Twice a Prince	3	126			17.30	4	4^5	4^{10}	3^h	2^h	3^{12}	$2^{½}$	B Baeza
3	My Gallant	3	126		b	12.40	3	3^3	3^h	4^7	3^2	2^h	2^{13}	A Cordero Jr
2	Pvt. Smiles	3	126		b	14.30	2	5	5	5	5	5	$4^{¾}$	D Gargan
5	Sham	3	126		b	5.10	5	2^5	2^{10}	2^7	4^8	$4^{1½}$	5	L Pincay Jr

Off Time: 4:50 Eastern Daylight Time **Time Of Race:** :23⅗ :46⅕ 1:09⅘ 1:34⅕ 1:59 2:24 (new track record)
Start: Good For All **Track:** Fast
Equipment: b for blinkers

Mutuel Payoffs

1	**Secretariat**	**$2.20**	**$2.40**
4	**Twice a Prince**		**4.60**
	No Show Mutuels Sold.		

Winner: Secretariat, ch. c. by Bold Ruler—Somethingroyal, by Princequillo (Trained by L. Laurin).
Bred by Meadow Stud in Va.

Start good. Won ridden out.
SECRETARIAT sent up along the inside to vie for the early lead with SHAM to the backstretch, disposed of that one after going three-quarters, drew off at will rounding the far turn and was under a hand ride from Turcotte to establish a record in a tremendous performance. TWICE A PRINCE, unable to stay with the leaders early, moved through along the rail approaching the stretch and outfinished MY GALLANT for the place. The latter, void of early foot, moved with TWICE A PRINCE rounding the far turn and fought it out gamely with that one through the drive. PVT. SMILES showed nothing. SHAM alternated for the lead with SECRETARIAT to the backstretch, wasn't able to match stride with that rival after going three-quarters and stopped badly.
Scratched—Knightly Dawn.

Owners: (1) Meadow Stable; (4) Elmendorf; (3) A I Appleton; (2) C V Whitney; (5) S Sommer

©DAILY RACING FORM/EQUIBASE

*Affirmed (inside) and Alydar: a
rivalry for the ages.*

- CHAPTER 21 -

Affirmed and Alydar

What we regard as the greatest race ever run in North America took place in 1978. It was the Belmont Stakes, in which Affirmed turned back the prolonged and prodigious challenges of Alydar. Neither relented, neither weakened, neither accepted defeat. Yet one, and only one, would win, so the other had to lose. A miniscule difference decreed Affirmed the victor. Was that difference in the stride, heartbeat, lung capacity, or racing advantage? Was it an erg of coordination, or of jockey strife, or luck? Hard to tell, but some invisible force thrust the nose of Affirmed to the fore, for the seventh time in ten eventual meetings against the slavering hunger of the implacable charger at his side.

We bow to the victor in gratitude for his definition of valor. We owe the vanquished nothing less.

A declaration of one race as the greatest invites challenge. Well, actually, it invites outrage. We shrink not.

If the Triple Crown is accepted still as the ultimate for the American Thoroughbred, then surely a pro-

longed stretch duel in one of the three classics presents more drama and consequence than virtually any other circumstance. That it be the denouement of a continuing rivalry of two horses linked since their earliest stardom elevates the race higher. That the Triple Crown itself is the one on the line through the struggle of the stretch is surely sublimity. Oh yes, the 1978 Belmont Stakes, in so many ways, stands up as the greatest of them all.

Compelling stories abound in the Affirmed-Alydar affair. Perhaps the most sentimentally rousing was that Alydar represented a resurgence of the beloved Calumet Farm. From the time Whirlaway won the Triple Crown in 1941 until well after the death of Calumet's owner, Warren Wright Sr., the devil's red and blue silks were seen as the non-pareil on American racetracks. Similarly, the voluptuous roll of green pastures, the sparkling barns, and gleaming white fences of the farm itself were the epitome of the Bluegrass country of Kentucky.

By the early 1960s, however, the magic had slipped away. The farm was still a jewel, and Mrs. Wright and her new husband, Admiral Gene Markey, were paragons of the sport. The stream of champions, however, was dry. Whereas, once, a Calumet foal crop of Twilight Tear and Armed might be followed in due course by a crop of Citation, Coaltown, and Bewitch — and then of Gen. Duke and Iron Liege or Tim Tam — the major victories faded. Forward Pass emerged as a classic winner in 1968, but he represented only a brief glimpse of days gone by.

By the middle 1970s Mrs. Markey had hired as her trainer young John Veitch, whose father, Hall of Fame trainer Sylvester Veitch, had authored his own glories with the stables of C.V. Whitney and then George D. Widener. In 1977 Veitch brought Calumet its first championship for many seasons, guiding Our Mims to an Eclipse Award as top three-year-old filly. Our Mims' younger half brother, Alydar, was an even more exciting prospect. To those who had revered Calumet as the New York Yankees of the Turf, the days of Derby roses wafted back, merging history with renewed possibility.

Intertwined with the heritage of Alydar was that of his rival-to-be, Affirmed. Alydar's sire, Raise a Native, was Affirmed's grandsire and had raced for Affirmed's owner and breeder, Louis Wolfson.

While Calumet was the apogee of the long-established supremacy of Kentucky's Thoroughbred tradition, Wolfson was among the most dynamic leaders in the upstart prowess of Florida's burgeoning breeding industry. He had established Harbor View Farm, near Ocala, a town south of Jacksonville, where Wolfson grew up. As a young man, Wolfson had set his sights on a professional sports career and was going along nicely as a University of Georgia football player, until he tackled the great Albie Booth of Yale one day and came up with a shoulder injury.

Directed otherwise by necessity thereafter, he instead scored his goals in industry, and by the time he was in his middle forties was so much a giant of American business that he had begun to cast about for diversions. Thoroughbred racing was his choice, and among the astute purchases he made early on were the brilliant two-year-old Raise a Native and the future Horse of the Year Roman Brother.

Raise a Native was a gleaming chestnut son of the great gray Native Dancer. Such were the market figures at the time that Raise a Native was a record-priced auction weanling when sold for $22,000. The following year, Wolfson bought him as a yearling for $39,000. In his four starts before injury at two in 1963, Raise a Native was so dominant that the renowned horseman Hirsch Jacobs declared him the most brilliant two-year-old he had ever seen.

While Jacobs' comment to that effect in the summer of 1963 might seem extraneous to the story of Wolfson and Raise a Native, it did not remain so. In the first place, Jacobs only three years before had trained a two-year-old of seemingly equal talent — at least in the eyes of his young daughter, Patrice, in whose colors the colt ran! This was Hail to Reason. Moreover, the self-same Patrice Jacobs would later marry Wolfson. Whether Mr. and Mrs. Wolfson ever engaged in Hail to Reason vs. Raise a Native debates, we know not, but either could have made some compelling points.

Raise a Native did not stand at Wolfson's Florida farm but was retired instead to Kentucky. He was ensconced at the Spendthrift Farm of Leslie Combs II, who, typically, had struck up a relationship with Wolfson when the racing newcomer appeared on the scene as an investor with resolve and resource. The horse's first crop included Exclusive Native, a Harbor View homebred who won the Sanford Stakes and Arlington Classic before joining his sire

est prolonged rivalry in American racing was thus germinated.

Alydar was a burnished dark chestnut, bold of eye, and powerful of build. Affirmed was a light chestnut, leaning more toward refined elegance than showy muscle. While one might strut, the other would stroll. It was always a mistake, however, to

Jockey Steve Cauthen affirming his colt's victory after the pair cross the wire first in the Belmont.

in the Spendthrift stallion barn.

In 1974, the year Mrs. Markey of Calumet sent the mare Sweet Tooth to Raise a Native, the Wolfson mares booked to the stallion's son, Exclusive Native, included Won't Tell You. The following spring the two mares foaled Kentucky-bred Alydar and Florida-bred Affirmed, respectively. The great-

suspect that Affirmed lacked either speed or inner ferocity when it came to competition.

Affirmed and Alydar first met at two on June 15, 1977, in the Youthful Stakes at Belmont Park. Trainer Laz Barrera had sent Affirmed out once before, and he won at first asking, but John Veitch was starting Alydar in a stakes race for his debut. Despite that unusual tactic, Alydar's works, looks, and aura were such that he was favored. It was the only one of their meetings in which they were not first and second. Affirmed won, and Alydar was fifth.

Through much of his rivalry with Affirmed, Alydar had a way of maintaining his fans, always running so well as to suggest that in some basic way he

Stretched to a mile for the Champagne Stakes, they caught a muddy track. Alydar came along on the outside and ran on by the rival he had not been able to get past in the Hopeful or Futurity. He won by one and a quarter lengths. Affirmed's victory might have indicated his superiority at a longer distance, yet at one and one-sixteenth miles in the Lau-

Alydar accompanied to the track by trainer John Veitch.

was the better. This was underscored by their second meeting, in which he defeated Affirmed by three and a half lengths in the Great American Stakes. They then went separate ways, both winning impressively, and hooked up again in the Hopeful Stakes. This race set the tone for what was to come. In a splendid effort by both, Affirmed prevailed by a half-length. The finish was much closer in their next encounter. In a splendid race by both, Affirmed prevailed by a nose in the Futurity.

rel Futurity, form reverted to what would be the recurring theme. Again, the chorus was repeatable. In a splendid race by both, Affirmed prevailed by a neck. Affirmed had won four of their six races. Alydar's loyalists were not dissuaded from their optimism as they looked ahead to the next spring's classics, but they had no credible argument against Affirmed's being voted the Eclipse Award for champion two-year-old.

Barrera and Veitch split the two, giving the racing

public plenty of time to conjecture and savor the thought of their resuming this youthful struggle. Affirmed and Alydar would not meet until the Kentucky Derby. Perfect.

In Florida and Kentucky, Alydar won the Flamingo, Florida Derby, and Blue Grass Stakes, the last by thirteen lengths. Moreover, he was a central figure in a sentimental Calumet moment when the aging Admiral and Mrs. Markey were taken by limousine to the rail at Keeneland, the better to see the colt, and jockey Jorge Velasquez brought him over to the outside rail. "Here's your baby, my lady," the jockey said to the grande dame, "Isn't he pretty?" The moment savored of springtime mint, with a touch of Derby rose. It was virtually impossible for Kentuckians to watch that wonderfully handsome, glistening colt, as he powered through the stretch a few minutes later, and not presume that this Whirlaway-look-alike was their Derby winner.

Meanwhile, on the West Coast, Affirmed was professionally competent in winning the San Felipe Stakes and Hollywood Derby by two lengths each, and more eye-catching in winning the Santa Anita Derby by eight.

Aura trumped cold form on Derby Day. Alydar was made the favorite to beat for a third time the colt that had already beaten him four times. The gentlemanly Wolfson masked any prickliness he might have felt over this interpretation of the two colts' histories:

"I realize that the name of Calumet Farm has a singular place in history, and with all Mrs. Markey has contributed to the sport, I can understand why Alydar was favored."

We have no hesitation in acclaiming the Affirmed-Alydar rivalry the best in American racing of the twentieth century. Nashua and Swaps were compelling, but they met only twice. Noor and Citation were draining, but it all happened so quickly and after Citation's best days were behind him. Man o' War-Sir Barton sounded good but turned out not to be competitive. Seabiscuit-War Admiral had drama by the quart, but they met only once. Damascus-Dr. Fager were breathtaking as were Sunday Silence-Easy Goer, but each of these pairings met only four times. Affirmed and Alydar met ten times. Bold Ruler, Gallant Man, Round Table, and Gen. Duke comprised an amazing foursome, but they never all got together in one race. Native Dancer and Tom Fool would have been wonderful, but they never actually raced each other. Silver Charm-Captain Bodgit-Free House had a wonderful spring, but not enough replays. Affirmed vs. Alydar was surely the greatest.

In that context it is ironic that of all their meetings in the most important echelon of races, it was the Kentucky Derby — the centerpiece of the sport — that was the least competitive. That and the messy disqualification in the Travers later that year would be the only two events that one might wish had been tweaked a bit as this unprecedented sequence played out.

Alydar dropped so far back in the Derby that his being able to win seemed a forlorn hope early in the race. Meanwhile, the teenage wonder, jockey Steve Cauthen, had the ultimate pro, Affirmed, in striking position. When it was time to strike, he struck, drawing away from a very good little colt named Believe It. Alydar made a powerful, but belated, run to be second, although he never seemed a threat to Affirmed, who was by then flicking his ears happily. Affirmed won by one and a half lengths.

ANNE M. EBERHARDT

Affirmed getting a visit from an old friend, Steve Cauthen.

leaders a year later. Yet, when the Triple Crown led back to its annual climax at Belmont Park, it was the rivals from the previous spring and summer's Youthful and Great America still at the head of their age group. Class, stamina, and that will-o'-the-wisp named soundness were prodigiously endowed to these two colts.

That the ninth meeting of two such horses would come in the Belmont Stakes and with the

The Preakness produced the replay of their juvenile duels that had been anticipated in the Derby. Affirmed that time was odds-on at 1-2, Alydar 9-5. Reality had sunk in, albeit belatedly. Alydar came along in the upper stretch with all his brashness and speed, and Velasquez found himself thinking he was going to pass Affirmed, as he had in the Champagne. "I'm going to get him, I'm going to get him!" he later repeated of the memory, but he did not. More apposite to the Preakness stretch run was the remark of third-placed Believe It's trainer, Woody Stephens: "When you come up to that one (Affirmed), you've hit a brick wall." Affirmed's margin was a neck, and the impression was that he could have held that neck for as long as Cauthen wished.

We are conditioned by experience when young prospects square off in spring juvenile stakes to doubt that we will still be talking of them as division

Triple Crown on the line was too much to ask, but there they were, bright and ready for another go. That the conclusion of the Triple Crown would summon forth their best race of all was a pipedream, but realism was apparently on an extended holiday.

Barrera knew that it was time for routine deworming of Affirmed, but postponed it in the fear that it might mean the difference between being 99.75 percent perfect and 100 percent. No margin was too small to concede. As the rivalry had unfolded, Barrera expressed as much admiration for Alydar as even the colt's most ardent fans. Maybe Affirmed was "a brick wall," but Alydar was convinced brick walls could be felled. He, and Veitch, still saw him as the wrecking ball. Now the two horses were doing something they had done eight times before — facing each other — and something they had never done before — racing one and a half miles.

In the custom popular in his father's generation, Veitch worked Alydar the entire distance of the Belmont. He knew that coming from behind had not worked, so it was widely conjectured that Alydar would gun from the gate and force Affirmed into a duel early. He had not been passing him in the stretch; maybe he could outstay him.

The Belmont was so magnificent that it is easy to recall it as having been just that — a battle from the start. In fact, the 6-5 Alydar did the 3-5 Affirmed the favor of letting him amble through six furlongs in 1:14. Then the real race began, and it was engulfing. Sixty-five thousand in the stands were swept up, as Affirmed and Alydar swept along. The two colts were in lock step part of the way, Affirmed on the inside, Alydar clinging to him and matching his every stride. As they turned for home, far up the stretch in a hazy afternoon of combat and history, Alydar made the supreme effort. He finally pushed his nose in front. Would his rival give in? No. This was Affirmed.

On they battled, and the end became near. To the horses, the furlongs must now have multiplied into a gauntlet of strife and withering effort. Still, they fought on, the blood of celebrated ancestry coursing through their potent bodies. Muscle and sinew and lungs said stop, but their eyes saw each other, and so their hearts said carry on.

Cauthen for the first time in all their battles switched his whip and hit Affirmed on the left. Whether that made the difference is doubtful, for Affirmed hardly needed to have it pointed out that an urgent sort of matter was at hand here. The finish was just ahead, and so was Affirmed. They swished under the wire. In one of those things jockeys do that amaze people who have never been jockeys, the youthful Cauthen stood immediately in the irons and raised his whip in triumph. The photo finish camera called it only a head, and yet he had known as they hit the wire!

ANNE M. EBERHARDT

As a stallion, Alydar far surpassed his old rival.

After the comfortable first six furlongs, the clock had reflected the fury that ensued. They pushed and tugged and prodded each other through a second six furlongs in 1:12⅗. The quarter-mile between the six-furlong pole and the half-mile pole was blazed in :23⅗, the next two furlongs in :24⅕. They then

Affirmed and Patrice Wolfson.

threw in a furlong in :11⅕, before slowing to :14 for the dizzy conclusion. Despite the slow start, the final time of 2:26⅘ was then the third-fastest time for the Belmont Stakes.

So, Affirmed had become the eleventh winner of the Triple Crown. As of 2001, he remained the most recent.

＞─◆─○─◆─＜

There have been many aspects to the epilogue of Affirmed vs. Alydar, some of them disheartening. They met only once again. Affirmed, with Laffit Pincay substituting for Cauthen, cut off Alydar on the far turn and, though Affirmed went on to win by daylight, his number came down, the Calumet colt inheriting the win. Thus, they stood at seven official wins for Affirmed and three official wins for Alydar.

The Calumet horse had been so tough that he continued after the Triple Crown and scored by huge margins in the Arlington Classic and Whitney. Affirmed, who had rested after the Belmont, twice lost to Seattle Slew (including one race in which Exceller beat them both) in the early autumn, in history's only meetings of Triple Crown winners. The magic of the current-year Triple Crown made him Horse of the Year, however. With Pincay having become his regular rider, Affirmed soared to new heights at four and repeated as Horse of the Year. A leg injury shortened Alydar's four-year-old campaign.

Alydar proved the greater sire, although Affirmed also had a distinguished record. For a time they both were at stud at Calumet.

After Mrs. Markey's death Calumet's management passed to a rather distant in-law, and such a wacky few years of management ensued that he was eventually imprisoned. There linger dark hints that Alydar's death in 1990 might have been at the hands of some criminal element in order to generate insurance money.

Calumet Farm was sold at auction in 1992, when Henryk de Kwiatkowski came in to rescue it and retain its charm. In another pleasant aspect, Veitch returned to the farm's employ as trainer in the fall of 2000. (His rival of long ago, Barrera, died in 1991.)

Affirmed stood the last decade of his life at the Bell family's Jonabell Farm, a few miles from Calumet. It was not until he was twenty-six years old, in the winter of 2001, that Mr. and Mrs. Wolfson received the news that his condition was such that he should be euthanized. Affirmed was buried at Jonabell, where, as if by magic, floral garlands appeared at his gravesite, placed by fans wanting no recognition but moved by their personal memories.

Someone tied a grouping of three flowers — a single rose, a black-eyed Susan, and a carnation — on a stone pillar at the Jonabell entrance, a silent reminder of a distant Triple Crown and of the greatest rivalry of them all.

Belmont Stakes
Purse: $150,000 Added

8th Race Belmont Park - June 10, 1978
Purse $150,000 added. Three-year-olds. 1 1-2 Miles. Main Track. Track: Fast.
Value of race, $184,300. Value to winner $110,580; second, $40,546; third, $22,116; fourth, $11,058.
Mutuel pool $1,186,662. OTB pool $1,389,646.

P#	Horse	A	Wgt	Med	Eqp	Odds	PP	1/4	1/2	1m	1¼	Str	Fin	Jockey
3	Affirmed	3	126			.60	3	1^{1}	1^{1}	$1^{1/2}$	1^{hd}	1^{hd}	1^{hd}	S Cauthen
2	Alydar	3	126			1.10	2	$3^{1 1/2}$	2^{1}	2^{5}	2^{8}	2^{12}	2^{13}	J Velasquez
1	Darby Creek Road	3	126			9.90	1	5	5	5	$3^{1 1/2}$	3^{4}	$3^{7 3/4}$	A Cordero Jr
4	Judge Advocate	3	126			30.10	4	$2^{1 1/2}$	$3^{2 1/2}$	4^{3}	5	4^{hd}	$4^{1 1/4}$	J Fell
5	Noon Time Spender	3	126		b	38.40	5	4^{1}	4^{3}	$3^{1/2}$	4^{hd}	5	5	R Hernandez

Off Time: 5:43 Eastern Daylight Time **Time Of Race:** :25 :50 1:14 1:37⅖ 2:01⅗ 2:26⅘
Start: Good For All **Track:** Fast
Equipment: b for blinkers

Mutuel Payoffs

3	Affirmed	$3.20	$2.10	.....
2	Alydar		2.20	.....
1	Darby Creek Road			.....
	No Show Mutuels Sold.			

Winner: Affirmed, ch. c. by Exclusive Native—Won't Tell You, by Crafty Admiral (Trained by Lazaro S. Barrera). Bred by Harbor View Farm in Fl.

Start good. Won driving.
AFFIRMED went right to the front and was rated along on the lead while remaining well out from the rail. He responded readily when challenged by ALYDAR soon after entering the backstretch, held a narrow advantage into the stretch while continuing to save ground and was under left-handed urging to prevail in a determined effort. ALYDAR, away in good order, saved ground to the first turn. He came out to go after AFFIRMED with seven furlongs remaining, raced with that rival to the stretch, reached almost even terms with AFFIRMED near the three-sixteenths pole but wasn't good enough in a stiff drive. DARBY CREEK ROAD, unhurried while being outrun early, moved around horses while rallying on the far turn but lacked a further response. JUDGE ADVOCATE broke through before the start and was finished at the far turn. NOON TIME SPENDER raced within striking distance for a mile and gave way.

Owners: (3) Harbor View Farm; (2) Calumet Farm; (1) J W Phillips; (4) O Phipps; (5) Miami Lakes Ranch
Trainers: (3) L S Barrera; (2) John M Veitch; (1) Thomas L Rondinello; (4) John W. Russell; (5) Antonio Arcodia

©DAILY RACING FORM/EQUIBASE

*John Henry (left) and The Bart
locked in "endless battle" in the first
Arlington Million.*

- CHAPTER 22 -

Steel-Drivin' Man

The era of the million-dollar Thoroughbred race began with the Arlington Million on August 30, 1981. Who could have guessed that this extravagant event would be won by a $1,100 yearling named John Henry?

In legend and song, John Henry was "a steel-drivin' man," with a wife named Polly Ann, who had a bit of steel herself and could stand in for him when he got sick. Prior to the 1981 Arlington Million, the most famous duel involving anyone or anything named John Henry was a contest in the West Virginia hills. The original John Henry was out to prove that human muscle, bone, resolve — and a sledge hammer — were better than a new-fangled steam drill at the specific railroader's task of driving blasting bores into rock. He made his point, but, as at least one version of the song has it, John "laid down his hammer and he died" shortly after winning the race. For all the bravado inherent in his name, the equine John Henry was a nondescript little fellow early in his career. The only

machismo attributed to him by his handlers was that he loved to trash his stall — something to put up with in the case of a well-bred sale yearling, or rock star, but just a nuisance in the case of a cheap son of Ole Bob Bowers.

According to *The Blood-Horse*'s late editor Kent Hollingsworth, in a 1983 article on the updated subject, the song, legend, and cheap yearling came together because "Woodsong Farm owner John E. Callaway likes to name his yearlings after songs. At the 1976 Keeneland January sale, Callaway bought a newly turned yearling, by Ole Bob Bowers— Once Double, by Double Jay, from the consignment of his breeder, Mrs. Robert Lehmann's Golden Chance Farm near Paris, Kentucky. Callaway paid $1,100 for this colt, bought him for a song more or less, and named him for the folk song 'John Henry.'"

There are many conflicting images at work here. For one, it is usually assumed that a yearling with a $1,100 price tag must spring from decidedly unfashionable circumstances. However, Golden Chance Farm was a pretty fashionable operation. Mrs. Lehmann's late husband, Robert, had purchased Dust Commander, with whom he had won the 1970 Kentucky Derby. After Lehmann's death in 1974, Mrs. Lehmann had built upon that foundation in continuing the farm. She won the Preakness with Master Derby in 1975 — the year she bred John Henry.

Insofar as pedigree is concerned, it is true that Ole Bob Bowers sired only nine stakes winners and twenty stakes-placed horses, but Callaway was on the lookout for something by that very stallion. "I had been racing over at Ellis Park, and kept getting beat by an Ole Bob Bowers colt," he told Hollingsworth, "and I decided I better get one by Ole Bob Bowers."

Although the name of the stallion might have an oblique flophouse sound to it (reminiscent of The Bowery), Ole Bob Bowers was sired by Prince Blessed, a stakes-winning son of the leading sire Princequillo. As a half brother to the sprint champion Decathlon, Prince Blessed had brought $77,000, top price of 1958 for an American yearling, when consigned by Hurstland Farm to the Keeneland July sale. Prince Blessed won two major California stakes, the Hollywood Gold Cup and the American Handicap. His son Ole Bob Bowers was out of a mare by the great Bull Lea and was himself the winner of the nine-furlong Tanforan Handicap in world record-equaling time. Ole Bob Bowers was also a half brother to two other stakes winners.

Then, too, the dam of John Henry, Once Double, while only a modest winner herself, was by the vaunted Claiborne Farm stallion Double Jay. Her dam was by Intent, and her second dam by the noted sire Mahmoud. All in all, it was one of those pedigrees that bargain hunters pray for — a touch of class, but so out of touch with fashion that drowsiness might befall other prospective bidders roaming the sale grounds. The colt, moreover, was offered not at one of the prescribed yearling sales, but as a shaggy weanling-cum-yearling at the Keeneland January sale. The yearlings by Ole Bob Bowers at the time had averaged $1,133 — or $33 more than John Henry cost — and two months before, the stallion himself had brought a top bid of only $900. After all, Princequillo, Double Jay, and Mahmoud could be found in a lot of pedigrees.

Callaway's experience was the reverse of the "middle class morality" foisted upon Alfred P. Doolittle of *My Fair Lady*. Doolittle was paid enough for his Eliza that he could not in good conscience blow the lot on a spree, whereas he would have preferred a less thought-provoking sum. Thus, his life underwent a stabilizing and socially elevating change not of his wishing. Callaway, on the other hand, had paid so little for John Henry that he had insufficient compunction about ridding himself of the colt.

He expressed rather poignantly the irony of having paid such a pittance for a horse: "If I had bid more, say $5,000, why I would have figured I had too much money in him to dump him, and probably would have kept him. My veterinarian didn't like him. He was small and back at the knee. He never seemed to be able to pick up his feet, kept stumbling all the time. He would stumble over a matchstick. And he was trouble in the stall, kept tearing up everything," although he was pleasant enough to deal with when out of the barn.

If one takes John Henry's bottom price, $1,100,

and juxtaposes it against his eventual earnings, $6,597,947 (thirty-nine wins in eighty-three starts), he comes off as statistically the greatest bargain race-horse of all time. However, the original buyer at $1,100 did not keep him and reap those riches. Nor

sale, having named him but not bothered to break the colt. Young Harold Snowden Jr. had a client who had had some luck with Ole Bob Bowers, so Snowden bought John Henry for $2,200. (To suggest that Callaway had scored handsomely by dou-

The Bart, with Eddie Delahoussaye aboard.

did the second buyer, nor the third, nor the fourth — who had already been the second. It took a fifth palm to hold this lottery ticket long enough for the numbers to pop up just right.

Here is the sequence:

Callaway relented to his vet's advice and put John Henry back in the next year's Keeneland January

bling his money would be a cruel joke.) Snowden, too, found John Henry destructive to his stall bedding, webbing, and feed tub, and he had him gelded to calm the horse down.

Despite his obstreperous stall manners, John Henry was tractable outdoors and was doing well enough that Akiko McVarish offered $7,500, pending her veterinarian's approval. This was not forthcoming. Veterinarians just did not seem to like the horse, the flaw of being back at the knee generally

PATRICIA McQUEEN

John Henry was a champion through the age of nine.

seen as a virtual guarantee of unsoundness. Snowden gave back the check, the deal not consummated. He then found a buyer in New Orleans resident Colleen Madere, at $11,000 (for John Henry and another two-year-old), that spring.

At two John Henry won a small stakes at one of Louisiana's lesser tracks, Evangeline Downs, and raced under claiming tags of $25,000 and $20,000

in New Orleans. The next spring, however, Madere became the fourth person to figure out a way to get rid of John Henry. The horse had appreciated, though, and she traded him back to Snowden for not one, but a pair of two-year-olds. Snowden ran John Henry once, at three at Keeneland, where the gelding was fourth. Thereupon, trainer Bobby Donato asked if Snowden had a prospect for a new client with maybe $50,000 to spend on two horses. Snowden sold the horse a second time (three if you count the take-back), this time for $25,000. John Henry had found a home, although he was to continue to have several more trainers.

The buyer was Sam Rubin, who raced as Dotsam Stable, named for himself and his wife, Dorothy (Dot). An earlier bargain horse beloved by American sports fans, Seabiscuit of the late 1930s, was owned by an entrepreneur who started out as a bicycle repairman (Charles S. Howard). Rubin was also a two-wheeler man, but was a bit more upscale at the time of his life when he bought John Henry. He owned the Sam Rubin Bicycle Corporation, with showrooms at a Fifth Avenue address, and was a lifelong racing fan.

For Dotsam, John Henry became a stakes winner

again and then a consistent stakes horse on grass, and by the end of his five-year-old year, he had won the first of his four Eclipse Awards on the turf. Lefty Nickerson had become his trainer on the East Coast, then sent him to Ron McAnally for his California campaigning. After the two sent him back and forth again several times, McAnally eventually stuck with John Henry wherever he went.

John Henry was six when Arlington Park — the proud Chicago track born at the end of the 1920s — instituted the first Arlington Million. The name revealed the total purse. (Fees for nomination, eligibility maintenance, and supplemental entries, plus final starting fees, reduced Arlington management's responsibility to $113,500 of the grandiose figure.) The winner's share was $600,000. For comparison, the Kentucky Derby that year, 1981, netted the winner $317,200; the Santa Anita Handicap, $238,150; and the Jockey Club Gold Cup, $340,800. (John Henry, at six, was not eligible for the Derby, of course, but he won the two other races.)

The reverence that the racing public would eventually have for John Henry was not yet at full flower — he had only been nationally prominent for a couple of seasons — but he was surely respected as one outstanding racehorse. The Million was his seventh race of the season, and he had already won five major stakes that year. He was coupled with Elmendorf Farm's good horse Super Moment, also trained by McAnally, and the fact that the entry was not odds-on attests to the quality of the field. The pair was the 11-10 favorite in a field of twelve, with big Rossi Gold second choice, the accomplished Key to Content third choice. The previous year's Washington, D.C., International winner Argument was back

in America after a couple of stakes wins in France, and although Mrs. Penny was past her glory days in England, she was another distinguished runner. Meanwhile, English champion Lester Piggott graced the scene aboard the European invader Madam Gay, although he missed by four pounds making her assigned weight of 113 as a three-year-old filly. John Henry, as one of the older males, carried 126 pounds.

During John Henry's championship seasons, the jockeys Darrel McHargue, Laffit Pincay Jr., Bill Shoemaker, and Chris McCarron all had extended stints as his regular rider. The 1981 Million came during The Shoe's phase, and, afterward, the admiring rider said repeatedly what a "professional" John Henry was and how that quality was what allowed him to win.

The Bart, a 40-1 shot owned by one of racing's newcomers at the top level, Franklin Groves of North Ridge Farm, prompted the pace of Key to Content early, and took over in the stretch. Ridden by Eddie Delahoussaye, The Bart also carried 126 pounds. One aspect that aroused Shoemaker's admiration so much that day was that the soft footing was something John Henry favored no more than, say, the webbing to his stall as a yearling.

"No, he did not like the going, and it took him a long time to get used to it," Shoemaker said. "We had to stay on the outside around the first turn, about four horses wide, but then he adjusted to the going and moved down on the rail going down the backstretch." John Henry was eighth in the early going and was about seven lengths off the pace after a half-mile. The climb into contention was a laborious endeavor, for man and beast, but Shoemaker arrived at the top of the stretch with a bit of confidence. The Bart at that point had taken over from Key to Content.

The Shoe had The Bart in his hip pocket, he assumed. He was wrong.

"At the eighth pole I thought we would catch him easily," Shoemaker admitted. "But then I noticed Delahoussaye had a lot of horse left. Then I knew it was going to take everything my little horse had. He is a professional, though. He may get beat sometimes, but he will try his very best every time."

Sports writer Pete Axthelm, involved in the telecast of the Million, was as enthralled as everyone else. He saw how John Henry charged down the lane, body stretched low to the ground, to cut down the lead; how The Bart belied his odds with one of those courageous efforts that seal the glory of the Thoroughbred. John Henry and The Bart raged on, digging and plunging, seemingly inseparable, and at length swept across the wire.

Axthelm was too game to fall back on the easy "too close to call." He had watched many a race and he called The Bart.

Axthelm, and The Bart, just missed.

To any viewer in the grandstand, the angle of vantage point might have seemed to tip the balance one way or the other. The presumably perfect eye of the camera caught John Henry's nose in front — perhaps by an inch.

Madam Gay was third, two and a quarter lengths behind. The time of 2:07⅗ indicated the holding nature of the turf, but equaled the course record; there had only been one other race at the one and a quarter-mile distance run over that strip.

"He just does the very best he can, all the time. No matter what the problem is, he goes to work. He is just a professional," Shoemaker repeated. "I don't know how else to describe him."

⊱ ⊰

Sent East again, and back to Nickerson a final time, John Henry flaunted his versatility as well as his professionalism by switching to dirt and winning the Jockey Club Gold Cup at one and a half miles. That time he did not cut it quite so fine; he defeated Peat Moss by a luxurious head. Once more across the country he trekked, winning the Oak Tree Invitational, but then finishing fourth in the Hollywood Turf Cup for his final start of the season. He had won eight of ten, on dirt and grass, that season and had twice won under 130 pounds. He was voted Horse of the Year, champion older male, and champion grass horse.

The twentieth century saw a number of geldings renowned for their longevity, versatility, and weight-carrying ability. Five stood out. At the end of the century, according to *Thoroughbred Champions: Top 100 Racehorses of the 20th Century*, Kelso was reckoned the best of them, Forego second, John Henry third, Exterminator fourth, and Armed fifth. John Henry, though, outstripped them all in one respect. He was the only one still strutting around at his best as a nine-year-old.

At seven and eight John Henry won only two races each, although they were major stakes and his eight-year-old season brought him a third Eclipse for turf male. Then, at nine, he defied all racegoers' and horsemen's experience by winning six stakes among nine starts — including his last four races — to reign yet again as Horse of the Year, as well as grass champion a fourth time. (The grass division was separated for championship balloting for the first time in 1953. Round Table and Fort Marcy won or shared three titles, but only John Henry has four.)

The little John with the big heart had won the first Arlington Million at six. He lost the race to Tolomeo by a neck at eight, but was back at nine to win it a second time by defeating eventual champion Royal Heroine and the 1982 Kentucky Derby winner Gato Del Sol. At one and three-quarter lengths, the second win seemed almost easy.

But it was the inaugural million that became a symbol of Arlington Park. After Dick Duchossois bought the track, saw it burn, and then rebuilt it in unexcelled splendor, he placed a large bronze statue by Edwin Bogucki in a prominent place. The bronze replicates the final moments of the first Million, two warriors stopped in flight — in endless battle.

Arlington Million
Purse: $1,000,000 Guaranteed

6th Race Arlington Park - August 30, 1981
Purse $1,000,000 guaranteed. Three-year-olds and upward. 1-1/4 Miles. Turf Course. Track: Soft
Value to winner $600,000; second, $200,000; third, $110,000; fourth, $60,000; fifth, $30,000. Mutuel pool $617,620.

P#	Horse	A	Wgt	Med	Eqp	Odds	PP	1/4	1/2	3/4	1m	Str	Fin	Jockey
12	John Henry	6	126			a-1.10	12	$8^{\frac{1}{2}}$	$8^{1\frac{1}{2}}$	$5^{\frac{1}{2}}$	5^{1}	3^{hd}	1no	W Shoemaker
5	The Bart	5	126			40.70	5	2^{1}	$2^{1\frac{1}{2}}$	$2^{1\frac{1}{2}}$	$2^{2\frac{1}{2}}$	1^{1}	2^{4}	E Delahoussaye
4	(S)Madam Gay	3	117			12.30	4	6^{hd}	$5^{\frac{1}{2}}$	$3^{\frac{1}{2}}$	3^{3}	4^{1}	$3^{\frac{1}{2}}$	L Piggott
6	Key To Content	4	126		b	6.80	6	$1^{\frac{1}{2}}$	$1^{\frac{1}{2}}$	$1^{\frac{1}{2}}$	1^{hd}	2^{hd}	4^{1}	G Martens
1	Match the Hatch	5	126		b	f-40.50	1	3^{hd}	3^{hd}	4^{2}	$4^{\frac{1}{2}}$	5^{1}	$5^{1\frac{1}{4}}$	J L Samyn
7	Argument	4	126			7.20	7	$9^{1\frac{1}{2}}$	9^{1}	8^{1}	$7^{\frac{1}{2}}$	6^{4}	6^{5}	A Cordero Jr
3	Mrs. Penny	4	121			f-40.50	3	12	12	12	$9^{\frac{1}{2}}$	7^{2}	7^{2}	D Brumfield
10	Rossi Gold	5	126			3.80	10	11^{hd}	11^{1}	$11^{2\frac{1}{2}}$	$6^{\frac{1}{2}}$	8^{4}	8^{6}	P Day
2	Super Moment	4	126			a-1.10	2	$4^{\frac{1}{2}}$	$6^{\frac{1}{2}}$	6^{hd}	8^{3}	10^{6}	$9^{1\frac{1}{2}}$	F Toro
8	Kilijaro	5	121		b	8.70	8	$7^{\frac{1}{2}}$	$7^{1\frac{1}{2}}$	9^{hd}	11^{6}	9^{1}	10^{13}	L Pincay Jr
11	Fingal's Cave	4	126			36.00	11	$10^{\frac{1}{2}}$	10^{1}	10^{hd}	$10^{\frac{1}{2}}$	11^{5}	11^{6}	S Cauthen
9	(S)P'tite Tete	5	126			41.00	9	5^{1}	4^{2}	$7^{\frac{1}{2}}$	12	12	12	S Hawley

a-Coupled: John Henry and Super Moment; f-mutuel field; (S) Supplementary nomination.

Off Time: 3:46 Central Daylight Time **Time Of Race:** $:25\frac{1}{5}$ $:50\frac{1}{5}$ $1:15\frac{3}{5}$ $1:42\frac{2}{5}$ $2:07\frac{3}{5}$ (equals course record)
Start: Good For All **Track:** Soft
Equipment: b for blinkers

Mutuel Payoffs

12	**John Henry (a-entry)**	**$4.20**	**$3.60**	**$2.80**
5	**The Bart**		**20.40**	**6.60**
4	**Madam Gay**			**4.80**

Winner: John Henry, b. g. by Ole Bob Bowers—Once Double, by Double Jay. (Trained by Ronald McAnally).
Bred by Golden Chance Farm Inc. in Ky.

Start good. Won driving.
JOHN HENRY was unhurried early, dropped inside leaving first turn, steadily improved position down backstretch, eased out leaving three-sixteenths pole and responded gamely to run down THE BART in final stride. The latter forced the pace for one mile outside KEY TO CONTENT, took a clear lead nearing eighth pole and just failed to last. MADAM GAY moved up along rail down backstretch, remained inside for stretch run, held on gamely in drive. KEY TO CONTENT rated kindly on the lead, gradually gave way leaving second turn. MATCH THE HATCH saved ground early, eased out between rivals on second turn but lacked needed closing response. ARGUMENT eased out between rivals after one mile but went evenly in drive. MRS. PENNY was outrun early, passed tiring rivals. ROSSI GOLD was not asked for early speed, swung wide after seven furlongs but failed to respond in drive. SUPER MOMENT gradually gave way between horses. KILIJARO was through after five furlongs. FINGAL'S CAVE showed little. P'TITE TETE was forwardly placed early outside horses, faltered nearing second turn.
Scratched—Bel Bolide, Ben Fab.
Overweight: Madam Gay, 4 pounds.

Owners: (12) Dotsam Stable; (5) F N Groves; (4) G Kaye; (6) Rokeby Stables; (1) Kathy M & Karen M Johnson; (7) Summa Stable & B Gordy; (3) E N Kronfeld; (10) L Combs II; (2) Elmendorf Farm; (8) Fradkoff & Seltzer; (11) J R Mullion; (9) P Wall
Trainers: (12) Ronald McAnally; (5) John Sullivan; (4) Paul A Kelleway; (6) Mack Miller; (1) Philip G. Johnson; (7) Maurice Zilber; (3) Thomas Skiffington; (10) Raymond Lawrence Jr; (2) Ronald McAnally; (8) Charles Whittingham; (11) John L. Dunlop; (9) Robert Frankel

©DAILY RACING FORM/EQUIBASE

*The inaugural Breeders' Cup Classic,
won by Wild Again (rail).*

- CHAPTER 23 -

Those Championship Saturdays

The concept of many breeders putting up a small amount of money to nominate a great number of foals for a race helped create a winner's purse of $40,900 for the first running of the Futurity Stakes. The year was 1888, when the Belmont Stakes, by comparison, netted its winner less than one-tenth of that amount. Not surprisingly, such a purse differential made the Futurity a key target, and for many years it was regarded as the most important race in America for two-year-olds.

Nearly one hundred years later, one of the contemporary leaders in racing, John R. Gaines, got to thinking about how to turn this collective financing concept into something really big. In a barnstorming tour that resembled a political campaign, Gaines described a new program of races called the Breeders' Cup, partly funded by annual nomination payments for stallions based on their breeding fees. Additional foal nominations and supplemental fees would help generate a super card of racing, seven races each with a purse of at least one million dollars.

It would be a sort of Super Bowl of American Thoroughbred racing and would be instrumental in naming champions in the key divisions. It would also promote international competition, for surely the rich purses and the late-season placement on the calendar would lure the best horses from Europe. An underlying goal would be to help popularize a sport that over the years had seen diminishing interest among a public surfeited with football, basketball, baseball, golf, etc.

Well, any deal this big, a concept this far-reaching, would have a great many hurdles. The benefit to those being asked to finance it was not immediate and, to a degree, required a leap of faith. Leaps of faith tend to be scratchy points in any negotiation. Nevertheless, when leading stallion managers such as Seth Hancock of Claiborne Farm signed on, the Breeders' Cup was headed toward reality. A diverting tweak to create a way for more levels of horsemen to perceive a benefit was the establishment of purse supplements for existing stakes races and new events around the country. Not all of the money, then, would go just for the seven-race super card.

The first Breeders' Cup was held on a bright, sunny day at Hollywood Park on November 10, 1984. The efficacy of the concept was apparent right away, as it turned out. Five of the seven winners were named Eclipse Award winners as division champions, and the international aspect was underscored when the Aga Khan's Lashkari defeated the defending Horse of the Year, French-based All Along, in the first Breeders' Cup Turf. The climactic race of the program, the Breeders' Cup Classic at one and a quarter miles, created one of the most tumultuous major races in American history. Jockey Pat Day kept a long shot named Wild Again going about his affairs with courage and professionalism while the champion Slew o' Gold was buffeted about by the eccentric colt named Gate Dancer. Decked out in ear covers to hold down noise dis-

traction, Gate Dancer, who had won the Preakness, squeezed Slew o' Gold enough to get himself disqualified. Meanwhile, neither he nor Slew o' Gold could direct his energies sufficiently to collar Wild Again. The Breeders' Cup was off to a sensational start.

Over the years the series has achieved all of its most grandiose aims save for measurably making the game more popular to the nation at large. Televised live by NBC, the annual feasts for the racing crowd have continued to bring stars from various countries together with America's best, and its winners have dominated Eclipse Award balloting for year-end championships.

There have been enough great Breeders' Cup races to fill a book, and they have already done so (*Breeders' Cup*, by Jay Privman, published by Moonlight Press.) For purposes of the present volume, we have singled out one performance for a separate

Dayjur (outside) jumped a shadow and let Safely Kept get home first in the 1990 Sprint.

chapter. This is the splendid effort of Personal Ensign to catch Winning Colors and Goodbye Halo in the 1988 Breeders' Cup Distaff. To the brilliance this event shares with many other Breeders' Cup moments, Personal Ensign added the unique aspect of its winner completing her career undefeated.

Trolling through other Breeders' Cup memories, we find many an engulfing stop along the way.

The event has moved to and fro among an elite few racetracks. In 1987 it returned to Hollywood Park, and two of the more memorable battles of high-class runners resulted. For the one and a half-mile two-million-dollar Breeders' Cup Turf, Trempolino arrived off his recent win in Europe's most prestigious prize, the Prix de l'Arc de Triomphe. He faced off with the serial grade I winner Theatrical. English jockey Pat Eddery brought the invader along nearing the stretch, and they were in combat with Theatrical and Pat Day to the wire, but Day won the battle of Pats as Theatrical scored by a half-length.

Even the brilliance of that race, however, was surpassed in the next race, the three-million-dollar Breeders' Cup Classic. In a duel of Kentucky Derby-winning colts, Bill Shoemaker, in the fifth decade of his remarkable career, finessed the older Ferdinand to a heart-check victory. Chris McCarron brought the three-year-old Alysheba along in a stretch-long crusade, but Ferdinand got home by a nose. It was a

Horse-of-the-Year nose. The following November, in the darkening autumn cold at Churchill Downs, Alysheba prevailed over Seeking the Gold to clinch his own Horse-of-the-Year campaign.

The 1989 Breeders' Cup Classic at Gulfstream

Lady's Secret in a superior performance in the 1986 Distaff.

Park also cemented Horse of the Year, in this instance for the Kentucky Derby-Preakness winner, Sunday Silence. That colt moved with cat-like quickness to take command, then staved off the withering challenge by his arch rival, Easy Goer (see chapter "Not Silent, nor Easy.") The race came a half-hour after Prized had staved off a trio of French runners to win the Breeders' Cup Turf by a head over Sierra Roberta in his first start on grass.

The 1991 Breeders' Cup Juvenile, at Churchill Downs, celebrated an instant hero in Arazi, a little American colt bred by Ralph Wilson Jr., the owner of the Buffalo Bills football team. Arazi was brought in by sporting owner Allen Paulson after already proving himself the champion two-year-old in

France. In an electric move, Arazi came from far back to catch the toiling front-runner Bertrando and then dashed right away to win by five lengths. The quickly induced image of a new Secretariat faded the following spring, but at the moment Arazi

In 1996 the Breeders' Cup was run out of the United States. It was hosted by the spacious and handsome metropolitan Toronto track Woodbine, in Canada. The Breeders' Cup Classic was the final race in the career of one of the 1990s' greatest he-

Arazi's electrifying Juvenile victory in 1991.

clearly had earned the sense of wonderment he fostered.

In 1993, at Santa Anita's Oak Tree meeting, fillies and mares staged two epics. In the Breeders' Cup Juvenile Fillies, big, rangy Phone Chatter outdueled Sardula by a head, and in the Distaff, the three-year-old Hollywood Wildcat dug in early in the stretch and kept the older champion Paseana at bay through a searching final furlong that earned a championship of her own.

roes, Cigar. Allen Paulson's grand champion had won the Classic in 1995, completing a bell-ringing campaign of ten wins in ten starts. This matched the campaign by the great Tom Fool as a handicap champion in 1953.

Cigar raced on in 1996, extending his winning streak over three calendars to sixteen. He had lost twice in recent starts before the Breeders' Cup, but such was his stardom that he was odds-on in the weight-for-age Classic. This raced produced the stretch drive depicted on the jacket of this volume, a stretch-long battle replete with breathless questions and a plethora of answers: could the Canadian colt on the rail, Mt. Sassafras, somehow fell the giants; could the Preakness winner, three-year-old Louis Quatorze, outrun his elders; could the gray with the kitchen-stove name of Alphabet Soup maintain the lead; could the great Cigar, perhaps a step off his peak at six, get his rally in gear in time?

The struggle carried to the wire, and the roan Alphabet Soup prevailed. Louis Quatorze was beaten by the length of that nose, Cigar was third, a head back, and the gallant Mt. Sassafras was but a half-length back. The winner, a son of the 1985 Breeders' Cup Mile winner, Cozzene, raced for Georgia Ridder, whose late husband had provided the second name in the renowned Knight-Ridder newspaper chain. (Ridder had been an avid California-based horseman who owned Cascapedia and Flying

Paster.) David Hofmans, trainer of Alphabet Soup, remained on the stage of high visibility when he won the Belmont Stakes the following year with Touch Gold.

The 1996 Breeders' Cup Classic was one of the best of the so-called blanket finishes in racing's annals. It bore strong resemblance to the 1956 Widener Handicap, in which the 1955 Horse of the Year Nashua made his four-year-old debut and somehow got to the wire with his head in front. On that occasion, it was Sailor and Find to the winner's left, while Social Outcast played the Cigar role in charging up on the outside.

In 1998 the Breeders' Cup returned to Churchill Downs. The field for the Classic was advertised as perhaps the best assembled in anyone's memory. It had a slightly disquieting result, for although Awesome Again deserved full marks for his rally between horses to win, it could be interpreted that the

Derby winners Ferdinand (inside) and Alysheba dueled in the 1987 Classic.

Flanders won the 1994 Juvenile Fillies over Serena's Song, but never raced again.

mirror the whole of the sport — dominating moments, great duels, the occasional tragedy, upsets, and astounding rallies.

Skip Away's six-length win in the 1997 Classic and Favorite Trick's five and a half-length victory in the Juvenile to secure Horse of the Year at two that same year illustrate one scenario. The seemingly impossible rallies from far back by the filly Epitome and the colt Tasso to wrest Juvenile races — and championships — out of seeming defeat illustrate another.

gray champions Silver Charm and Skip Away were no longer quite at top form; meanwhile, the distinguished European Swain drifted so far to the outside under Frankie Dettori that reporters were sent back to Pythagorean geometry to try to figure out how much ground he actually lost.

Perhaps that Breeders' Cup card's signature moment was the victory of Da Hoss in the Breeders' Cup Mile. The highly intense British trainer Michael Dickinson had won the Mile with this gelding at Woodbine two years before, and now he was trying to win it again after just one race in the interim. In a virtuoso performance of horseman and horse, Da Hoss came back after giving up the lead and edged Hawksley Hill by a gallant head margin.

The Breeders' Cup has been graced by many marvelous performances that

Lure and Miesque both won back-to-back Breeders' Cup Miles; majestic, gray Daylami's Turf triumph eased the nettle for jockey Dettori; Flanders' gallantry in her Juvenile Fillies win over Serena's

Miesque in her second consecutive Mile victory.

Song resulted in an injury, presumably within a fraction of a fracture of real tragedy; Lady's Secret toured so majestically in superiority that her 1986 Distaff made her Horse of the Year.

Then, too, there was Arcangues, the French horse who gained a place in history in 1993. Jockey Jerry ments, though, occurred in the 1990 Sprint. The eventual European sprint champion Dayjur had proven able to adapt to the dirt and speed of an American sprint in the first half-mile. He was confident and closing on the gallant filly Safely Kept. Dayjur had her measured; he was going to win.

Theatrical holding off Trempolino in the 1987 Turf.

Bailey had never ridden him before and couldn't understand the instructions of French trainer Andre Fabre, but the communication of man and horse has never been restricted to spoken language. In the stretch, here came Bailey and Arcangues to win at the fantasy odds of 133-1.

Perhaps the most bizarre of Breeders' Cup mo- Then, he saw shadows across the track, and he gathered himself, not once, but twice, for prodigious leaps across those frightful things. The loss in momentum made the difference, and so the filly's victory was, barely, safely kept.

As envisioned from the start, the Breeders' Cup has it all.

E. Martin Jessee

*A desperate charge on the outside, and
Personal Ensign retires undefeated.*

- CHAPTER 24 -

A Personal Perfection

The Kentucky Derby winner turned for home. A wondrous roan, a rawboned Amazon of a racehorse, Winning Colors had become only the third of her gender to win the Run for the Roses, and that was not the only time she had defeated colts. Now, in a climactic, one-million-dollar race, she was about to face a challenge from another outstanding three-year-old filly, the consistent Goodbye Halo. Another battle was shaping for the long stretch and the long history of old Churchill Downs, a grand lady in her own way.

Why then, was such a sense of letdown washing over the crowd, a mood to accompany the darkening grayness of an unforgiving autumn afternoon?

The crowd was about to come up empty because Personal Ensign was coming up empty. Unbeaten in a dozen races, the fans' darling had gone into this Breeders' Cup Distaff as her farewell. Now, as she struggled in the mud, it seemed woefully apparent that her unbeaten status was slipping away. "Not today," her trainer, Shug McGaughey, muttered to

himself, and many in the crowd would have echoed the thought. The professional horseman quite likely had already begun to retool his goals just to hope the filly would get through the goo and come back sound, when somehow an eight-length deficit began to shrink.

Personal Ensign had kicked into high gear — and high theater.

><del>•</del><del>•</del>O<del>•</del><del>•</del><

Although she was a well-bred and impressive filly from one of the staunchest and most enduring of breeding programs, Personal Ensign had not achieved her unbeaten status through some airy entitlement. True, she had had her days of flowing unchallenged to the wire, but she had also had her struggles. An injury at two was so severe that McGaughey found himself skeptical of even one of the most renowned veterinary surgeons when it was suggested the filly might get back to the races.

Personal Ensign was bred and raced by Ogden Phipps, whose connection to high-class horses dated from the middle 1920s. It was during that decade that his mother, Mrs. Henry Carnegie Phipps, and uncle, Secretary of the Treasury Ogden Mills, formed Wheatley Stable. Within a decade, Phipps had started his own stable. Add another decade-plus, and, after wartime service in the Navy, Phipps had incorporated breeding and racing as serious pursuits to accompany his investment/banking career.

Phipps had been an early fan of the female family launched by Colonel E.R. Bradley's importation of the French mare La Troienne. He had bought into the family, and, upon Bradley's death in 1946, Phipps had eagerly signed up to be one of the buyers of Bradley's blue-ribbon broodmare band. Along with Robert Kleberg Jr. of King Ranch and John Hay Whitney of Greentree Stable, Phipps acquired the mares. The three sold off drafts and divided what they wanted to keep via the highly sophisticated method of drawing straws over lunch. Greentree got La Troienne herself, but there were already enough of her descendants to go around.

In due course, the essence of La Troienne wafted down to Buckpasser, a Phipps homebred of exceptional power who was Horse of the Year in 1966 and a champion every year he ran. Buckpasser's first crop included Numbered Account, whose female line sprang from La Troienne as well — at a genetically acceptable distance to avoid radical inbreeding — and who was the champion two-year-old filly of 1971. Numbered Account, daughter of the 1966 Horse of the Year, was bred to Damascus, the 1967 Horse of the Year, and thus foaled the high-class stakes winner Private Account, destined to sire Personal Ensign.

While the top part of Personal Ensign's pedigree was replete with Phipps directives for several generations, the bottom half represented one of the infrequent and judicious purchases Phipps has made over the years. Her dam, Grecian Banner, was a homebred by Hoist the Flag, but the next dam, Dorine, was an outstanding Argentine-bred mare that Phipps had purchased. Dorine was a daughter of the Hyperion stallion Aristophanes, destined to be the sire of the spectacular Argentine and American stakes winner Forli (in turn the progenitor of the great Forego).

The Private Account—Grecian Banner filly of 1984 was named Personal Ensign. Earlier names with such a naval motif were among those favored by Phipps, as per Buckpasser's dam, Busanda (Bureau of Supplies and Accounts). Phipps also has shown deft use of show business names (Broadway, Great White Way, Queen of the Stage, Will Hays); names with specific reference to society or style (Fashion Verdict, Dapper Dan, Beau Brummel, Ward McAllister), and names with a wry personal connection. Cadillacing was named for the word used by an employee to describe things going exceptionally well.

Personal Ensign came to McGaughey's barn as a two-year-old in 1986. A young Kentuckian who had worked for Hall of Fame trainer Frank Whiteley and was about six years into his career as a head trainer, McGaughey had been recommended to the Phipps family by Seth Hancock. By then, three generations of Phippses had a long-standing relationship with three generations of Hancocks, owners of Claiborne Farm in Kentucky.

McGaughey did not bring Personal Ensign to the races until September 28 of her juvenile year. She had worked like a good thing and was 4-5 for a maiden race of seven furlongs at Belmont Park. The track was muddy, and she was hesitant at the break but soon took the lead under jockey Randy Romero and soared home by twelve and three-quarter lengths.

It was a debut to bring back memories of past champions' extravagant introductions to racing, fillies such as her own ancestress Numbered Account. It is also true, however, that many an impressive first-time starter makes no further headlines. That Personal Ensign would not be one of the latter was quickly established. On October 13, Personal Ensign had her second assay under colors, and such was the impression of her debut that she was 3-10 although taking the huge step up into stakes company, and grade I stakes company at that. Moreover, she was asked to race a mile in the Frizette. (Such campaigning is not McGaughey's normal progression, but the filly's debut had come too late to afford gradual steps and still make any of the East's traditional targets for the division.) For the first of only three times, she hit the wire with a rival lapped on her, digging in through her inexperience to beat Collins by a head.

McGaughey was annoyed at the suggestion that she had been disappointing. After all, here was a second-time starter racing a mile in top company, and she had won! He soon had more to fret over than the nuances of press coverage, for Personal Ensign broke the pastern bone in her left hind leg during a workout. Suddenly irrelevant were decisions about whether to push for a late claim to an Eclipse Award. Just caring for the animal became the sole consideration.

Personal Ensign's maternal grandsire,

Hoist the Flag, had been a sensation fifteen years earlier, moistening the mouths of all who yearned for a Triple Crown winner. Then a serious hind leg fracture had put his life at risk, and his recovery for stud duty underscored the advances of veterinary procedures to address injuries of a degree so recently associated with inevitable demise of their victims.

Fifteen years had passed, and, McGaughey said, Personal Ensign's injury "never was a life-threatening situation." It surely seemed a racing career-ending affair, however. Dr. Larry Bramlage placed five screws in the pastern.

"We never thought she would race again," McGaughey said, thinking back to that time from the vantage point of her retirement. "I thought the vets

Personal Ensign and trainer Shug McGaughey.

were crazy when they told me a week after the operation that she had a chance to run again."

It was almost a year later that McGaughey had her all the way back. She won again the first time out, in an allowance race, then added another overnight race. The margins were three and three-quarter lengths and seven and three-quarter lengths. She stepped up to win a grade II race, the Rare Perfume, against other three-year-old fillies at a mile, by four

Winning Colors had achieved her own immortality by holding off Forty Niner in the Kentucky Derby.

and three-quarter lengths. Back in grade I company, she next faced older fillies and mares at a mile and quarter in the Beldame Stakes and won by daylight, two and a quarter lengths. For the second year, she had presented credible evidence of being the best of her age group, but for the second year had too limited a campaign to be voted a championship. This was to change when she was four.

Few projects in sports can be as pressure-filled as bringing an unbeaten competitor — team or individual — back for a new season. This was the task facing McGaughey in the spring of 1988. Personal

Ensign was six for six, and, as it turned out, had slightly more than half of her races ahead of her. She went immediately into stakes company this time and was under a drive to win the grade I Shuvee by one and three-quarter lengths. Next came two lovely waltzes, by seven lengths in the grade I Hempstead Handicap and eight lengths in the grade II Molly Pitcher Handicap.

Stepping up the level of challenge rather than ducking pressure, Phipps and McGaughey let her face a bellwether moment in the career of a Thoroughbred filly: She next challenged males. The track at Saratoga was sloppy for the Whitney Handicap, but Personal Ensign handled it adroitly, beating the high-class colt Gulch by one and a half lengths.

Next came the Maskette. She was back to facing only fillies this time, but this hardly rated as dropping down to an easier task. At a mile, she chased the Derby winner, Winning Colors, for a long way and was under pressure to wear her down and win by not quite a length. Then, in her farewell to New York, Personal Ensign coasted home by five and a half lengths to win her second Beldame. Despite the quality of the Whitney, Maskette, and Beldame, she had been odds-on for each, at 4-5, 3-10, and 1-10. (How impressive must another filly be to go off at 3-10 against a Winning Colors?)

Personal Ensign had now run a dozen times over three seasons, twice with long interruptions, and had won them all. Fans, and historians, naturally were sent rummaging for reference points among that short list of horses unbeaten in their entire careers. As for racing in America, the search seemed to point toward Colin as the most applicable precedent, he a champion of an even eighty years before who raced at two and three and was fifteen for fifteen. As for Europe, the great Ribot, at sixteen for sixteen, presented himself most recently for recollection.

Personal Ensign would retire unbeaten, thirteen for thirteen, if she could win the Breeders' Cup Distaff, but the race was to bring out the toughest field of her own gender she had ever faced. Not a stable to duck the competition is this Phipps-McGaughey duo.

Winning Colors raced for Eugene Klein and had become the first of four (through 2001) Derby winners trained by D. Wayne Lukas. Prior to winning the Derby, she had warmed up against colts by winning the Santa Anita Derby by seven and a half lengths. She, like Personal Ensign, has since been elected to the National Museum of Racing's Hall of Fame. Despite her personal slant on the phrase "gender bashing," Winning Colors was not without challenge among three-year-old fillies. That division in 1988 also included Alex Campbell's and Arthur Hancock III's Goodbye Halo, trained by Charlie Whittingham. Like Personal Ensign, Goodbye Halo had stirred some thought of an Eclipse Award at two, but her late season form in the East did not eclipse Epitome's amazing stretch run to win the Breeders' Cup Juvenile Fillies. Now, at three, Goodbye Halo was not racing against late-season timing, but a filly Derby winner. Nevertheless, she had won such major distaff races as the Kentucky Oaks, Mother Goose, Coaching Club American Oaks,

and Las Virgenes. If she were to win the Breeders' Cup, it would be tough for even the magic of a Winning Colors' Derby victory to deny an Eclipse Award for Goodbye Halo.

Six others faced the three top stars, and there was plenty of quality among them. Personal Ensign was 1-2, again a numerical measure of her aura. Winning Colors and entrymate Classic Crown were 4-1, Goodbye Halo 11-2, and the Jonabell Farm entry of Epitome and Spinster Stakes winner Hail a Cab at 10-1. None of three others were shorter than 20-1, but Breeders' Cup fields by their inherent quality often mean that major stakes winners are consigned to extravagant odds.

>—◦—<

The excitement of an unbeaten career seemed to be waning, as the field turned out of the backstretch. McGaughey thought Personal Ensign was "hopelessly beaten at the three-eighths pole." What gratification the crowd would get — and it would have rallied to become enthralled — would be from the sight of seeing the Derby winner hooked by the one three-year-old filly who could challenge her.

Then, Personal Ensign began to pick it up. It became a race with two focuses, a duel brewing up front and a belated rally being generated from eight lengths back. Such a vista is not the easiest thing for the human eye to follow, but presents one of the pulse-surging situations that elevate Thoroughbred racing to surpassing drama.

Jockey Romero had ridden Personal Ensign in all but one of her races. "She's not a filly that really takes a lot of stick," he said later, "but every now and then I tapped her." He added as sweet a tribute as a jockey can give: "Every time I rode her, I rode her like she was the best in the world."

The ultimate test of all that confidence was in the offing, and it was an urgent thing. Personal Ensign hated the going, but she apparently hated even more the thought of being outrun. Winning Colors was strong, and she was up to the task of holding off Goodbye Halo, although it was not easy. At the quarter pole, Winning Colors still had daylight over Goodbye Halo, and Personal Ensign was forcing her way into the fray. Romero angled the unbeaten one to the outside. Now there was a clear path, and the only question was whether there were time and distance enough for her will to prevail. Goodbye Halo closed on Winning Colors, but the leader had her measure. What was coming toward her farther out, though, was another matter. That least expected of phenomena, an unbeaten racehorse, now presented herself once again as the Derby winner's adversary.

Phipps had seen this before, when his great Buckpasser had seemed well and honorably beaten in the 1966 Flamingo and 1967 Suburban and then, as if by sleight of hand, had gotten his head in front at the wire each time. The owner's Dapper Dan, on the other hand, had fallen short by a neck of catching Lucky Debonair on this same Churchill strip in the Derby of twenty-three years before. In Personal Ensign's final trial, the margin was dwindling, but like those predecessors, she was not running over dying leaders. Her assailants were headstrong on their own agendas, too, and each meant to win.

McGaughey said it best: "I didn't think she had a chance until maybe five or six strides before the wire."

The rally was frenzied, the will inflamed, and Personal Ensign continued to close. The wire now became the enemy, but she converted it at the last possible instant. They burst through the light of the photo finish camera, and some few who were watching from perfect vantage points felt a weight released. It would take some minutes for the stewards' verification, but these in the crowd were correct. The unbeaten career had been preserved.

"She didn't want to get beat," Romero said, admiringly. "She was determined to get the job done."

The official margin was a nose, and Winning Colors still preserved a half-length of her lead over Goodbye Halo for second. Sham Say was fourth, five lengths behind, appropriately non-intrusive.

Lukas and Whittingham were respectful of the class and courage that had beaten them. Lukas looked to a basketball analogy and likened the nose defeat to "getting beat at the buzzer by a 30-foot shot." The salty Whittingham, paragon of a sport whose jargon deems "runnin' hussy" a compliment, remarked "my little ol' filly did pretty good against that big cow (Personal Ensign). Look how big she is. She's a runner."

Night fell, not many minutes after Alysheba won the Breeders' Cup Classic to put an end to the hour or two in which Personal Ensign had appeared a potential Horse of the Year instead of only a slam-dunk Eclipse Award distaff champion at last. The segue from racehorse to broodmare prospect was rapid. Personal Ensign was not going back to Belmont, but to Claiborne Farm, her birthplace. The pressure passed from McGaughey to Seth Hancock, who fretted over a delayed van. Then that drama, too, eventually found all well with Personal Ensign. She went into that night, as all her nights, an undefeated racehorse.

There is no such thing as an undefeated broodmare, but Personal Ensign has excelled as a breeding animal, as well. As of early 2001, she had six foals old enough to race. Three were grade I stakes winners and two others were stakes-placed, all bred and raced by the Phipps stable. Her first foal, Miner's Mark, by Mr. Prospector, won the Jockey Club Gold Cup and other stakes. Her fourth foal, My Flag, by Easy Goer, won the Breeders' Cup Juvenile Fillies at two and added the historic Coaching Club American Oaks and other major victories at three in 1996, when Personal Ensign was named Broodmare of the Year. In 2001, Traditionally, by Mr. Prospector, be-

came the mare's third major winner when he won the grade I Oaklawn Handicap. Two other Mr. Prospector—Personal Ensign foals, Our Emblem and Proud and True, placed in graded stakes.

For all her success, Personal Ensign has had her troubles, and in four years she has either lost her foal or been unable to be bred. Still, in 2000, she was back in good health and foaled an A.P. Indy filly that was given a name that would seem optimistic for most pedigrees, but understated in her case. The filly was named Possibility.

Breeders' Cup Distaff
Purse: $1,000,000

6th Race Churchill Downs - November 5, 1988

Purse $1,000,000. Fillies and mares. Three-year-olds and upward. 1-1/8 Miles. Main Track. Track: Muddy.
Total purse, $1,000,000. Value of race, $913,000. Value to winner $450,000; second, $225,000; third, $108,000; fourth, $70,000; fifth, $50,000; sixth, $10,000. Foal awards, $43,500. Stallion awards, $43,500. Mutuel pool $744,804.

P#	Horse	A	Wgt	Med	Eqp	Odds	PP	St	1/4	1/2	3/4	Str	Fin	Jockey
6	Personal Ensign	4	123			.50	6	8	6^1	$5^{1/2}$	5^2	$3^{1/2}$	1no	R P Romero
8	Winning Colors	3	119		b-4.00		8	2	$1^{2/2}$	$1^{2/2}$	$1^{2/2}$	$1^{1/2}$	$2^{1/2}$	G L Stevens
2	Goodbye Halo	3	119			5.50	2	1	$2^{1/2}$	3^4	$2^{1/2}$	$2^{2/2}$	3^5	E Delahoussaye
3	Sham Say	3	119	b	30.60		3	7	5^2	2^{hd}	3^4	4^1	4^2	J Vasquez
9	Classic Crown	3	119	b	b-4.00		9	5	8^6	7^1	6^5	5^5	5^4	A Cordero Jr
4	Hail a Cab	5	123		a-10.30		4	9	9	9	7^1	7^2	6^2	C J McCarron
1	Epitome	3	119		a-10.30		1	4	$7^{1/2}$	8^5	8^2	8^6	$7^{1/2}$	P Day
5	Willa On the Move	3	119			22.20	5	3	$4^{1/2}$	4^2	4^1	6^{hd}	8^9	C Perret
7	Integra	4	123			83.30	7	6	3^1	6^{hd}	9	9	9	J Velasquez

a-Coupled: Hail a Cab and Epitome; b-Winning Colors and Classic Crown.

Off Time: 3:18   **Time Of Race:** :24⅖   :47⅕   1:12   1:38⅖   1:52
Start: Good For All   **Track:** Muddy

Mutuel Payoffs

6	Personal Ensign	$3.00	$2.20	$2.10
8	Winning Colors (b-entry)		2.80	2.20
3	Goodbye Halo			2.40

Winner: Personal Ensign, b. f. by Private Account—Grecian Banner, by Hoist the Flag (Trained by Claude McGaughey III).
Bred by Ogden Phipps in Ky.

Start good. Won driving.
PERSONAL ENSIGN, caught in close quarters between horses racing to the first turn, commenced to rally after going six furlongs, angled out approaching the stretch and finished determinedly to wear down WINNING COLORS in the final stride. WINNING COLORS sprinted away soon after the start, raced well out from the rail while making the pace, settled into the stretch with a clear advantage and just failed to last. GOODBYE HALO moved to the outside of WINNING COLORS while racing forwardly into the backstretch, remained a factor to the stretch and continued on gamely while drifting out slightly into PERSONAL ENSIGN during the late stages. SHAM SAY edged out into PERSONAL ENSIGN racing to the first turn, remained well out from the rail while racing forwardly to the upper stretch and gave way. CLASSIC CROWN, outrun for six furlongs, moved a little closer along the inside nearing midstretch but lacked a further response. HAIL A CAB was always outrun. EPITOME saved ground to no avail. WILLA ON THE MOVE tired badly while racing wide. INTEGRA showed brief speed while racing wide.

Owners: (6) O Phipps; (8) E V Klein; (2) Campbell Jr & Hancock III; (3) Evergreen Farms; (9) Star Crown Stable; (4) J A Bell III; (1) J A Bell III; (5) R Lamarque; (7) G J Aubin lessee
Trainers: (6) Claude McGaughey III; (8) D Wayne Lukas; (2) Charles Whittingham; (3) William B Cocks; (9) D Wayne Lukas; (4) Philip Hauswald; (1) Philip Hauswald; (5) Leon J Blusiewicz; (7) William R Helmbrecht

©DAILY RACING FORM/EQUIBASE

DAN JOHNSON

Sunday Silence and Easy Goer in perfect sync at the finish of the 1989 Preakness Stakes.

- CHAPTER 25 -

Not Silent, nor Easy

The two equine gladiators named Sunday Silence and Easy Goer came from backgrounds rich in contrasts, but also similarities. Arthur Hancock III recalled that, had they been so inclined, the two as young horses could have seen each other across pasture fence lines. The lanky, almost black Sunday Silence was foaled, and frolicked, at Hancock's Stone Farm, which neighbors the Claiborne Farm of his family. The extravagantly handsome chestnut Easy Goer began his life at Claiborne, run by Hancock's brother, Seth. Both farms spread across the copious lushness of Bourbon County, Kentucky.

Both young prospects were sons of leading sires, and yet when it came to fashion, contrast came into play. Sunday Silence was a son of Halo, whom Arthur Hancock's friend and associate Tom Tatham had arranged to be moved from Maryland to stand at Stone Farm. Halo was already the sire of a Kentucky Derby winner, Sunny's Halo, and had led the sire list in 1983. Despite such a background, Sunday

Silence when sent to auction fetched a modest $17,000. Hancock, assuming the breeder, Tatham, and his Oak Cliff Stable associates would not want to let him go for that amount, bid on the lanky colt himself. Apprised of this move, Tatham turned down the chance to hang on to a colt that had been dangerously ill as a foal and then would have to survive a frightening van accident en route to another sale opportunity.

Hancock thus owned the colt he had raised, and for which apparently nobody had much appetite. He later sold half-interest to the great West Coast trainer Charlie Whittingham, who had trained the star filly Goodbye Halo for Hancock and Alex Campbell Jr., and who respected Stone Farm's way of raising rugged horses in large pastures. Whittingham then sold half of his half to Dr. Ernest Gaillard, although he quipped later that he would not have made that deal had he seen the colt breeze a time or two beforehand.

Easy Goer was not by a leading stallion, technically.

Turning for home, Sunday Silence and Easy Goer engaged in their stretch-long duel.

His sire, Alydar, did not rank first in any year in progeny earnings until 1990. Nevertheless, since his flashy racing days Alydar had been recognized as a heroic sort of individual and was well established as an outstanding sire soon after his first crop came to the races at two in 1983.

In the female side of their pedigrees, both Sunday Silence and Easy Goer were foaled from stakes winners, but there the similarities ended. Wishing Well, dam of Sunday Silence, won a half-dozen stakes, several of them graded, but she was one of only two stakes winners sired by Understanding, and her own dam was a non-winner and her second dam was unraced.

Easy Goer, in contrast, was out of the champion mare Relaxing, she a daughter of the champion runner and prominent sire Buckpasser. Everything about this family was steeped in repetitive generational success.

Easy Goer was not exposed to the yearling market. He was bred by Ogden Phipps, whose family for several generations has epitomized the sporting band of horsemen who breed to race their own and who have at hand the stock to put into reality the old cliché "breed the best to the best." The Phippses long have been patrons of Claiborne, and in Easy Goer the combine had contrived to produce another in a succession of superlative racehorses.

There may be some question as to whether Easy Goer as a sale yearling would have beckoned a price in keeping with his exalted heritage, for he had rather short pasterns, and not particularly handsome ones, at that. When the Phipps stable's trainer, Shug McGaughey cranked him into competition, however, the colt soon confounded those who hold strong opinions about longer, elegant pasterns and ankles being required for efficient, easy running action and continuing soundness. Stubby or not, those pasterns were part of an arrangement of bone, muscle, and tendon that helped propel Easy Goer across his paths of contest with symphonic fluidity.

Defeat by a nose in his debut deprived Easy Goer of being unbeaten in his first five races. The final two of these were in the Cowdin Stakes and the great Champagne Stakes, which he won by four lengths. He was already hailed as a champion. A disappointing struggle to be second to Is It True in Churchill Downs' off going in the Breeders' Cup Juvenile did nothing to snatch an Eclipse Award from him.

Sunday Silence again presented a contrast. Whittingham likened him to a tallish teenager who had yet to grow into his frame. He did not make a start until October 30 of his two-year-old season, at which time he, too, was narrowly beaten in his debut. Then followed a runaway ten-length win and a close second in an allowance race. In the latter, the $17,000 yearling was beaten a head by the $2.9-million Seattle Slew yearling, Houston. It may have seemed otherwise at the time, but it was not far from Houston's greatest moment in retrospect, although this was a high-priced yearling that did not fail to become a stakes winner.

Whittingham then gave Sunday Silence three months off, sent him out for his three-year-old debut on March 2, and watched him win by daylight over six and a half furlongs. This was a gawky kid no longer. Victory in his first stakes attempt, the San Felipe, then led to a needlessly gaudy, eleven-length victory in the West's key Kentucky Derby indicator, the Santa Anita Derby. Whittingham quipped that he lectured jockey Pat Valenzuela that a key reason "the Good Lord made your neck turn"

was to look behind him and avoid just such unnecessary effort and winning margin. Nonetheless, as Sunday Silence prepped in the final days before the Derby, the cold Kentucky spring put a bounce in his step to match that of his master trainer. The colt clearly felt so fine that Whittingham was unable to mask his confidence.

Meanwhile, Easy Goer had been as spectacular at three as he had been at two. An eight and three-quarter-length win in the Swale Stakes was followed by a thirteen-length win in the Gotham (maybe even the devout Pat Day forgot about that God-given neck swivel, too, in the exultation of being on such a horse). He then used less of himself in winning the Wood Memorial by three.

Whittingham had tried the Kentucky Derby to no avail with Gone Fishin' back in 1958 and again with Divine Comedy two years later, after which he famously declared he had no intention of coming back until he had a real chance to win. True to his word, he started his third Derby horse twenty-six years later, and the winning of it with Ferdinand gave him an increased appetite. By the end of his life, Whittingham had made up for lost time enough to have run seven horses in the race.

McGaughey, raised in Kentucky, had finished sixth and sixteenth with the entry of Pine Circle and Vanlandingham in 1984 and had sent out Seeking the Gold to finish seventh in 1988. He dreamed of coming back with a top contender. In Easy Goer, McGaughey had just that, and he sent him out with another legitimate contender. This was the Flamingo Stakes winner Awe Inspiring, racing for Phipps' son, Ogden Mills (Dinny) Phipps, who tended to refer to his colt as "1-A" in recognition of Easy Goer's pride of place. The Phipps entry was 4-5,

Sunday Silence second choice at 3-1. Their quality did not dissuade so many hopefuls to keep the field smaller than fifteen. The 115th Derby was the coldest on record, temperatures dipping into the forties, with snippets of snow settling briefly upon already frosty julep glasses.

Houston led for a long way, while both Sunday Silence and Easy Goer were well up in contending positions. For all his past awkwardness and his lingering tendency to run greenly, Sunday Silence was deceptively nimble, and he seemed to relish the muddy track as he burst to the fore in the upper stretch. Despite doing a quick swerve, he was clear at the time and in control through the final furlongs, and he won by two and a half lengths. Day finally got Easy Goer flying along in time to catch stablemate Awe Inspiring to be second by a head.

The chestnut handsomeness of Easy Goer and his facile victories had prompted some timorous hints that he looked more than a bit like Secretariat. A horse that generates such feeling pre-Derby and then fails might be subject to an irrational resentment that sports stars of all species have to face. In Easy Goer's case, though, there were many unable to let go of their most exalted fantasies. Their confidence to "wait 'til next time," leaping upon the fact that he once again had faced a muddy track at Churchill Downs, the crowd at Pimlico engaged in some Derby nullification. The beaten 4-5 choice with a stablemate at Churchill Downs was 3-5 while going it alone at Pimlico!

McGaughey undoubtedly harbored hopes that all this confidence would be justified by sundown, but he expressed the thought that his rival Sunday Silence ought to have been favored. The Derby winner was 2-1.

Sunday Silence and Easy Goer met four times. The Preakness was their one duel that matched the best and brightest of the duels that Easy Goer's sire, Alydar, used to lose so frequently, but so gallantly, to Affirmed.

The 114th Preakness was like a basketball game in which one team storms to a stunning early lead, then the other comes back in a twinkling, but neither can shake ahead of the other from there.

Neither colt got away well in the eight-horse field, but both recovered nicely. Northern Wolf and then Houston led early, and then in a swoop that demonstrated Easy Goer's power of hypnotism, the wonderful strides took him from fifth to first. The Secretariat imagery had come back to life, and he was several lengths ahead of Sunday Silence two furlongs after having sat a couple of lengths off him.

Valenzuela by then was supremely confident, but admitted his surprise at the timing of Easy Goer's sudden move. No matter, he let out a notch and his athletic partner reeled in Easy Goer as quickly as he had let him go.

McGaughey's description captured the flabbergasting jerk of emotions: "One moment, it flickered through my mind, 'how far is Easy Goer going to win by?' But then the other horse caught up so quickly that I thought 'how far is *he* going to win by?'"

Sunday Silence had a neck on Easy Goer turning for home, and Valenzuela "thought I was going to put him away right there," but the pattern of running off from and up to each other in turns had been exhausted. From there to the wire, it would be two gallant and perhaps truly great colts matching strides, matching speed, matching courage.

Easy Goer was along the rail, and while Sunday Silence performed no dramatic tricks this time, he did close over enough that Day had little hope of using his whip on the right. Day knew he was perilously close to the rail. Sunday Silence did not squeeze him further, but neither did he drift out. Valenzuela at one point hit his own horse on the right, and if Sunday Silence had flinched left from that, a great horse race might have tumbled into a horrifying tragedy.

They battled on, they did, and at one point it occurred to Day that since there was little he could do with his whip, maybe a bit of finesse would tip the scales. He canted Easy Goer's head toward Sunday Silence, hoping that looking him in the eye from such harrowing intimacy might prompt the merest cleft in the other's bravery. It was not to be. The battle raged unabated, and the spirits of those who saw them soared. The two colts were locked virtually together, but "virtual" is not "exact," and so one of them would win and the other would lose. The wire mercifully blinked over them, and the winner was Sunday Silence, by a scant nose.

The time was 1:53⅘, only two-fifths of a second over Tank's Prospect's stakes record.

The two stout hearts had raced straight and true, with neither impeding the other, but the impression — part frightening, part claustrophobic — of intimidation justified claiming foul in Day's mind. The stewards had the treat of watching the race again, but with the need for dispassion. They quickly voted to leave the finish order as it was.

>━◆━○━◆━<

We have spoken before of differences involving Sunday Silence and Easy Goer. A sad contrast of that day involved their jockeys. Pat Day's drug problems were behind him, but Valenzuela's were in front. While Day, a born-again Christian, has restrained

whatever demons might haunt him and taunt him as a former substance abuser, Valenzuela — P. Val was once his affectionate nickname — has been knocked down by temptation over and over. He soared to an extraordinary success with Arazi in the colt's five-length Breeders' Cup Juvenile win in 1991, and he

Trainer Shug McGaughey with Easy Goer.

has had several start, stop, restart sequences in his career. As of early 2001, he was trying once again to be reinstated, but California authorities — as racing jurisdictions as far afield as Italy had been — were unwilling to take him back without more prolonged proof of discipline.

After the Preakness, Sunday Silence, of course,

was but one trip around Belmont Park — two sweeping turns — from becoming the first Triple Crown winner since Affirmed. He was, finally, favored, at 9-10. Those sweeping turns at Belmont, though, were said by many to favor, somehow, the specific mechanics of Easy Goer's conformation/soundness equation. After the Belmont had been run, we heard that theory expounded upon by various levels of observers — even van drivers were talking about it — and the theory had taken on some strength, for Easy Goer soared through the stretch and avenged his earlier losses by eight lengths.

The two met one more time, in the Breeders' Cup Classic at Gulfstream Park. In the intervening five months, Sunday Silence had lost again, rested, then won the Super Derby. Easy Goer had done nothing but win, starting with the Belmont. He toured the history of New York racing, following with wins in the Whitney, the Travers, the Woodward, and the

CANDACE RUSHING

Sunday Silence receiving a treat from his trainer, Charlie Whittingham.

Jockey Club Gold Cup.

Twice beaten, once victorious, Easy Goer was nonetheless the favorite over Sunday Silence. This was not a few pennies to the dollar in difference, either. The aura of Easy Goer, and his winning streak, made him a 1-2 choice with Sunday Silence at 2-1. (The dark colt's proponents might have joked that 2-1 meant "two wins to one.")

The deftness of Sunday Silence, his sheer athleticism to go along with an inherent quality, put him in the lead in the stretch. Chris McCarron was aboard that time. In the final furlong, Easy Goer threw his knockout punch yet again, but Sunday Silence the nimble had already ducked it. He was too far in front to be passed. For the third time, the dark horse beat the bright red chestnut. The margin was a neck.

Sunday Silence, with three wins in four meetings, was voted Horse of the Year.

Both colts raced briefly, and successfully, at four, before injuries prompted retirements. They did not meet again after the Breeders' Cup Classic of their three-year-old days. Resonating from the Affirmed-Alydar battles, when Alydar was seen (and proved to be) the better sire prospect despite their records on the racetrack, Easy Goer was clearly the more fashionable young stallion. He moved into Claiborne Farm, occupying the stall of Bold Ruler and Secretariat of earlier years. Arthur Hancock III, meanwhile, found so little enthusiasm among American breeders for Sunday Silence that he had little choice but to accept an offer from Japan for ten million dollars. (In a baffling history, the Halo stock never did become as fashionable as it deserved to be, despite the stallion leading the sire list a second time in Sunday Silence's championship season.)

Again, contrast has been wrought. Easy Goer

died young, long before it could be ascertained whether such high-class stakes horses as My Flag and Will's Way would become a pattern. In the meantime, Sunday Silence has become such a success in Japan that his progeny's earning figures dwarf most other stallions' of the world. In recent years, the Japanese owners of his offspring have ventured to such ports as Europe and Dubai, and the evidence is beginning to come in that the best of the Sunday Silence runners are competitive anywhere in the world.

In Japan, Sunday Silence has become so much a public icon that apparel is sold with no logo, only an uneven vanilla stripe down black fabric. The marking on his handsome head has become as recognizable as a Nike "swoosh."

Preakness Stakes
Purse: $500,000 Added

10th Race Pimlico - May 20, 1989
Purse $500,000 added. Three-year-olds. 1-3/16 Miles. Main Track. Track: Fast.
Value of race, $674,200. Value to winner $438,230; second, $134,840; third, $67,420; fourth, $33,710. Mutuel pool $1,491,333.

P#	Horse	A	Wgt	Med	Eqp	Odds	PP	St	1/4	1/2	3/4	Str	Fin	Jockey
7	Sunday Silence	3	126			2.10	7	5	$4^{1\frac{1}{2}}$	3^{1}	$3^{1\frac{1}{2}}$	1^{hd}	1no	P A Valenzuela
2	Easy Goer	3	126			.60	2	8	$5^{\frac{1}{2}}$	$5^{\frac{1}{2}}$	1^{hd}	2^{4}	2^{5}	P Day
4	Rock Point	3	126			22.80	4	6	7^{4}	7^{6}	5^{1}	3^{hd}	3^{2}	C W Antley
5	Dansil	3	126			28.30	5	3	$6^{1\frac{1}{2}}$	$6^{1\frac{1}{2}}$	$4^{1\frac{1}{2}}$	$4^{4\frac{1}{2}}$	$4^{3\frac{3}{4}}$	L Snyder
1	Hawkster	3	126			53.60	1	7	8	8	8	6^{12}	$5^{1\frac{1}{2}}$	M Castaneda
6	Houston	3	126			5.40	6	2	$2^{1\frac{1}{2}}$	$1^{2\frac{1}{2}}$	2^{2}	5^{hd}	6^{26}	A Cordero Jr
3	Pulverizing	3	126		b	70.00	3	1	3^{hd}	$4^{\frac{1}{2}}$	$7^{\frac{1}{2}}$	8	$7^{1\frac{1}{4}}$	A T Stacy
8	Northern Wolf	3	126		b	33.70	8	4	1^{hd}	$2^{\frac{1}{2}}$	6^{4}	7^{7}	8	C J Ladner III

Off Time: 5:35 **Time Of Race:** :23$\frac{2}{5}$:46$\frac{2}{5}$ 1:09$\frac{3}{5}$ 1:34$\frac{1}{5}$ 1:53$\frac{4}{5}$
Start: Good For All but Easy Goer **Track:** Fast
Equipment: b for blinkers

Mutuel Payoffs

7	**Sunday Silence**	**$6.20**	**$3.00**	**$3.20**
2	**Easy Goer**		**2.40**	**2.40**
4	**Rock Point**			**3.60**

Winner: Sunday Silence, dk. b. or br. c. by Halo—Wishing Well, by Understanding (Trained by Charles Whittingham).
Bred by Oak Cliff Thoroughbreds Ltd in Ky.

Won driving.
SUNDAY SILENCE, bumped by NORTHERN WOLF after the start, was bumped lightly again by PULVERIZING racing into the first turn, then remained close up while well out in the track into the backstretch. He was steadied when EASY GOER moved by him nearing the end of the backstretch, then caught that rival with a rush approaching the stretch. SUNDAY SILENCE held a narrow advantage into the stretch while under left-handed urging, then outgamed that rival while brushing repeatedly with him after his rider switched his whip to the right hand inside the final furlong. EASY GOER quickly reached a striking position after breaking in the air and eased to the outside of horses at the first turn. He moved boldly from the outside to catch HOUSTON racing into the far turn, but was replaced by SUNDAY SILENCE while dropping to the inside nearing the stretch. EASY GOER came again under left-handed urging to gain a brief lead approaching the final sixteenth and narrowly missed while brushing with the winner. A foul claim against SUNDAY SILENCE by the rider of EASY GOER, for alleged interference through the stretch, was not allowed. ROCK POINT, unhurried early, made a run from the outside approaching the stretch, remained within easy striking distance to the final furlong but lacked a rally while lugging in during the drive and brushing with DANSIL. DANSIL, reserved while saving ground into the backstretch, eased out while moving on the far turn, then was brushed by ROCK POINT while weakening under pressure. A foul claim against ROCK POINT by the rider of DANSIL, for alleged interference after entering the stretch, was not allowed. HAWKSTER, outrun to the far turn, raced wide into the stretch and passed only tired horses while being carried out slightly by HOUSTON. HOUSTON, prominent from the outset, sprinted clear while racing slightly out from the rail into the backstretch, was steadied along the inside after being replaced by EASY GOER before reaching the stretch, then bore out while tiring. PULVERIZING, away alertly, was steadied along behind the leaders racing into the first turn, eased out bumping SUNDAY SILENCE lightly and was finished soon after entering the backstretch. NORTHERN WOLF came over after the start bumping SUNDAY SILENCE, raced outside HOUSTON while showing speed into the backstretch and stopped badly.
Scratched—Awe Inspiring.

Owners: (7) Gaillard-Hancock III & Whittingham; (2) O Phipps; (4) Brookmeade Stable; (5) John Franks; (1) Mr-Mrs J S Meredith (6) Beal-French Jr-Lukas; (3) A A & Sylvia E Heft; (8) Deep Silver Stable
Trainers: (7) Charles Whittingham; (2) Claude McGaughey III; (4) Sidney Watters Jr; (5) Frank L Brothers; (1) Ronald McAnally; (6) D Wayne Lukas; (3) John J Robb; (8) Harold A Allen

©DAILY RACING FORM/EQUIBASE

- INDEX -

Index (continued)

- ABOUT THE AUTHOR -

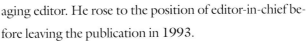

Edward L. Bowen is considered one of Thorough-bred racing's most insightful and erudite writers. A native of West Virginia, Bowen grew up in South Florida where he became enamored of racing while watching televised stakes from Hialeah.

Bowen entered journalism school at the University of Florida in 1960, then transferred to the University of Kentucky in 1963 so he could work as a writer for *The Blood-Horse*, the leading weekly Thoroughbred magazine. From 1968-70, he served as editor of *The Canadian Horse*, then returned to *The Blood-Horse* as managing editor. He rose to the position of editor-in-chief before leaving the publication in 1993.

Bowen is president of the Grayson-Jockey Club Research Foundation, which raises funds for equine research. In addition to *At the Wire*, Bowen has written eleven books, including *Man o' War* and *Dynasties: Great Thoroughbred Stallions*. Bowen has won the Eclipse Award for magazine writing and other writing awards. He lives in Lexington, Ky., with his wife, Ruthie, and son George. Bowen has two grown daughters, Tracy Bowen and Jennifer Schafhauser, and one grandchild.

- OTHER TITLES -

from Eclipse Press

Baffert: Dirt Road to the Derby

Cigar: America's Horse (revised edition)

Country Life Diary (revised edition)

Crown Jewels of Thoroughbred Racing

Dynasties: Great Thoroughbred Stallions

Etched in Stone

Four Seasons of Racing

Great Horse Racing Mysteries

Investing in Thoroughbreds: Strategies for Success

Lightning in a Jar: Catching Racing Fever

Matriarchs: Great Mares of the 20th Century

Olympic Equestrian

Royal Blood

Thoroughbred Champions:
Top 100 Racehorses of the 20th Century

Thoroughbred Legends series:

Citation: Thoroughbred Legends

Dr. Fager: Thoroughbred Legends

Forego: Thoroughbred Legends

Go for Wand: Thoroughbred Legends

John Henry: Thoroughbred Legends

Man o' War: Thoroughbred Legends

Nashua: Thoroughbred Legends

Native Dancer: Thoroughbred Legends

Personal Ensign: Thoroughbred Legends

Seattle Slew: Thoroughbred Legends

Spectacular Bid: Thoroughbred Legends

EP
ECLIPSE
PRESS